NEGOTIATOR'S FACTOMATIC™

H. William Koch, Jr.

PRENTICE HALL
Englewood Cliffs, New Jersey 07632

Prentice-Hall International (UK) Limited, *London*
Prentice-Hall of Australia Pty. Limited, *Sydney*
Prentice-Hall Canada, Inc., *Toronto*
Prentice-Hall Hispanoamericana, S.A., *Mexico*
Prentice-Hall of India Private Limited, *New Delhi*
Prentice-Hall of Japan, Inc., *Tokyo*
Simon & Schuster Asia Pte. Ltd., *Singapore*
Editora Prentice-Hall do Brasil, Ltda., *Rio de Janeiro*

© 1988 *by*

PRENTICE-HALL, Inc.

Englewood Cliffs, NJ

10 9 8 7 6 5 4 3 2 1

Library of Congress Cataloging-in-Publication Data

Koch, H. William,
  Negotiator's factomatic.

  Includes index.
  1. Negotiation in business—Handbooks, manuals,
etc. I. Title.
HD58.6.K63 1988   658   88–5990
ISBN 0–13–611393–1

ISBN 0-13-611393-1

PRENTICE HALL
BUSINESS & PROFESSIONAL DIVISION
A division of Simon & Schuster
Englewood Cliffs, New Jersey 07632

To Becky, Sarah, Bissie, Geoff, Katie, Colin,
and Christopher

ABOUT THE AUTHOR

H. William Koch, Jr., brings unique experience to his insights on successful negotiating skills that have worked so well for others. During 30 years of heading his own confidential consulting business, he has worked closely with more than a thousand top executives and has had ready access to the operations of major firms of all sizes in 50 states and a dozen foreign countries.

His work has made him a leading expert on what it takes to reach the top, and his first top selling book, *Executive Success*, was praised for its special help to the individual in a progressively more competitive and demanding world. He has authored seven other management skill books for Prentice Hall before turning his full attention to *Negotiator's Factomatic*™. Of his new book, he says: "It has the widest application to a person's total life success and personal goals. It distills the best of what has worked for others in gaining their achievements. I have told it like it is—no holds barred—in order to help the reader avoid a lot of all too common problems and mistakes. Hopefully, it will provide a shot of success throughout all parts of the reader's career and personal life."

A *cum laude* graduate of Princeton University, Mr. Koch was himself a top corporate achiever and was early elected to the Young Presidents Organization. Appropriately, for his insights on high skill negotiating methods, he has matched his business activities with participation on key boards and committees of civic and educational institutions.

INTRODUCTION

This book describes almost 200 challenging, sometimes difficult, negotiating situations and prescribes tactics for not only surviving but thriving throughout the negotiating process. *Negotiator's Factomatic™* is divided into 13 sections, which makes it easy to locate the information you need. Quickly, conveniently, you can find examples of how veteran deal makers react to situations similar to those you now face.

WHY INTELLIGENT PEOPLE SOMETIMES BLOW IMPORTANT NEGOTIATIONS: AN EXAMPLE

Over a relaxed luncheon setting in an old English inn near Cambridge University, academic leaders from across Europe assembled to negotiate. Their task was to determine how much their respective universities would pay and what their authority would be in an innovative project to pool computerized information and exchange key findings in scientific research.

Despite the intelligence and enthusiasm of all parties, the negotiation was a disaster. While part of the problem stemmed from language and cultural barriers, what really caused talks to falter were some problems all too common in negotiation. For example, negotiators let pride and ego interfere with good judgment. They enlisted the support of experts who quibbled over the computer system to be used. They failed to organize the negotiation around a mutually agreeable agenda, and all of them lacked final deal-making authority.

What this shows us is that no matter how intelligent or educated we are, we are never too smart not to blow a negotiation. Most people would do well to examine their negotiation style, because most of us could stand some, if not a lot, of improvement. Hence, this book.

WHAT *NEGOTIATOR'S FACTOMATIC™* CAN DO FOR YOU

Negotiator's Factomatic™ is an innovative, convenient tool to use before, during, and after any negotiation. The techniques described in this book are equally effective for individuals or negotiating teams. In fact, you can use *Negotiator's Factomatic*™ daily, because most of us engage in informal negotiations every day of our lives. Since negotiation is so fundamental, we often achieve career advancement, higher productivity, and many of our personal goals as we improve our ability to negotiate. This book can show you how, so keep it by your side before, during, and after negotiations!

The advice in this book works regardless of the size and stakes of a negotiation. One of its most important benefits you'll discover is that by practicing the strategies you'll become a more confident, more seasoned negotiator. Here is a sample of what you'll learn:

- What to do if your opponent enlists a host of experts to confront you at the negotiating table.
- Why you should insist on an opponent with final deal-making authority.
- What excited, anxious opponents are telling you about themselves.
- Why it's sometimes wise to concede a point to your opponent, because a bigger victory may be in store for you.
- The importance of having both parties feel as if they've made a good deal.
- How to use timing to your advantage.
- The hazards of third-party influence on negotiations.
- Why you should anticipate surprise situations and how you can react to surprises in ways that reverse your opponent's strategy.
- What to say to yourself to prepare for negotiations.
- How to keep going when the odds seem stacked against you.
- How to balance intuition and experience for a winning approach.

Negotiator's Factomatic™ also provides helpful checklists to summarize important topics. Key Tactics is a feature which highlights special problems and basic principles for easy reference.

Appendix A, What Do You Say When . . . A Negotiator's Script Book, gives word-for-word dialogue that can be used to deal with common obstacles and challenges you may face in specific negotiating situations. The content also serves to show what your opponent might say in 19 negotiating situations. Appendix B, A Treasury of Quick-reference Checklists for Negotiators, is particularly helpful as you prepare for a challenging round of bargaining sessions with a new opponent.

Negotiator's Factomatic™ can guide you to more satisfying, more effective negotiations. Take the time now to skim the Table of Contents so that you will become familiar with the many situations addressed in this book. Then, refer to these pages throughout your career as you apply your skills.

H. William Koch, Jr.

TABLE OF CONTENTS

SECTION 3—THE ADVANTAGES OF BEING CAUTIOUS WITH THIRD PARTIES.   55

SECTION 4—TECHNIQUES FOR SIZING UP AN OPPONENT   89

SECTION 5—WHAT TO SAY TO YOURSELF ABOUT A NEGOTIATION

SECTION 1

WHAT TO DO IN SURPRISE SITUATIONS

SECTION 1

WHAT TO DO IN SURPRISE SITUATIONS

In today's business world, negotiators must be ready for surprises. You cannot assume that you know enough about the people sitting across the table. You cannot assume that you understand their motives, and you can't expect them to always adhere to simple, old-fashioned ethics.

As you strengthen your negotiating skills, you must learn to expect surprise and to use it to your advantage. You can turn a surprise to be an asset in your favor. You can learn to limit the effect surprises have on you, and you can become a better negotiator by becoming more familiar with the surprise situations described in this section.

WHAT TO DO WHEN YOUR OPPONENT IMPOSES A SURPRISE DEADLINE

Most deadlines are based on emotion rather than logic. Because of this, such limitations may or may not be real. Successful negotiators learn to look beyond the words of any deadline to discover what it means. The words, "I have to have an answer to my proposal by tomorrow," impose a time restriction, but they can have one of several meanings:

1. A childlike impatience with the way things are going, which is an emotional demand.

2. A parent-like desire to put you in your place by playing on your fear of failure; a rebuke to you from an opponent who wants to exert authority over you.

3. A logical, adult appeal based on circumstances which do make time critical.

Childhood habits are hard to break, as are parenting habits. Many people grow up believing that the tantrums that worked in their childhood are still appropriate. Other people try to use the authority role of a parent to handle most situations. When either of these types of people issue time demands, they tend not to be serious about them. They are simply relying on habits based on emotional patterns. The trick is to never respond to your opponent with childlike anger or parental authority. Always respond as an adult.

HOW TO RESPOND TO THE DEADLINE YOUR OPPONENT DICTATES: A CHECKLIST

- *Never smile, laugh, or grimace.* Opponents may interpret this body language as a put-down to their demands.

- *Do look seriously pensive.* A sharp negotiator might write down the deadline and say, "Let me make a note of that." Your objective is always to indicate to your opponent that you take the demand seriously. At this point, do not try to change the deadline.

- *Say to yourself, "There it is, that old, familiar deadline."* This conditions you not to panic or become even mildly affected by a surprise time limit.

- *Having responded to your opponent's time demand on an adult level, continue negotiations on any other area.* Avoid further discussion of the new deadline. Use body language and quicken the tempo of your voice to suggest that you are speeding things up.

- *Whether a time demand involved days, weeks, or even months, don't put your response tactics to work until just before the designated deadline.*

WHAT TO DO AS THE DEADLINE APPROACHES

Let your opponent expect you to honor the demand until just before the time runs out. About an hour before the deadline, request a postponement of your meeting. Blame the postponement on something unrelated to the negotiation. You could, for example, arrange to be called to the phone or have someone call you out of the meeting to talk about an urgent matter. One negotiator simply looks at his watch and says, "Excuse me, I was asked to return an urgent call before now; I'll be right back." He goes to a phone, but always one that is out of earshot.

Outside developments such as these allow you to request a postponement without overtly challenging the deadline. You give the appearance that circumstances are beyond your control, but you are, of course, testing your opponent. By granting a postponement, your opponent puts you in control of the time matter. Until your unrelated crisis is handled, negotiations can't go forward, and only you know when you want that to be.

KEY TACTIC: Two Special Situations and How to Cope with Them

Two situations require special tactics:

1. If your request for a postponement fails, or

2. If your opponent's original surprise deadline took the form of, "Right this minute. Now!"

When facing an ultimatum, your tactic is simple. With a smile on your face, always prepare to leave. Make sure your opponent sees and understands that you are leaving. Usually, an opponent will back down, perhaps saying, "Hold on, I was only kidding." If the person doesn't back down, always leave, but be pleasant about it. Remember, you can always walk back into the meeting. Until you test, though, you'll never know if the deadline is really necessary. Often, if you do not return immediately after walking out, your opponent will have second thoughts and contact you to resume negotiations. Never make a bad deal just because time is running out.

HOW A DEADLINE CAN BECOME A NEGOTIATING ADVANTAGE

Let your opponent think you are trying to meet the deadline. From time to time throughout negotiations, make statements such as, "In view of our time problem, this is the best I can do." Or, "To hit your deadline, you'll have to help me by. . . ."

Many opponents will have feelings of victory when they think they have you on the run from a deadline. This can make them careless, and often they will be quite giving and make concessions based on their pressure on you. It isn't logical, but it is often the case.

HOW TO REACT TO ACCUSATIONS FROM YOUR OPPONENT

We have been called the most litigious nation on earth. Surely, we have more lawyers per capita than any other society. To understand why a negotiator might blame an opponent for everything that goes wrong, we must remember that blaming is truly woven into our social fabric.

WHY YOU SHOULD EXPECT ACCUSATIONS

Our political processes reek of competition between political parties, between states, between towns, and between agencies. If Congress threatens to cut budgets, special interest groups scramble to push the reductions off on someone else.

Things are not much different in other segments of our society. We often see competing products side-by-side on television, with Brand A accusing Brand B of some defect. Half of our marriages end in divorce, which usually involves both negotiations and accusations. Considering our problems with such things as cars, insurance, and utility bills, who in this country has not at one time or another been a party in negotiations that involved blame? Why, then, should anyone ever be surprised when someone accuses us of something?

A SEVEN-STEP TECHNIQUE TO REDUCE THE NEGATIVE EFFECTS OF ACCUSATIONS

1. *Expect blaming accusations and never take them personally.* We are a nation hard at work blaming one another. If you remember how entrenched our blaming habits are, you will not feel guilty or personally insulted when the blame is directed at you. You will also learn to minimize your feelings of fear.

2. *Remember that your accusers are counting on you to lose emotional control due to guilt, anger, or fear.* They are counting on your

emotions to reduce your ability to think clearly and logically. Instead, take three deep breaths the next time someone hurls blame your way during negotiations.

3. *Notice that, often, the very people who are trying to upset you are already out of control themselves.* When this happens, try to set up a cooling off period. This also gives you time to think and to plan your strategies, based on what you have just heard from your opponent. Often, when others lose their cool, they will tip their hand in some way to reveal their needs and fears. Try to gauge whether the other person's anger is real or a calculated tool designed to throw you off balance. Either way, you can't go wrong with a cooling off period.

4. *Be creative in finding excuses for a cooling off period.* Consider these examples:

   • Look at your watch and say, "Excuse me for a moment. This is the time I was supposed to call the man back from the IRS." For some reason, everyone forgives you when you have a call from the IRS.

   • Accidentally spill the contents from your briefcase or your handbag, and then take a long time picking things up and sorting them out.

   • Suddenly remember that you left your car engine running, that you are illegally parked, or that you have to feed the meter.

   • When some negotiators are on their own turf, they have someone interrupt them on a preplanned signal. The other person's excuse could be something like, "You have a phone call in the outer office." You might also have a visitor in the lobby, a spouse on the phone with a small emergency, or an urgent call to get back to the plant.

     If you have more than one person on your negotiating team, plan a signal in advance to use if necessary. One person leaves the room briefly and then returns to announce some sort of minor emergency outside the room. You must excuse yourself for as long as necessary to let emotions cool.

5. *After a cooling off period, return to the accusation against you by openly making a record of it.* You might say, "Just a minute, I want to make a note of your charges." Or, "Hold up a second while I write down exactly what you are claiming." This works to your advantage in three ways:

- It makes your opponent think you are taking the accusation seriously.

- It causes your opponent to wonder why you are writing down the accusations so exactly. Is it for our lawyer? To tell the accuser's boss? To go public with it?

- You are also buying more cooling off time for both of you, plus time for you to plan what you want to do next.

6. *Remember that often an accusation against you carries the threat or opinion of an expert, thus making it a form of double teaming.* (See page 68.) You must immediately stop negotiations until you have matched their expert with an expert of your own.

    Here are some examples of how the strategy works:

- If they say, "My lawyer says you're in trouble," you say, "Hold on a minute, let me call my lawyer right now."

- If they say, "Our records prove that . . . ," you say, "Let me consult my records before this goes any further."

- If they say, "Everyone tells us you're wrong," you say, "I know a lot of people who disagree with you, and this is the time for me to get them into this discussion."

- If they say, "Our policy strictly states our right to . . . ," you say, "I have knowledgeable people with valid questions about your policy, and I need to be in touch with them right now."

7. *Any time things seem to be getting ugly, seek an adjournment.* Keep your opponent uncertain about what you're thinking and what your next step will be. One technique is to ask to use the phone out of your opponent's earshot. Immediately, this makes the other person wonder what hidden power you may have on the other end of the phone.

HOW TO REWRITE YOUR OPPONENT'S LOADED AGENDA

Before Socrates drank his fatal hemlock, he faced a choice: to die or to accept an agenda to bargain on subjects he considered nonnegotiable. By drinking poison, he terminated negotiations in the one way available to him.

No one has to negotiate, and this is your ultimate weapon against a loaded agenda. Your opponents may forget that you have an option to just walk away, and they may prepare a loaded agenda to use against you. They will be counting on greed, fear, or plain stupidity to drive you into negotiations despite their loaded agenda.

HOW TO RECOGNIZE A LOADED AGENDA

All of us have faced a loaded agenda at some time. The trick in dealing with this type is first to recognize it as a loaded agenda. Do these situations sound familiar?

- Your opponent's lawyer smiles, offers an agreement to you, and says, "To protect everyone against any misunderstandings in the future. . . ." What the lawyer is really giving you is a loaded agenda for future negotiations on your opponent's terms. Of course, you will always have your lawyer look things over before you agree to or sign anything.

- Your banker pleasantly asks you to sign a so-called routine form, which according to the banker is required by law. All too often, such a routine form is a loaded agenda which may haunt you in the future. Unexpected events could cause you to negotiate against the loaded agenda you long since forgot you signed. There is no such thing as a routine document that cannot be changed if you take the time to review it with your experts before you sign.

- All routine sales contracts or customer agreements may contain a loaded agenda which limits your negotiating rights in the event of a problem. Pause to review who does what to whom. What happens if the parking lot loses your car; the child care center loses your child; the broker loses your securities; or the post office loses your insurance premium?

KEY TACTIC: Question Even Routine Contracts

All routine contracts can be modified by something else in writing. You can put an agenda for future claims negotiations more in your favor. Talk this idea over with your lawyer if it makes you nervous.

WHAT TO EXPECT FROM A LOADED MEETING AGENDA

Agendas for actual negotiation meetings may be written or unwritten. In either case, your opponents may try several controlling tactics.

1. They may try to set the priorities for what will be decided, and in what order.

2. They will often try to control the time negotiations start and end. As in a poker game, your opponents' idea is to win a few pots, and then leave the game while they are the winner and you are the loser. Becoming unavailable to an opponent is a widely used negotiating tactic.

3. They may try to make you feel you've gotten a good deal. This helps them avoid the possibility that you'll try to upset the arrangements later.

4. They may try to control the information that is available to you. To use a real estate analogy, this is like buying a house before you have seen the cellar.

5. They may try to intimidate you so you will be afraid to complain, if and when you find that you have been taken. Methods of intimidation can be artful, playing on anything from fear of legal action to fear of embarrassment.

A STEP-BY-STEP METHOD FOR REWRITING A LOADED AGENDA

1. When your opponent's priorities are different from yours, insist on a package deal. Simply stated, no one wins anything until

all the items agreed to be negotiated are in fact negotiated. This prevents negotiators from unexpectedly leaving the game with their winnings.

2. When deciding when to start and end negotiations, allocate a large block of time to use if necessary. Also, state a wide range of check points, those issues you need to check with your lawyer, accountant, or other concerned people, such as appraisers, engineers, bankers, your spouse, or friends.

    Never agree to any agenda which limits your time, your right to get more information, or your ability to walk away completely before the agreements are finalized in writing.

3. When preparing to finalize the deal, always include nonperformance contingencies on your agenda. Examples of these musts are—

    • What if payment isn't made in the time and manner specified?

    • What if the product or service isn't provided in the method, quality, value, or time provided?

    • What if the present negotiators are unavailable later? Who will replace them?

    • Who will prepare, review, and sign agreements related to nonperformance? Never rely on your opponent's people exclusively in these matters.

    • Who will arbitrate differences concerning the definition of nonperformance to be applied to your agreement?

HOW TO RESPOND TO A FIRE DRILL

A fire drill is a would-be crisis that is unrelated to the terms of an agreement. Fire drills are objectionable for two reasons:

- They interrupt concentration on the main parts of an agreement, and
- They are attempts to get you to go more or give more than originally agreed.

The following example illustrates the effect of constant fire-drill maneuvers.

Jan's new boss hired her after a long process of negotiation, because Jan was a highly qualified sales talent. She had a top flight mind and ample experience, plus she was a motivated, success-oriented person and a team player. Jan's new compensation package could have doubled what she earned at her previous job, but her compensation was tied to performance.

Jan would have had little trouble reaching her sales quotas had her boss left her alone. Instead, he kept interrupting Jan with one crisis after another.

After ten months, Jan realized what was happening. Her boss had been escalating their original agreement. She had been asked to do many tasks unrelated to her sales job. As a result, her earnings were far below what she had expected.

HOW TO SPOT A FIRE DRILL: A CHECKLIST

Have you ever purchased something and the seller delivered more than requested? The seller might say something like this, "The plant may be going on strike, and I thought you would want as much as possible just in case." Such a delivery is done in a great hurry and a mood of crisis.

In this case, the fire drill has interrupted your deal by altering its basic terms, such as how much you agreed to buy and when. The possible strike is unrelated to your responsibility as a customer. But now you are asked to do more than you bargained for. As in a real fire drill, the strike was a false alarm, but you are stuck with extra inventory.

Your boss agrees to give you a raise with the understanding that your workload will increase by 50 percent. The next thing you know, you are chasing one fire drill after another. You end up working 70, not 50, percent more. The constant interruptions distract you from the primary job activities you took over in return for your wage increase. If the distractions continue, your work will suffer, or you will be working longer hours and weekends to do what is asked of you.

You sell and deliver something to someone. Per the agreement, you will be paid in person on Wednesday. On Tuesday night, the buyer calls you at home to say, "I'm going into the hospital tomorrow morning for a few days to see how sick I really am."

You are a nice person, and you agree to wait until the buyer's crisis is over to get paid. A week passes. You still have not been paid. His wife phones to say, "He's at home, and we expect him to be back at work in ten days."

Three weeks later, the buyer calls, not to apologize but to complain. "Those things I bought," he says in a highly agitated tone, "are not working the way I hoped. I'm trying to avoid a crisis, but I'll need more time. I'll get back to you."

The buyer never says thanks for waiting to be paid, and he does not mention when you can expect payment. He is a master of the fire drill. He has already pulled two false emergencies on you with his sickness and product problems. Surely, he is looking for another drill to delay payment. Through his tactics, he has—

1. Interrupted your original payment agreement, and

2. Gotten more time from you by creating false crises.

HOW TO WIN DESPITE A FIRE DRILL

The old adage, "Fight fire with fire," fits perfectly in the case of a fire drill. Always counter the other person's fire drill with one of your own immediately. Consider these responses to the situations we've discussed.

1. The buyer calls to say he cannot pay because he is going into the hospital. You call back within minutes to say you have a bank overdraft, and one of your people is racing over to his house to pick up the check.

2. Your boss has been taking advantage of your original employ-

ment contract. Now the boss is on the phone telling you to go to an out-of-town convention. The convention is not directly related to your job duties, but it will draw you away from work you are responsible for completing. You call your boss back within minutes and say, "I just came home to start packing and, guess what, there is an IRS notice at the house. I have to be available during the convention week. Sorry!"

3. A supplier asks you to enlarge your order because a strike is threatened. You call back and say you have two other sources who have no apparent labor problems. You think a price reduction is in order to justify your loyalty in light of the risk of parts stoppage. You deliberately sound very upset because you are replacing the seller's crisis with your own.

HOW TO RESPOND WHEN AN OPPONENT TESTS YOU WITH WAY-OUT OFFERS

A private chat with an experienced negotiator will often reveal that he or she won some outlandish victory in the past based on a wild offer which an opponent accepted unexpectedly. Such surprises occur when the person making the offer does not know or understand what is on an opponent's mind. Long after winning with a wild offer, the negotiator may not know the reasons it worked.

KEY TACTIC: When to Use a Wild Offer

Wild offers tend to be most successful in two negotiating situations: hiring and promoting. Here are some examples:

- "I didn't need to pay him more money. I gave him an outside window to make him happy."
- "I told her that she could be president in six years, and she grabbed it. I would have agreed to one."
- "I told him he'd have to take a wage cut to come to work for me, and he agreed. I really would have doubled what he was getting at the competitor if I had to."
- "I got her to sign a noncompetition agreement before she came to work for us. I never dreamed she would!"

WHAT TO REMEMBER ABOUT WAY-OUT OFFERS

- Most negotiations include one or more way-out offers because your opponent is guessing that you have a weakness.

- A buyer will always receive a way-out offer to test his or her impatience to buy.
- A seller will always receive a way-out offer to test the seller's need to sell.
- Way-out offers use much more than money to probe your weaknesses.
- A person who accepts a way-out offer is never permitted to know that an opponent is astounded to have won so easily. Opponents take care to make all way-out offers appear reasonable in case they are accepted unexpectedly.

HOW TO COUNTER A WAY-OUT OFFER: AN EXAMPLE

Suppose a small business owner offered to sell the company for twice what it was worth. The buyers knew this was a way-out offer designed as a test, but they did not let on that they knew. Instead, one of them said to the seller, "Before we talk a final price, let's talk terms. I need no money down, 40 years to pay, and an interest rate half of the prime rate on the day we sign the contract."

The owner of the business responded, "I could agree to that, but I can't reduce my price one cent."

"Of course, we bought it," one of the negotiators said, "because we had no risk up front. In 40 years, the business would be worth ten times what we paid even including the low interest charges for 40 years. The seller was so intent on the ridiculous price that he didn't pay attention to our ridiculous terms. It often works that way."

FOUR RULES FOR RESPONDING TO A WAY-OUT OFFER

Rule 1: Act as if you do not know you have been given a way-out offer. Do not emote in any way. Simply listen in a mood of serious concentration.

Rule 2: Try to find an equally way-out proposition to better the deal, even if you are considering taking the wild offer, as did the buyers in our small business example.

Rule 3: If your opponent turns down your matching or bettering way-out offer, ignore your opponent's offer by directing negotiations to another area on the agenda.

Rule 4: Later, when the way-out offer comes up again, say, "I thought you were kidding, so I didn't bother to respond. Of course, if you're not kidding, we've been wasting our time."

Usually, your opponent will admit that there is still room to talk and will reveal a desire to keep negotiations going.

HOW TO REACT TO AN OPPONENT'S FLAT PRICE ULTIMATUM

A take-it-or-leave it, flat price ultimatum is not negotiation. An ultimatum is important, however, and it means that you must quickly look for anything that is negotiable to keep talking in the face of an impasse.

When facing a price ultimatum, you gain nothing by attacking the price head on. You gain everything by re-examining what your opponent means. Start with little issues to loosen up your opponent emotionally as well as rationally.

A THREE-STEP TECHNIQUE FOR EXPLORING A FLAT PRICE ULTIMATUM

In a simple, familiar negotiation example, a car dealer stands up to declare a flat price ultimatum. How should you respond?

Step 1: Respond with a series of questions whose answers you already know to be yes.

- "Can I get it in other colors?"
- "Is it reasonable on gas mileage?"
- "Have you had good reports from the owners of this model?"
- "Can it be financed?"
- "Does your service department have a record of satisfied customers?"
- "Will it give me a good trade in value?"

At this point, the dealer may feel that the chances of selling you the car are good. Plus, the dealer already answered yes to your last six questions without losing a dime. The yes answers help shift the dealer's frame of mind from demanding an ultimatum to a more giving mood. This lowers the dealer's guard, which was your original objective.

Step 2: Move to another series of questions about little issues which may not have a clear-cut yes answer. For example, ask—

- "Could you save me a few hundred dollars by taking out the radio?"
- "Could you give me all-weather tires for the same price?"
- "Can you see your way clear to throw in rust proofing at no extra charge?"
- "How about free service for the first 10,000 miles?"
- "Could you throw in a roof rack at no cost?"

Your first set of questions with yes answers led the dealer to believe you were close to accepting the flat price ultimatum. Your second set of add-on or nibbling questions is designed to test the dealer's flat price ultimatum. Feeling victorious about your apparent acceptance, the dealer may begin to yield on little issues.

Step 3: Keep the dealer guessing about how you are reacting to the answers to your second set of questions. After each answer, ask your next question without reacting to the dealer's earlier answer. Now you have your opponent guessing about your position. The dealer thought you were sold, but now is not quite as confident about having made the ultimatum.

Then: At this point, smile and start to walk out as you say, "Thank you very much." That's all you say! In almost all instances, the dealer will come after you to try to learn more about what you are thinking. Particularly, the dealer is wondering how you have reacted to the answers to your second group of questions. Remember, you were careful not to react to the answers. Of course, the dealer is worried that you may be heading off to a competitor.

If the dealer comes after you, you now have a real negotiation, no more flat price ultimatum. If the dealer does not come after you, you are still in a flat price ultimatum situation, and this setting can never be one of negotiation. So, you might as well leave. You can always return later if you want to accept the price but, again, this is not negotiation.

A CHECKLIST FOR RESPONDING TO A FLAT PRICE ULTIMATUM

- Do not contest the price head on.
- Start talking about issues to which the other person can say yes. This won't cost the seller any money!
- After your yes questions, start asking what-if questions. These give you add-ons for no extra cost.

- Never react to your opponent's answers to your what-if questions.
- Smile, say thank you, and start to leave without tipping your hand.
- Watch and listen carefully to what your opponent does next.

WHAT TO DO IN A DEADLOCK

A particularly numbing feeling can set in after a difficult, trying negotiating session, and the situation can quickly deteriorate into a deadlock. Neither party can or wants to say anything else.

Often when this occurs, neither party has planned for talks to fall apart. Indeed, until the moment that both parties go numb, they may be trying to work something out.

When a deadlock occurs despite both parties' best efforts, the only hope is to let time pass. This waiting period should be days or weeks, not a few hours or a single day.

To overcome a deadlock in a now-or-never situation, seek a third-party mediator, provided that time is running out and further delay carries an equally high risk for both parties. For example, two partners in a small business grew to hate one another. Finally, they agreed to negotiate for one partner to sell out to the other. After several months, their negotiations ended in a seemingly impossible deadlock.

In the midst of their earlier negotiations, the two partners had closed the doors of their business and announced publicly that it would soon be reopened under new management. Even after reaching a deadlock, the partners sensed that keeping their business closed much longer would ruin it. So, they agreed to call in a professional mediator. Their banker, whom they both trusted, was to select the mediator.

The mediator began unravelling the deadlock with these instructions, "We'll use six sealed bids over two hours."

"You've been arguing for months. Let's not waste any more time negotiating. Let's start bidding. Tomorrow, I want each of you on hand with arrangements to have certified checks made payable to one another in whatever amount the final bid is.

"The bidding will begin at 9 A.M. At that time, I will receive your first bid in a sealed envelope. Only I will see the bids. I will tell you who has the higher bid, but you will not know its amount.

"We will repeat the process until one person remains unchallenged as the high bidder. Only then will the other person know the price of half of the business. Obviously, neither of you will bid more than you think 50 percent of the company is worth. So whoever wins, no one will have a complaint position."

As it turned out, one of the partners paid many thousands of dollars more than the other partner's last bid. Even so, the buyer expressed a feeling of having received a fair value. The seller also indicated that the compensation was fair. Both partners later told us that without the mediator they would have watched their company go down the drain.

AVOIDING PROBLEMS WITH LAST-MINUTE CHANGES TO A DEAL

Many negotiators assume that, once a deal has been formalized, the deal making is over. Not so. Your opponents may well surprise you by continuing their negotiations in unorthodox ways after the deal is set. Consider these examples:

- "How could I have been such a fool," the small business owner told us. "The day after I spent almost $1 million on new special machinery on the basis of a big order, the would-be buyers called to cancel. One of their vice presidents had a cousin in Taiwan whose firm cut our price 50 percent. Now I'm stuck because I counted on their assurances."

- "They hired me as executive vice president, and I gave up a good job I had for 20 years," the executive said. The next month, they sold the company and I was asked to leave, almost before I had set up my new office. All the promises they had given me went right out the window."

- "It was the biggest sale I had ever made, and my commission would have been six figures. But at the last moment, they cut me out of the deal entirely. I had failed to protect myself legally. I believed in them and counted on their promises. How could I have been so blind?"

- "The deal went through like clockwork," the company president told us. "We did everything carefully and legally because we were selling them our most profitable division. The payment arrangements were for quarterly installments that would match our critical cashflow requirements."

  "Then, before the second quarterly payment came due, they called us to say they couldn't come up with all of the money. By the third quarterly payment date, they cut the amount of their payment back again. When we threatened legal action, they simply smiled and said, 'Sorry, sue us.' There was a complete change in character in these people. I'm convinced now that they planned it all along.

"Sure, we'll sue them, but in the meantime our cashflow problem may put us out of business before we get things straightened out."

We provide these horror stories to illustrate that last-minute additions to a deal can occur after an agreement has been formalized, and often in spite of all kinds of promises. Even so, you can counter these tactics and get the deal back on target.

SUCCESSFUL FALLBACK POSITIONS TO DIFFUSE LAST-MINUTE CHANGES

Unfortunately, the best way to stave off surprise changes after the deal is made is to always be slightly paranoid beforehand. In each of our examples, the people who were hurt had one thing in common: they relied on performance from the other party. They failed to look beyond the deal to what comes next—performance. If they had, they would not have burned all of their strategic bridges behind them. They would have provided fallback positions. Here are some strategies for creating fallback positions:

- If you get a big order, even one that is legally binding, do not spend large sums of money in anticipation of the customer's performance. Let the customer build a solid track record before you decide that the performance is in fact what you expected.

- If you make an important career change, anticipate nonperformance by your new employer. Arrange to have some kind of "Golden Parachute," that is, a legally binding statement explaining what happens if terms of your employment are not met. This will protect you just in case the new employer is unable to perform on the assurances given you. A good way to approach this subject with a potential employer is to say, "You're the top people in your area. It will be a privilege to be associated with you, but suppose you're hit by a bus tomorrow. Where would that leave me?"

- If you are involved in contingency fee or commission arrangements, never leave a deal in verbal form. Get your terms legally recorded before you bring the buyer and seller together or before you perform your fee service. Before you bring a buyer and seller together, both parties need you, and they know it. Once

they meet each other, they may overlook your value or resent
your commission.

• Whenever your arrangement involve delayed payment, installment payments, balloon notes, or similar terms, never rely on
the legal right to sue. Of course, lawsuits are necessary to protect
yourself legally, but do not rely on your legal recourse in making
related decisions. In other words, do not leave yourself vulnerable
in the event that the other person fails to perform. Anticipate
nonperformance, and avoid spending the money before you have
it in hand.

FIVE TIPS FOR HANDLING SURPRISE ADDITIONS TO A NEGOTIATION IN PROGRESS

So far, we have discussed changes made to a completed deal.
Changes are just as likely to crop up during negotiations. Use these
ideas to help reduce their impact:

1. *Never show resentment or lose your cool.*

2. *Always trade time for any surprise addition.* "I'll need some time to
   think that over." Or, "Why don't we adjourn for now, so I can
   consider this new development."

3. *Treat any surprise addition or demand as if it is a big issue, even if it
   is not.* When you do this, you slow down the pace of negotiations,
   and your apparent concern makes your opponent pay a psychological price every time he or she injects a surprise into your
   negotiations.

4. *Always match a surprise demand with a surprise of your own.* Do
   this artfully. Never appear to be saying, "If you do that to me,
   I'll do that to you." Instead, as you take time to review the
   unexpected demand before you, develop a new strategy based
   on what has just happened.

5. *Sometimes you can deliberately yield to a new demand to make your
   opponent think he or she has a good deal.* In this case, you yield
   strategically to speed up a close, and you match the new demand
   with something such as, "Oh well, if that will put this thing to
   bed now, then I agree." Do this only after you let some time
   go by, and act reluctant rather than appear anxious.

SECTION 2

STRATEGIES FOR COPING WITH TROUBLESOME TACTICS

STRATEGIES FOR COPING WITH TROUBLESOME TACTICS

As you read in Section 1, surprise situations call for the right response. Sometimes the best response, however, is to ward off the surprise in the first place by knowing how to anticipate and spot tactics that might otherwise throw you off track. In other words, your foresight prevents you from being taken by surprise, and you can react cooly, calmly, and correctly every time.

RECOGNIZING AND HANDLING MISINFORMATION

Misinformation has nothing to do with outright fraud, yet the results can have equally damaging effects. The president of a large casualty insurance company reports, "The single best example of misinformation is what the two parties to a two-car accident usually tell us happened when they negotiate for a claims settlement. Often, you'd swear they were each involved in separate accidents because their perspectives are so different."

In any negotiation, the other person's perspective may be quite different from yours. Sometimes there is a distortion of information which is not clear to the other person. Often, there is deliberate distortion designed to influence your perspective in your opponent's favor. In either case, you must watch for misinformation throughout negotiations.

WHY MISINFORMATION CAN BE HARD TO SPOT: TWO EXAMPLES

Misinformation in real estate: A couple visiting a vacation resort for the first time became interested in buying a second home there. With little knowledge of local prices and no real conviction to buy, they stopped into a local real estate agent's office.

The agent graciously took them to lunch at a yacht club and introduced them to many locals as "my new friends." The next morning, she invited them to her home for brunch and introduced them to people she wanted them to meet. A day later, she took them to a dinner party at a private club. Between social events, the agent showed the couple what she called "just the right kind of house for your kind of people, and in the right area for people like you."

By this time, the six-figure cost of the "right kind of house" seemed secondary to the wonderful social world that the buyers would be joining. By now, of course, they considered the real estate agent a close, trusted friend, whom they would be seeing on many future occasions.

By stretching financial resources, the couple bought an expensive home. Sadly, circumstances did not turn out as they had expected. The yacht club had a five-year waiting list, and the private club did not have a list at all. Prospective members were invited to join, but these buyers were not among them.

The cruelest cut of all was that over the next two years their real estate agent was never available to them socially. She was always too busy, out of town, or ill. At least, that is what she said.

Everything the buyers had hoped to be getting with their real estate turned out to be a pipe dream. After two years, the couple sold the home at a loss to rid themselves of the emotional pain caused by social isolation.

In negotiating for the house, the real estate agent distorted the buyers' perspective with misinformation that led to a false dream. What a pro!

Misinformation in business: A middle-aged man owned all of the stock in a rapidly growing computer accessory firm in the Southwest. His background was in science. He had little knowledge of finance. Even so, his working capital position was quite good; he had few financial pressures on his daily laboratory routines.

One day, a risk capital expert from out of town visited the owner unexpectedly, saying, "I came to learn about all of the exciting things going on here." Before the expert left town, the very flattered business owner agreed to an expense-paid visit to New York to meet the expert's associates.

At the airport in New York, a uniformed chauffeur met the owner, carried his bags to a sleek limousine, and drove him to a building in the Wall Street area for a luncheon appointment. The chauffeur escorted the owner to a private elevator which whisked him to a private club on the sixtieth floor. The club manager greeted him by name and led him to a lavish private dining room overlooking the harbor. As he entered, everyone stood up to show respect.

Among the eight people assembled were experts in law, banking, marketing, accounting, finance, underwriting, and public relations. Everyone seemed to hang on every word the small company owner spoke. Three hours later, the risk capital expert scheduled a meeting with them again the next day. Until then, the risk capital expert had arranged for the owner to have dinner and see a new smash hit musical. The limousine and chauffeur continued to be at his service.

Before the week was over, the small business owner had new business partners who owned 40 percent of his company. Three years later, he told us, "The whole thing made me lose my perspective. I thought

I had joined a powerful team with values the same as mine. I thought I had joined a shiny new world that I had been missing."

The once proud sole owner was sitting in a dingy plant office of the company, which was now controlled by outsiders. "If I'm lucky, I get invited to their New York meetings once a year. I'm an accessory—seldom considered, often ridiculed. Worst of all, they have me on a long-term employment contract. Sure, I'm making good money, but no more than I would have on my own. I can't walk away from this bunch that looks down their noses at me. I'm some negotiator."

FOUR DEFENSES AGAINST MISINFORMATION

1. *Remember the two examples you just read.* Our infatuation with an idea can quickly turn to pain when an opponent upsets our perspective for his or her own short-term gain. Stay alert.

2. *Never rely on figures or numbers alone.* Remember the adage, "Figures never lie, but liars figure." Many people assume that watching numbers is protection enough. Not so! Watch for both quantitative and nonquantitative misinformation.

3. *Recognize fads.* When certain practices such as merging, job hopping, going public, or buying real estate are popular, opponents may use them to influence negotiations. The idea is to get you on a bandwagon before it is too late. This is a poor reason to be beaten in a negotiation.

4. *Resist and privately question all information that relies on the authority of certain technologies, methods, or people.*

KEY TACTIC: 14 Phrases That Often Signal Misinformation

- "The computer says. . . ."
- "A spreadsheet analysis proves. . . ."
- "Our experts have concluded. . . ."
- "Industry figures tell us. . . ."
- "They are the best in the field and they say. . . ."
- "This is confidential information available only to us."
- "The boss has confided in me about how it is supposed to be."
- "Our survey proves. . . ."
- "Our lawyers can assure you that. . . ."

- "Ask our bankers what they think of us."
- "We have inside information that proves. . . ."
- "Take a look at our bank account to see how strong we are."
- "Talk to our accountants; they're an impartial source."
- "That's one person you can trust."

HOW TO RECOGNIZE AND AVOID SHORTCHANGE ARTISTS

A shortchange negotiator's bag of tricks most often consists of seven types of ploys. Learn to spot them, and you'll save yourself time, money, and grief. Here is a checklist:

- *The ten-to-one syndrome.* This is a memory tool to remind us of the customer who asks for a price on 1,000 units, then orders 100 units based on the high volume price.
- *The time warp.* This term characterizes people who take a 10- or 30-day discount weeks or months after it has expired. A variation on this theme is the *check-is-in-the-mail* ploy, which keeps your money earning interest in their bank account long after the negotiated payment date.
- *The lost message.* We use this term to refer to the surprise changes in agreements people try to make without approval. When you say, "But you agreed to do so and so," their response is, "But didn't you get my message? We assumed we had your approval when you didn't get back to us."
- *The professional cop-out.* This term reminds us of agreements we have seen altered in the name of professional excuses. We have heard such things as:
  "Our lawyers wouldn't let us do that."
  "Our accountants say it's not possible."
  "Our engineers found that we simply could not."
  "My doctor tells me that I have to change my arrangements for health reasons."
- *The up-in-smoke syndrome.* If someone fails to live up to all parts of an agreement by saying, "I have no record of that, and I've looked everywhere," then this term applies!
- *Amnesia.* Closely related to the Up-in-Smoke Syndrome, amnesia occurs when, long after your negotiation ended, someone says,

"I have absolutely no recall of any agreement on that, nor do my people. Absolutely no recall!"

Amnesia sufferers never actually call you a liar, but they imply that it is your mind, not theirs, that is impaired.

• *I-need-your-help pleas.* In such cases, everything promised, agreed to, and in any way formalized—even legally formalized—becomes subject to review in the name of humanity.

KEY TACTIC: Be Specific

Never become cynical about negotiations or distrustful of most people. Better to continue to like people. Instead of cynicism, become much more specific about the issues and terms to which you agree and the cost of nonperformance. This will help people resist taking the easy way out if they are tempted to change your deal.

HOW TO AVOID BEING EXCLUDED FROM MEETINGS

Being left behind in negotiations is a tricky subject, because the people who are left usually do not realize what has happened until it is too late. Consider this situation.

WHAT HAPPENS WHEN SOMEONE IS FROZEN OUT: AN EXAMPLE

Three division heads of a rapidly growing company had been meeting with their president all morning. The agenda covered the next year's budget. The president seemed to enjoy hearing the division leaders negotiating for larger pieces of the operation's financial pie. The president believed that a little competition among people kept them sharp.

The meeting adjourned for lunch, with the final budget allocations up in the air. Mike, the oldest and most conscientious of the three division heads, used the break to work in his office downstairs.

The other division managers went upstairs to the corporate dining room. Within ten minutes, the company president arrived. They had not planned to have lunch together; it just happened. When Mike rejoined the group an hour later, the president opened and closed the negotiation session with one statement: "We kept going during lunch, Mike, and things are pretty much wrapped up. I have to leave the office in a few minutes for my Chicago trip, but they'll tell you what's been decided."

What had been decided during lunch left Mike with a sharply restricted budget. The other two division leaders had increased funding.

"That one meeting," Mike said several years later, "turned my career around. I've been low man on the totem pole ever since."

FIVE WARNING SIGNS OF BEING LEFT BEHIND

Mike was left behind for one reason: he failed to consider that it might happen. If he had, he could have arranged to stay with his coworkers during lunch. The next five examples will show you some situations to be careful about, but these are by no means all of the ways you might get left behind during negotiations.

- You bring a potential buyer and seller together, expecting your normal commission. You permit them to have a meeting during which you are not present.

  Warning: They may agree to a final deal and also agree to cut out your commission.

- You have been developing an account for several months. The customer agrees to give you the order next week. You have to be out of the office next week, and your boss agrees to handle your calls.

  Warning: Your boss could take the call in your absence and somehow rub your customer the wrong way. The big order could go out the window.

- The president of your organization is an avid golfer. You are so-so at golf, but you do not really like the game. Whenever possible, you find excuses not to play.

  Warning: Your career might slow down unexpectedly. Other people may get close to the boss and negotiate their best interests during the golfing sessions you are missing.

- You are a top expert in your field. Everyone in your organization recognizes your strong talents in your area. You work harder and harder in that area to build your reputation. Consequently, you pass up many chances to mix and mingle with your peers in other areas of the organization.

  Warning: You risk losing touch with the politics of the company, and you forfeit many chances to be part of ongoing, spontaneous negotiations. You may be pegged as a specialist with whom others cannot identify. You may stall at the midmanagement level.

- You have a sharp mind and a strong, outspoken personality. Other people respect you, but frequently rub you the wrong way during negotiations. You win most negotiations, but people feel bruised by their dealings with you. You have never learned to let your opponents win anything or enable them to save face.

  Warning: You may find yourself cut out of more and more formal and informal negotiating opportunities, both in and out of your organization. Your delegating skills could reach an all-time low, because good delegation requires the give-and-take of continuing negotiation with people on all levels. Over time, you could become less valuable and less promotable in your organization.

KEY TACTIC: Stay Alert to Negotiating Opportunities

For every formal negotiating session, there are hundreds of informal negotiating opportunities. If we are not alert, we can lose a lot. Even failing to maintain good manners with people on all levels can be costly. For example, if we throw a work assignment at someone or take someone for granted, we lose their willingness to negotiate with us on anything we need.

WHY YOU SHOULD RESIST YOUR OPPONENT'S FRIENDLY OVERTURES

Many people believe that they will get more of what they want from others by forming a bond with their opponent. This means trying to make an opponent like you, and therefore more likely to give you what you want. Attempts at bonding may include—

- Flirting with the opposite sex.
- Unctuous manners and speech.
- Offers of favors unrelated to the negotiations.
- Name dropping to show how nice you are.
- Self-testimonials to show how fine you are.
- Subordination of all the negotiating logistical details with comments such as, "Whenever you want," "At your convenience," or "Whatever you say."

FIVE REASONS TO AVOID GETTING TOO CLOSE TO YOUR OPPONENT

1. Your opponent may regard your friendly overtures as a weakness.
2. Your opponent may regard your attempts at bonding as a tactic, which would put him or her unduly on guard.
3. Your behavior may seem strange, which casts doubt on your credibility.
4. Your opponent may think your behavior is dangerous or that you do not stand for anything, either of which would make the other person nervous.
5. Your behavior may be regarded as comic, which causes you to lose your opponent's respect.

HOW SHARP NEGOTIATORS CAN EXPLOIT OFFERS OF FRIENDSHIP: AN EXAMPLE

"Whenever someone tries to butter me up or even flirts with me," the bank president said, "I know the negotiation is going to be a piece of cake.

"I growl because I know I can keep them off balance as they try to find new ways to get me to smile and like them. Usually, they're so busy thinking about pleasing me that they can't concentrate on their real negotiating objectives.

"Then, when I close a deal that is good for me, I smile. They're so relieved that they walk away pleased at the bum deal I've given them."

Does this sound vicious and brutal? It is! But it is also a reality of winning to be used against people who confuse negotiating with pleasing.

Never openly seek your opponent's favor. There is a great difference between being diplomatic and being obvious. After all, the art of negotiating is to avoid being obvious about anything.

WHY HABITS LIMIT YOUR NEGOTIATING SUCCESS

Nature reminds us of the dangers of inbred habit. A herd of cattle will continue charging across a flooding river even after hundreds of animals have drowned. They will stampede over a cliff to their deaths, so strong is their habit of following.

In like fashion, many people negotiate from habit most of the time. This is why top negotiators always take time before negotiations begin to learn how the opponent usually plays the game, to learn his or her habits. An opponent who knows your habits can plan surprise strategies and win by exploiting the things you can be counted on to do.

HOW HABITS WORKED AGAINST ONE UNION

The president of a large company wanted to sell the firm quickly, before an industry profit downturn became obvious to everyone. The president had an annual labor contract bargaining session coming up and, knowing the union's habits very well, he threw heavy surprise demands before them. As expected, the demands drew threats of a strike. In the midst of this reaction, the president issued statements to the financial community explaining that he had never planned to sell the company but would consider doing so in the wake of union problems. Three weeks later, a buyer took the bait, forgot to study industry profit projections, and bought the company. Consequently, the new buyer closed half of the company plants. Half of the company's union members lost their jobs.

By habit, the union reacted to negotiation issues exactly as the president had expected. Union negotiators never asked themselves why the president was hitting them with surprising demands at a time when the company was profitable. Instead, their habitual response cost half of their people their jobs.

Equally careless of the union negotiators was their refusal to spot a change in the president's habits. Never had he escalated his demands in such a surprising fashion; never had he demonstrated such a take-it-or-leave-it attitude. Why, they might have asked, did the president abandon his old habits?

A CHECKLIST FOR ANALYZING AND OVERCOMING NEGOTIATING HABITS

- You know your opponent's negotiating habits, but he or she suddenly breaks out of them. Ask yourself why.
- An extreme demand is placed on the negotiating table. You have tested the demand, and it stands. Ask yourself why.
- When you face illogical requests for delays or accelerated schedules, look for hidden reasons.
- When a normally vigorous opponent shows fatigue or loss of concentration, find out why.
- When new faces suddenly appear around the negotiating table, ask questions. Who are they? How much authority do they have? Why are they here now?
- When additions or a shift in emphasis suddenly alter the agenda, find the cause.

KEY TACTIC: Stop and Think about Surprises

Events such as war, peace, market fears, market rallys, national disasters, industry crises, or government crises can suddenly influence negotiations. Whatever the situation, pause to reexamine your new negotiating climate.

When you face a surprise that might require new strategies, seek explanations of the situation immediately, and consider its consequences. If a surprise from an opponent is sharply out of character for that person, look for answers. If you cannot find them, halt negotiations. Use any excuse, but do not resume until you make sense of things.

HOW TO DIFFUSE YOUR OPPONENT'S EMPTY-POCKETS APPEAL

One type of negotiating opponent can put the greatest Shakespearian actor to shame. Such individuals have a thousand nuances of body language to emphasize their lines. They almost cry, and then laugh through tears. They may grimace as if you are slowly inflicting a wound, or they may utter a sudden cry of agony as if from a swift blow. Their predictable encore is a quick change of attitude. They start to sympathize with you despite their earlier words.

And what did their earlier words boil down to? Always the same line, "Oh, we could never afford to agree to that." Because their message is the same, we refer to it as the "Empty-pockets Appeal."

Think of how often you have heard, "We could never afford to do that," during a negotiation. Think how powerful that one line can be in the hands of an experienced actor. People tend to fold immediately upon hearing these words from an opponent, as if the negotiation door is slammed shut before their faces.

AN OSCAR-DESERVING NEGOTIATOR IN ACTION: AN EXAMPLE

We once spent two hours sitting next to a customer complaint counter at a large retail outlet. Behind the counter was a small, frail, grandmotherly woman. She greeted each arriving complainant with a smile and rich, loving concern. During the two hours, we watched her handle 11 complaints about 11 different matters.

She was a marvelous actress. In each case, she found many opportunities to say, "Oh, we could never do that." She never said it the same way twice to the same person. Instead, she acted out a variety of moods, depending on how forceful her opponent was. Each time she repeated the line, she followed up with something like, "Oh my dear, if only I could." This woman was saving her store a fortune!

SEVEN TACTICS TO NEUTRALIZE AN EMPTY-POCKETS PERFORMANCE

1. *Don't let yourself get caught up in the play.*

2. *During negotiations, imagine that your opponents are actors, and look forward to hearing how they deliver their big line, "Oh, we could never afford to do that."*

3. *Look for variations on this line.* Someone may have found a new way to say the same thing. Perhaps they will use anger, insults, pathos, regret, or incredulity.

4. *Remember that what you are hearing is acting.* Discount it 100 percent.

5. *If a chorus chimes in on the same line, you know it is preplanned.* If everyone around the table gives you almost simultaneous performances of, "Oh, we could never afford that," ask yourself why they rehearsed. Perhaps they see themselves in a weak bargaining position.

6. *Call for a break right after the great performance.* Respond immediately to an empty-pockets appeal in one of these three ways:

   • Ask for a break in the meeting without saying why.

   • Change the subject to a completely different area of negotiations.

   • Excuse yourself, saying something like, "I am due to make a phone call right now!"

   It is important not to react to the great performance at the time it is presented.

7. *After your intermission, you can start repackaging the same demand.* This means retalking and rephrasing the very proposal that your opponents said they could never afford. The key is to let them save face by pretending that now we are talking about something different.

HOW TO HELP YOUR OPPONENT SAVE FACE: TWO EXAMPLES

• A car dealer offers a "best deal" price to a young couple, and they respond with an immediate Empty-pockets refrain. The dealer calls an intermission by leaving to answer a phone call. Then the dealer returns after three or four minutes and says, "I could save you money if we left out the rear speakers; they're a pain for our people to install."

This sounds like a new deal, but it is really not. The money saved on speakers will produce a slightly lower price, but for less product. Even so, everyone saves face through artful use of repackaging.

• An important customer angrily recites the empty-pockets routine and threatens to cancel an order because you proposed a three percent price increase. You arrange a long intermission to serve as a cooling-off period.

After the intermission, you say to the customer, "You've been paying us on a 30-day net basis. Why not move it to ten days and earn our two percent discount? That will cover most of the price increase."

This sounds like a new deal, but it is the same deal, because any customer can receive a two percent, ten-day discount. Nevertheless, you have enabled the customer to save face.

Sometimes you may have to sweeten a deal to make it sound new. For example, on a $1 million order, the method of shipment, the rate of delivery, the variety of color, or the warehousing arrangements may be phrased to sound like a big, new deal. Yet, the arrangements may cost you only a few dollars more than the original proposal.

Similarly, an offer to do a paint job on a house worth $500 for free may be a new deal to the house purchaser, but if the house's value is six figures, the deal really has not changed. You've just made it sound like a whole new offer.

WHEN TO IGNORE A PROMISE

Everyone makes promises in negotiations, but some are best ignored. You can learn to spot four kinds of promises that often hamper effective negotiations. They all come wrapped in indefinite suggestions. Nothing specific is ever promised, but the tone of what is said encourages you to let your dreams run wild. We call these kinds of promises the "Big Four." They fall into these categories:

- *Indefinite conspiracy promises.* "Protect me on this budget," the production head says to the treasurer when the two are alone, "and no one will ever need to know we're golfing buddies."

- *Indefinite secrecy promises.* "Give me that price," the customer winks, "and no one will be the wiser."

- *Indefinite opportunity promises.* "Vote with me, and we'll go a long way together," the president says to the directors.

- *Indefinite threat promises.* "Let's all agree to this," the office manager says to her staff, "to avoid any misunderstandings upstairs about our loyalty."

TIPS FOR EVALUATING AN INDIRECT PROMISE

Always assume there could be a divorce, and then measure the cost to you. What will happen if one of you breaks the promise? How disappointed will you be? How much money will it cost you? How much will it cost you in terms of ethics, peace of mind, or anger?

On the other hand, it costs you nothing to go along with a Big Four promise if you understand that what is promised may not materialize. For example, a board chairman promised a senior executive the company presidency during a company showdown. The chairman needed support right at that moment. The indefinite promise was, "If we can get through this together, I'll do my darndest to get you the presidency." Of course, it never happened but, as the senior executive told us, "My main objective was to get three more years under my belt before retirement. I never wanted the presidency, and I certainly never counted on it."

Just remember that, when you count on indefinite promises, you are agreeing to something now to gain something indefinite. Problems are always possible. For a classic example of promise tactics, consider the many recent mergers and acquisitions. A lot of people changed their expectations when the ink dried on the merger agreements.

Indefinite promises have caused disappointments in many ways. Here are some examples of how they can go sour:

- Career promises that never materialize.
- Financing that is full of contingencies and that never materializes.
- Friendship that evaporates after your would-be pal gets what he or she wants.
- Vows of secrecy that, when broken, leave you exposed.
- Promises for additional orders that are forgotten after you lower your price.
- Service promises that are never kept.
- Mutual support alliances that dissolve when your partner loses interest in your long-term goals.
- Protection promises that leave you vulnerable when support is suddenly withdrawn.
- Social contacts who fail to open doors for you as promised.
- Promises to swap information which turn out to be one-way exchanges.

THREE KEYS TO GETTING WHAT YOU ARE PROMISED

1. If the promise is crucial to your future needs, get it in writing in a form which states what you get and when you get it. Demand specific, not contingent, terms.

2. Get a written agreement that describes a significant penalty that will result if the promise is not kept. For instance, a broken promise concerning your career might provide for handsome severance pay. A broken future order promise might provide renegotiation of contract price. A broken service contract might provide financial compensation for services not rendered.

3. When accepting indefinite promises, whether they involve secrecy, friendship, best efforts, protection, social contacts, or information exchanges, try to take the future aspects out of the transaction. Now, while the other person still needs you, ask, "Where

does this leave me if you get run over by a car today?" Think twice if your opponent cannot answer with specifics that protect you.

It pays to keep indefinite promises out of a negotiation. Such promises may come true, but never put yourself in a position to need or rely on them.

HOW TO RECOGNIZE AND ADJUST TO SUDDEN CONFRONTATION

This is a troubling situation wherein—

- You have not been involved in negotiations with the person or group involved.
- You have not agreed to negotiate with the opponent.
- You have not prepared an agenda for possible negotiations with this group.
- You are involved in other things when the confrontation occurs.

EXAMPLES OF SUDDEN CONFRONTATION

The unexpected confrontation is usually highly emotional or crisis-laden. This is why your opponent has not observed the usual prenegotiation protocol, as in these cases:

- The phone in your office rings. A customer is in a rage and shouts that, unless you meet a list of demands, all future business is cancelled.
- The truck driver finds you in the plant cafeteria and pleads, "I drove all night to get this stuff to you, and now they want me to lay over until they can unload tomorrow. I just wanted to tell you I'm pulling out of here in 30 minutes one way or another."
- You look up from your work and see your biggest creditor standing in the doorway with a second man. The creditor brushes into your office grimacing and sounding gruff as he says, "We're here for my money, and if we don't get it, John here has the authority to put a padlock on your door."
- Late one evening, you are riding downstairs on an elevator with a subordinate, who suddenly blurts out, "I need a raise. I think I'm being taken advantage of."

- The union business agent catches you in the hallway, and six other employees soon surround you. "Hey," the business agent says, "This has got to stop, right this second, or everyone goes out on strike before lunch!" Of course, you have no idea what the problem is.

- A key assistant storms into your office and says with clenched teeth, "Unless that so and so is transferred out of my area, I will leave before quitting time today!"

SIX GUIDELINES FOR COPING WITH SUDDEN CONFRONTATIONS

1. *Smile, with your face and with the tone of your voice, and say, "I'm ready to talk."* Never respond to confrontation with confrontation.

2. *Act in a reasonable manner as you start to change the negotiation location.* Never negotiate on the turf your opponents thrust upon you. Wherever you find yourself in a face-to-face confrontation, whether in the plant, your office, the cafeteria, the elevator, or elsewhere, start moving yourself to some other location as soon as you have smiled and said, "I'm ready to talk." Tell your opponent, "Come with me, where we can have a better place to meet."

3. *Whenever possible, assemble a team on the way to your new location.* Thus, you might arrange to pass a person who can help you in this unexpected confrontation. As you pass this potential ally, say, "Come along, we have an important matter to discuss." Let your opponent hear what you say to the other person. Refer to the talk as "an important matter." Never use words such as problem, crisis, or emergency. Such terms might inflame your opponent or inflate your opponent's concept of how much the confrontation has shaken you.

   In a one-on-one confrontation late at night or in a remote location, you obviously cannot use the team tactic.

4. *Go to a site that you select.* You have told your opponent you are ready to talk, you have possibly assembled a team, and you have chosen new physical surroundings. This shows that you plan to have some control of the discussion, too. Plus, you have bought some time for your opponent to cool off.

   Now, suddenly excuse yourself for a harmless reason and say, "I'll be right back; I just want to be sure we are not interrupted." This provides more cooling off time just when your opponent may be getting worked up by anticipating the start of your meeting.

5. *Insist on a written agenda.* Smile once again and say, "Okay, I'm ready to talk, but let's get an outline down on paper to be sure I get everything that's on your mind." At this point, ostentatiously produce pad and pencil and get ready to write. This is a great control technique. If everyone gets on you at once in a group confrontation, you can say, "Hey, slow down; one at a time. I can't hear what you are saying." Because you are the one writing the agenda, you control the pace. As you slowly write, read back each sentence.

   Your physical act of writing things down will worry opponents. "Why," they will wonder, "make such a careful record?" This tactic goes a long way to eliminate random threats, expletives, and silly demands.

6. *Try to get a break or an adjournment after completing the written agenda.* Say, "I need to think about all of this." This is a dangling carrot. They may interpret "think about this" as a sign that you are going to give them what they want.

   With or without an adjournment, following these steps helps you establish an orderly negotiation climate. It also gives you an opportunity to negotiate every step of the way on your terms.

KEY TACTIC: How to Handle Telephone Confrontations

Use a variation of face-to-face tactics in sudden confrontations on the phone.

1. *Change the setting by calling back on another phone.* Pleasantly say, "I'm ready to talk," and explain that you can't talk on the present phone because it is not private enough.

2. *Take the opportunity to assemble a team before you call your opponent back.* Announce someone new with you or say, "I just dug out some new files."

3. *Allow something (real or otherwise) to interrupt you for 30 seconds or so.*

4. *Announce that you want to write everything down.* Read each point back to the caller.

5. *If you can, ask, "May I call back after I have a chance to go over all of this?"*

6. *The best way to prolong a phone conversation is to offer to write a letter outlining the agenda.* Say, "I need to be sure I've gotten everything right about what you have told me and what you want." At this point you are not agreeing to anything. Your task is to keep things clear.

   In some cases, you might ask the caller to write a letter. But first, ask yourself what problems might result. For instance, writing a letter might get your opponent in a legal mood or force that person to copy the letter to others who could make it difficult to back off later.

HOW TO HANDLE VERBAL AND EMOTIONAL ABUSE

When someone hurls verbal and emotional abuse at you, remember a fundamental fact. People who regularly resort to verbal and emotional abuse are usually the world's worst negotiators. They tend to think less clearly than other opponents, and they advertise their negotiating positions for all to see and hear. Beware, though, for this generalization does not apply to some clever negotiators who feign a high emotional state to test you for fear or to cause you to lose control. For these people, verbal abuse is an act which they will quickly abandon when they see you are not falling for it.

When you come under verbal or emotional abuse, smile and say, "I am willing to talk." Explain that you will be writing down the person's positions to make sure that you understand them. Your writing helps cool down the situation. Usually, the person confronting you will retreat a little out of fear of being recorded in a bad light. After all, who can be exactly sure why you are writing this down?

Two additional tactics to remember are to arrange a cooling off period to give your opponent time to regain control and to never fight fire with fire. Never return verbal and emotional abuse in a way similar to what is being heaped on you.

You can prepare yourself for encounters with abusive negotiators by reviewing two sections in this book. "How to React to Accusations from Your Opponent," (page 6), will remind you not to feel singled out when someone blames you for something. After all, we come from a society in which many people are well practiced at this tactic. The section, "How to Recognize and Adjust to Sudden Confrontation," (page 46), will remind you of ways to buy time, how to exercise your control of the negotiation location, and reasons to write down the other person's demands.

KEY TACTIC: *Avoid Being Goaded into a Lawsuit*

In recent years, a disturbing new tactic has come to light. It has nothing to do with a particular negotiation, but everything to do with getting something from you. We call this the "Liable-and-Damages Syndrome," and it goes like this.

Your opponent deliberately goads you to go on record in some fashion for which you can later be sued. It's all planned! For example, a multimillion dollar suit was filed against an individual member of a town's real estate zoning board. The suit alleged that the individual, by what he said and how he said it, damaged an applicant whose zoning proposal was ultimately turned down by the board. The suit is backed by the recorded transcripts of the zoning meetings.

WHAT TO DO WHEN A BLUFF FAILS

There used to be something macho about a good bluff. Even today, many people boast about their bluffing victories. "I said to them, 'Take it or leave it'." "I put my foot down and said, 'That's the way it is!'" "I drew the line and dared them to cross it."

Many of the bluffs that were once effective are now passé, yet people continue to use them and fail completely. Such people tend to be poor negotiators who cannot comprehend why their tactics do not work.

Of course, when someone tries a passé bluff on you, it increases your negotiating opportunities. It sends you a signal that your opponent is relying on old habits. Because the bluff no longer fits contemporary conditions, it often can be artfully turned against the person using it.

SIX PASSÉ NEGOTIATING BLUFFS

- *A bluff based on limitations of women.* This might take the form of, "You had better mind your place around here and not get any women's lib notions." Or, "We seriously doubt that under certain circumstances you could keep your objectivity." And in yet another version, "Somehow, our people feel more comfortable having it come from a man."

- *A bluff based on company, product, service, or skill uniqueness.* "If you want what only we can give you, you've got to expect to pay more." You might also hear, "You'll find that I'm the only one who can really handle your problems," or in another situation, "When you buy our company, you'll find there is no competition anywhere that can touch us." Or, "Our people are so loyal that you could never have a union here."

- *A bluff based on promotion that requires 100 percent dedication and loyalty.* Show us that you're with us on this, and we'll take care of you." "Forget what they're trying to get you to do. They haven't been around as long as we have." You might also hear, "We can't match their offer, but we know how dedicated you are to our organization," and "I'm going to deny your request, but I know I can count on your loyalty to me."

- *A bluff based on conforming to values.* This one sounds like this, "Unless you agree with us, I'm afraid we'll have to assume that your values are in doubt," and "We can be sure of one thing, you wouldn't want to do business with those people with their ethics." Two other variations: "I don't have to give you any reasons. You know my values and that should be sufficient," and "You'll change your mind when you think it over because we see eye to eye about the things that count."

- *A bluff based on social hierarchy.* Have you ever heard, "I can't go along with your plan because it wouldn't be fair to my peers"? Here are some variations of the same bluff: "You had best do it our way, or you'll be drummed out of the club." "We can't go along with that demand because it would upset the social order around here." "You can't ask that of our kind of people."

- *A bluff based on restricted information.* With this type of bluff, you might hear, "If you knew what we know, you'd understand why you have to agree." Or, "Believe me, you can rest easy on this because there are invisible powers at work." "Go along with this, and I'll see to it that the right things go into your personnel record." "Don't ask me to tell you that. You wouldn't want to know. Just trust me."

THREE WAYS TO HANDLE A BLUFF THAT FAILS

Whether a bluff that fails is yours or your opponent's, these three steps can help everyone save face and get on with negotiations:

1. *Check the social values and attitudes related to the bluff.* Determine if the failed bluff no longer matches social values or realities. If your bluff has been out of step with today's world, back off. Never be trapped with an obsolete image about yourself. If your opponent's bluff fails because it is clearly passé, use humor to highlight the person's weakness. Here are some possibilities:

   - "Your company has no competition, but that's what they said about the Edsel."

   - "There are hidden forces at work on your behalf? That's what went wrong in Watergate."

   - "You say she's not objective enough to handle the job? That's what they said about Madame Curie."

2. *Back off from intimidation.* When a failed bluff was based on passé intimidation, real problems can arise. If you seemed to threaten your opponent with a currently unpopular attitude, you had best try to convince the person that you were only kidding, as in these instances:

- "Hey, I have a wife who knows twice as much as I do. I would never try to put down any woman."
- "Hold on. You misunderstood me. I never meant to imply that you were not my equal. I worked my way through night school."
- "Wait a minute. I never meant to imply that we are keeping anything back from you."

   If an opponent tries to intimidate you with passé attitudes or values, never lose emotional control. Hit back with implied embarrassment from outsiders. For example,

- "What would they say upstairs if they thought you were acting so macho?"
- "Can you imagine how it would look if it came out that you're so bigoted?"
- "Imagine how it would look to my customers if they thought you threatened to cut your quality and jeopardize their safety to hold your price."

3. *Assume that any failed bluff does some damage to the negotiator who tried to use it.* If this happens to you, expect negotiations with this opponent to get tougher. If it happens to an opponent, act as if you were not making much of the exposed weakness, but test the opponent on everything from that point forward.

SECTION 3

THE ADVANTAGES OF BEING CAUTIOUS WITH THIRD PARTIES

SECTION 3

THE ADVANTAGES OF BEING
CAUTIOUS WITH THIRD PARTIES

Imagine trying to complete a merger without a lawyer, or try getting yourself through an audit without an accountant! We need a certain amount of third-party involvement in our negotiations. This is a fact of life. But just as true is the reality that third parties can overstep their authority. The result is a detrimental influence on your deal making.

This section presents 13 types of situations in which you might encounter third parties. We discuss guidelines for dealing with necessary third parties, uninvited intruders, and well-meaning loved ones. Your goals are to recognize and limit harmful effects of third parties and to learn what to do to get maximum benefit when you do rely on outsiders.

TECHNIQUES FOR REDUCING OUTSIDE MEDDLING

Countless negotiations are ruined when a third party suddenly injects new concerns into a discussion. Of course, many negotiations require a lawyer, accountant, banker, or other expert to implement what has been decided. This type of third-party involvement is usually not a problem. What is troublesome is a third party who refuses to simply implement a deal and instead intrudes as if he or she were one of the negotiators.

HOW THIRD PARTIES CAN DERAIL NEGOTIATIONS: THREE EXAMPLES

- A lawyer sits down with a buyer to draw up a routine contract. Soon, the attorney is talking about similar sales and market values. The conversation has nothing to do with the lawyer's function, yet it causes the buyer to have second thoughts. Eventually, the deal falls through.

  Lesson: Limit who talks about what.

- An accountant is consulted to help set up employee stock option plans relative to a nearly consummated merger. The accountant knows nothing about the specialized machinery used in a small capital-intensive industry, but nonetheless starts to raise questions about the production methods one of the two merging companies uses. The accountant's questions bring negotiations to a halt because they antagonize one of the owners.

  Lesson: Watch for personality clashes.

- Two bank presidents nearing completion on negotiations for an intrastate merger decide to meet socially with their spouses. During their evening together, one of the spouses drinks too much and says, "How can you folks live in such an urban area? Doesn't the traffic get you down?"

  The other couple laughs defensively, and one of them says,

"We couldn't bear to be out of the mainstream." In their home that night, the city-dwelling president's spouse asks, "Do you really think we have much in common with them? They may be a little too provincial for us." The deal never materializes.

Lesson: We can only guess how many negotiations go sour because a spouse suddenly provides a new perspective on negotiations. Be careful!

SIX RULES TO REDUCE MEDDLING

Rule 1: Pick negotiating times and places which limit the chance that third parties will interrupt or otherwise change the climate you have established.

Rule 2: When terms of a negotiation are final but not yet signed, sealed, and delivered, sign papers as soon as possible. This allows less chance of other people second guessing the deal.

Rule 3: Always insist on privacy and confidentiality during all stages of a negotiation. This reduces the chance that your opponent will discuss negotiations with third parties who might influence your opponent's positions with their own viewpoints.

Rule 4: When follow-up activities are necessary after a negotiation, always offer to do the detail work. Many people are lazy and will be pleased to let you tend to details which you deliberately have made appear unimportant. Say, for example,

- "I'll be happy to run that past the tax people."
- "I'll be happy to get the legal boilerplate together."
- "I'll be happy to pull this all together on our word processor."
- "I'll be happy to take the trip out there to pick up those records."
- "Let me handle the details; you're too busy and I really don't mind."

The more details you handle to help a deal go through, the less chance that outside sources will mess things up.

Rule 5: Anticipate possible meddling before negotiations start. Then carefully monitor problems during negotiations. Watch for—

- Personality conflicts.
- Overly talkative or rambling people who might upset the direction, mood, or clarity of the issues you consider central to negotiations.
- Unduly loyal, agressive, or defensive people whose well-meant assistance may do more harm than good when their actions appear to speak for you in ways you don't intend.

- People who are too expert. Some people try to dazzle with their expertise. This can sidetrack negotiations because the dazzler may raise peripheral issues related to his or her expertise, but unimportant to the negotiations.

Rule 6: Be very careful about mixing business and pleasure until negotiations are final. Otherwise, you risk personality conflicts and off-handed remarks which can have a negative influence on negotiations. This includes social get-togethers where spouses or others are present.

WHAT TO DO ABOUT A BIASED REFEREE

Most people know that, if you get a tough judge in a lawsuit, you can appeal. If you get a bad call in a sporting event, you can appeal to another official. Employees may try to go over their bosses' heads when they feel wronged.

But bias in negotiation is much trickier to identify. This is because the ultimate outcome of negotiation is an agreement to which you consent. Unless negotiations are related to legal proceedings or government agencies, they probably won't have formal referees. Instead, they often involve experts whom both parties allow to become part of the negotiations.

The problem is that too many experts are biased, and negotiators may overlook this fact until it is too late. Then, when they realize what has happened, they find there is no certain route for appeal.

HOW BIASED EXPERTS CAN SLANT NEGOTIATIONS

Presumably impartial experts can lose their perspective for many reasons. You will win more in negotiations if you learn to spot bias caused by—

- Opportunity
- Incompetence
- Revenge
- Power

Bias caused by opportunity: Typically, this type of bias involves money, as in this example. The buyers of a new house selected an independent appraiser to help them prevent paying a broker's price that might be overvalued.

What the buyers failed to note was that the independent appraiser had only one chance to collect a fee from the buyers. The broker, however, was a potential lifetime customer for the appraiser. Thus, although the broker never asked the appraiser to do anything wrong, the appraiser adjusted the value of the house to a figure that would be favorable to the broker.

Bias caused by incompetence: A small manufacturing company president decided to purchase an expensive computer system, but the president's banker refused to negotiate a loan until the company hired an impartial expert to help select the system.

"This seemed reasonable," the president said, "but I got careless and permitted the bank president to select the expert because I knew I needed the bank's blessing to get the loan.

"In our town, there is one accounting firm that stands head and shoulders above all the others. Our banker knew the accounting firm was heavily into computers and called one of the partners to arrange to have their top computer specialist assist me in my purchase decision. It seemed logical to me at the time. In our first brief meeting, this expert told me I should go with the same large computer manufacturer that the accounting firm used, and that was what I did."

The small manufacturing company ended up paying twice as much as it might have for a computer system that was not half as good as other new products that had come on the market in recent years. Yes, the company negotiated its bank loan, but at tremendous unnecessary cost due to the incompetence of the expert.

Bias caused by revenge: A small but rapidly expanding electronics company in New England sold 20 percent of its stock to a venture capital firm in the Southwest. A legal agreement drawn up at the time of purchase gave the new investor a two-year option to purchase another 15 percent of the stock at a value to be decided by an impartial expert who was named in advance in the agreement. As it turned out, the impartial expert was a partner in a large New York investment banking firm. Both parties knew and respected the New York firm.

Ten months after the option period began, the small company landed an enormous order from an aircraft company in California. The option holder elected to buy immediately because the company's future had no where to go but up. So, the New York expert went to New England to set a price. He did, and the stock sold for $2 million less than it was worth.

"We were shocked," the small company chairman said, "and we were curious how it could have happened. It took us another two years to get the true story. Now we know that our friend in New York hated the president of our big new California customer. It was a clash that went way back to when the aircraft company unexpectedly backed away from a deal with the New York group and caused them a lot of embarrassment. So, when he saw that one of our new products would save a bundle for our customer, he tried to hurt them by slowing down our growth. He knew we could use the stock sale money to really gear up our limited production facilities. This would have helped our customer, though, and he really hated them."

The small company management learned this conclusion from a confidential source and had no way of proving the information. The sale stuck. "If I had it to do over," the company's president said, "I would have insisted on a price determined by a panel of at least three experts. This would have prevented the problem."

Bias caused by power feelings: This type of bias refers to an expert who unfairly sides with one party to a negotiation merely to demonstrate the expert's power over the other negotiators. Bias caused by power feelings is not to be confused with opportunity bias, in which an expert favors one party in hopes of getting some future benefit, such as a favor or financial gain.

Bias caused by experts' power feelings is perhaps the single most damaging factor in negotiations. Because of it, careers have been shot down, professional negotiators have all but abandoned logic, and dire consequences have resulted, as the following examples indicate:

- A personnel consultant is asked to select an executive vice president from a field of three presumably equally competent vice presidents who run departments. The candidates agree in advance to accept the expert's opinion without rancor.

     When interviewing the three candidates, the personnel expert is surprised that the one female candidate has a very sharp sense of humor. This trait has helped her rise to the vice presidential level. People seem to like to work for her and to produce more for her. This is a considerable asset for the company. Yet, the personnel expert does not select her because he feels uncomfortable with her. He loses his feeling of power around her. So, he decides to teach her a lesson by passing her over for the promotion.

- The company money expert votes against a young marketing specialist's budget because the older employee wants to exert power over someone. Of course, the money expert knows nothing about marketing.

- A legal expert claims to be killing a merger for legal reasons. The real cause is the expert's personality conflict with the owner of one of the firms. The expert fears losing power to the new owner. Of course, loss of the potential merger sorely hurt both firms.

Effective consultants serve a valuable role in many types of negotiations. The secret is to be aware of problems that can accompany an outside expert and take steps to minimize them. These guidelines can help.

FIVE RULES FOR BRINGING EXPERTS INTO NEGOTIATIONS

1. Even when you are selecting the expert, expect and recognize—

   • Opportunity bias.
   • Incompetency bias.
   • Revenge bias.
   • Power-feeling bias.

2. In complex matters requiring expert opinions, insist on at least two, if not three, opinions.

3. Limit expert opinions to a narrow range. Don't permit accountants to call the shots on a marketing plan.

4. Closely examine an expert's credentials and make sure they match your needs. Don't accept someone as a computer expert simply because the person has experience with one aspect of computers. Do not accept an engineering expert whose primary experience is not related to your needs.

5. Avoid having related third parties pick your experts. Your banker may try to help you find your expert. Your lawyer may have a college classmate who is an expert. Or, your accountant may have "a client who is absolutely tops in the field." Avoid such well-meant recommendations. You take the time to locate and screen possible expert candidates, and then you decide.

THREE RULES FOR AVOIDING OUTSIDERS' DIRTY TACTICS

- If you are discussing a promotion with your boss over time, expect someone in your organization to resort to dirty tactics to influence your negotiations.
- If you are negotiating to establish power and authority in an organization, expect someone within your organization to use dirty tactics to limit you.
- If you are negotiating about any kind of money, always expect dirty tricks. Whether you are discussing mergers, fees, commissions, banking control of funds, loans, bonuses, whatever, someone will be tempted to horn in on your business. This temptation may be too much for anyone even remotely related to the money involved, and the result will be dirty tricks.

No one wants to be the victim of someone's manipulative ploys. You won't be if you follow these three rules.

RULE 1: KEEP YOUR MOUTH SHUT

What others don't know, they can't attack. Your best defense against outside dirty tactics is privacy in your negotiations. Watch out for busybodies, the people who spend their time trying to find out what is going on. Some busybodies act out of curiosity, while others are more calculating. Whatever their motive, their chatter can jeopardize your negotiations. Loose lips sink ships!

RULE 2: PLANT FALSE CLUES IF NECESSARY

If someone is going to use dirty tricks against you, a strategically placed false clue can turn their ill will into your good luck. These examples illustrate why:

- A sales manager was planning to offer a potential customer a major price reduction. The manager has reason to believe that someone in his industry trade organization was in clandestine contact with his principal ·competitor. So, he dropped into the trade association's office, mentioned the prospect, and said, "I want the business, but I really can't do much on price."

Sure enough, the competitor offered the prospect a modest price cut. The sales manager won the order with the price cut he had planned all along.

- Two department heads were competing for the same promotion. Over and over, one candidate told close associates how he would win the day. Through the office grapevine, the other department head heard the "win the day" remark. She, in turn, sent another message through the grapevine: she too was plotting to win and would go all out to show up her opponent.

  This caused the first department head to step up his campaign to win the promotion. His opponent, on the other hand, cooly arranged to have top management discover the other department head's office politics. At the same time, she conveyed the attitude that she really couldn't think about the promotion because she had to concentrate on her people and the company. Of course, the team player got the promotion.

RULE 3: GUARD THE SECURITY OF YOUR NEGOTIATIONS

Take precautions about both prenegotiation planning meetings and actual negotiating sessions. You can be low key and still protect your best interests. Here are some guidelines.

- Do not talk business over lunch if you might be overheard.
- Do not confide in people who are not connected with the negotiation over the phone, in public, or in writing.
- Check out the peripheral people around your negotiation, such as waitresses, clerical people, hotel staff, and strangers.
- Check out communications security, including phones, computers, messengers, and beepers.
- Pay attention to all paper records, such as notes, computer printouts, and reports. Make only a few copies, number them, and know who has what at all times. Do not leave papers lying around, especially during meeting breaks.

HOW TO HANDLE ESCALATING DEMANDS FROM REMOTE PLAYERS

The buyer says to the seller, "I would have signed our agreement today, but now the bank says you have to do this for me." So begins an escalating demand from a remote player. Such demands usually come—

- Unexpectedly and at the last moment.
- From an authority you have little chance to control.
- In a take-it-or-leave-it message.

Negotiators' knee-jerk reactions to escalating demands tend to be either panic or instant agreement, but you have other options.

HOW TO RECOGNIZE DEMAND ESCALATION FROM REMOTE PLAYERS

Demand escalation from remote players can take a variety of forms. At the last moment your opponent can dredge up any outside authority. Demands can be based upon real or imagined requirements of—

- the law
- the bank
- the board
- accounting practices
- safety
- engineering
- public relations
- inflation
- the labor contract
- time
- availability
- government regulations

Remember, a remote player who dictates a take-it-or-leave-it escalating demand is counting on you to panic. Be ready when you hear phrases such as these from an opponent:

- "The law says there is no other way."
- "The bank insists!"
- "Labor contract terms mean that . . ."

- "Time has run out; it's now or never."
- "The rules leave us no alternative."

FIVE TIPS FOR RESPONDING TO DEMAND ESCALATION WITHOUT PANIC

1. *Smile or look pensive.* Never show emotion, especially anger or fear.
2. *Request an adjournment.* Say something like, "I need to consider this development with my people." Do not say which people you have in mind. Let your opponent wonder.
3. *Request some pause in the meeting if an adjournment is not possible.* The break may only last 15 minutes, or it could be longer if you want to keep your opponent in suspense.
4. *Rely on your negotiating skills.* Is this situation more like a surprise deadline (see page 3) or a last-minute addition (see page 12)? Size up the situation and decide which response tactics best fit your present needs. Take time to plan your course; there is no reason to panic.
5. *Respond in an appropriate manner.* Here are some helpful hints:

   - Test your opponent. Send signals that if that's the way it is, maybe the deal is off.
   - If your test fails to produce an alternative from your opponent, match authorities. Insist on calling experts of your own to examine the position of your opponent's remote player.
   - Be nice. Don't let a mood of acrimony set in.
   - Remember, you have every right to insist on starting negotiations over. Your opponent raised the new issues, so take your time to make a deal that is what you need.

WHAT TO DO WHEN YOU'RE DOUBLE-TEAMED

Ask any landlord, sales person, broker, builder, customer service manager, car mechanic. They'll all agree that no situation is tougher than being double-teamed when negotiating to buy, sell or adjust something.

Double-teaming is a fact of everyday business life. Here's one horror story from a furniture store owner: "First *she* wants a blue carpet at a discount," he says. "Then after I break my price and cut the carpet, they both come into the store and start screaming—*he* hates blue and *he* never agreed to blue. *They* say they won't pay me a penny for the carpet piece I've prepared for them."

It's the same story in the brokerage business: "*He* calls me up and takes a put option on 600 shares," the broker tells us. "I buy the options and charge their account $3600 plus my commission. Then the market goes up, and *she* comes charging into the office threatening to sue the firm for the loss of *her* money. 'I told him the market was going to go up,' she says, 'and you knew the market was going up. I want *our* money back in 24 hours, or I go to the SEC.'"

HOW TO SPOT THE DOUBLE-TEAM

Your first step in tackling the double-team is to spot it at the outset. Train yourself to look for the double-teaming method in any of several different forms.

THE GOOD COP/BAD COP

This is the most common and easily recognized form of double-team. It occurs when two people go against one—in a negotiation—by playing carefully contrived roles of "good guy" and "bad guy."

The purpose is to keep the negotiating opponent under pressure from conflicting emotional appeals. Examples are—

- Daddy threatens to spank the child unless the child complies with his request. Then, Mommy hugs and kisses the child and begs the child for compliance "so that Daddy won't spank you."

- The husband and wife sellers of a property take opposite roles with a buyer. The husband says, "Take it or leave it. I'm all out of patience." Then his wife takes the buyer aside and says, "I want to help you get what you want. Let's see if we can't figure something out."

- A boss calls in an employee and introduces him to an expert. The expert tells the employee that his work level is way below the average. The boss takes the employee aside and says: "Never mind the expert. I'll take care of you, *but* can you possibly take on more work so I can be sure he doesn't put his feelings in writing to our superiors?"

Note: Putting it another way, one team member brings the good news while the other team member brings the bad news. The pleasure and pain is always balanced to create compliance in the individual upon whom this negotiating tactic is used.

KEEP A SHARP EYE OUT FOR THE INVISIBLE OPPONENT

While the good cop/bad cop method of double-teaming is common, it is also the easiest kind to handle because you can see and talk to both of the parties teamed up against you.

More difficult is the invisible double-team. Just as you think you're negotiating with only one person and nearing agreement, your opponent says, "I've got to check this with my boss," or, "Excuse me while I go upstairs to get approval."

In situations like these, you can see only one opponent, but you're really negotiating with two. And they can play you like a fish on a long line while they take turns giving and withdrawing their offers.

SPOTTING THE INANIMATE HALF OF A DOUBLE-TEAM

Even tougher is the situation where the second member of the team is not a person but a thing, an inanimate object that carries the weight of authority.

Look for authority symbols like these. You'll know you're being double-teamed in a negotiating situation when you hear remarks like these:

- "Let me punch that into *the computer* to see how it looks."

- "Let me look up those prices in our company *price list* to see what they say."

- "Let me look up the *legal precedent* for this."
- "Let me check our company *policy manual* on this."

The inanimate opponent is the most insidious type, because most people tend to accept such symbols of authority without question. In reality, they can be the most powerful weapons in your opponent's negotiating arsenal.

HOW TO FIGHT THE DOUBLE-TEAM BY EVENING THE ODDS

As soon as you recognize the double-team, whether it is visible, invisible, or inanimate, you can fight back by creating a second member of your own team.

Here's how: Let's say, for example, that your opponent surprises you by bringing along his lawyer, acountant, banker, engineer, or other expert. Your strategy is to match expertise by calling in an expert of your own—or at least calling one on the telephone.

Create an invisible ally: The same approach works well when you're up against an invisible opponent.

- If your opponent says, "I'll have to check that out upstairs, *you say*, "I understand. I've got to run this by my people, too."
- If your opponent says, "I've got to check this with our experts," *you say*, "I wonder if they'll agree with what my experts have told me."

Introduce your own authority symbol: Here again, when confronted with an inanimate symbol of authority, your strategy is to even the odds by introducing an authority symbol of your own.

- If your opponent says, "I've got to see how this fits our company policy," *you say*, "I'll be interested to see how it compares to the other companies I've been in touch with."
- If your opponent says, "I've got to run these numbers by the computer," *you say*, "That's a good idea. Let me take them to our own data processing people, too."

KEY TACTIC: Get It In Writing

When you finally reach agreement in a situation in which you've been double-teamed, insist on putting the terms of your agreement in writing, and have the document signed by all the persons authorized to make the agreement with you.

Your written agreement can range from a simple memo of understanding to a full-blown legal document, but your object in every case is the same: to prevent an invisible opponent from showing up at the last minute to say "I never approved that," or, "He didn't have the authority to make that arrangement."

To protect yourself, make sure your written document includes your opponent's signature, his job title, and language to the effect that he has the authority to make this agreement. Check with your lawyers for the precise wording.

WHY IT'S WISE TO LIMIT OUTSIDERS' INFLUENCE AT YOUR NEGOTIATING TABLE

Who of us has not seen groups of negotiators assembled for the benefit of television cameras just before negotiations start or upon concluding a negotiating session. Traditionally, the media gave newsworthy pre- and postnegotiation coverage to key national or governmental negotiations. More and more, however, we see local newscasts about negotiations of local teachers' salary scales, plant union contracts, and fire department wages. This increasing coverage of local bargaining sessions is not restricted to television. Radio stations and newspapers are expanding coverage as well.

BEWARE OF THE IMAGE SPECIALISTS

Whether you run a small local company, a large national firm, or an international organization, you are aware of your image and its importance to your business. So, too, are the people on both sides of union negotiations, as well as the politicians who must all appeal to local constituencies, the sales people who have some product or service to promote, and the lobbyists with their professional or industry cause to represent. Even the arms negotiations meetings of the world's superpowers are bombarded with outside propaganda designed to influence negotiations.

A trend today is that older types of specialty businesses designed to assist lobbyists, such as statistical and legal research services, are giving way to a new type of business that can also influence negotiations. These new businesses are the image specialists, and they include pollsters, direct mail experts, fashion and makeup consultants, TV camera and format technicians, even jury selection experts. The key effort is no longer to influence negotiations by logic. The focus now is to bring emotion to bear on negotiations. While the image specialists are making this practice big business, they are by no means the only ones using emotional appeals.

Now, negotiating groups from many camps are learning the lessons of television. Some examples follow.

HOW EVERYONE IS GETTING ON THE IMAGE BANDWAGON

- Eighth grade students in a small town went on a one-day strike the day before the negotiations between local teachers and the school board began. "The purpose," one student told a television news team, "is to show that we believe our teachers need more money."

- Female employees of a small rural bank ended up on a national talk show to explain why they picketed their bank to protest unfair treatment of working women.

- As the President of the United States negotiated with Congress for more aid for the Contras in Nicaragua, more than 30 Catholic bishops marched through Washington, D.C., to meet on the Capitol steps. Arrests of some marchers were splashed before the nation on the evening television news. Who would doubt that members of Congress re-examined their positions in light of the publicity and its impact on their constituents?

HOW TO MINIMIZE THE INFLUENCE OF UNEXPECTED SPECTATORS AT YOUR NEGOTIATIONS

- When environmentalists try to influence federal or state agency negotiations with a local plant by staging sit-ins at the plant, we know that someone has made the internal negotiating sessions widely known in order to bring outside pressure.

- When lawyers go public with a case, we recognize that they are inviting the outside public into the internal legal negotiations in an attempt to influence juries, judges, or regulatory agencies.

- When nonunion employees go public with a symbolic outside demonstration concerning internal employee/employer negotiations, we perceive an appeal for negotiating pressure from the outside.

All of these tactics come down to appeals to outside opinions as pressure sources. Here is a three-step plan to reduce the risk of emotional appeals to outside opinions.

Step 1: To minimize the risk of outside spectators at your negotiations, try to diffuse the emotions of everyone at your negotiating table.

Step 2: Insist that all parties to your negotiations agree not to go public, or else you do not negotiate. Do this before any word of your negotiation leaks. Once someone goes public, it is too late to refuse to negotiate, because the whole world is watching.

Step 3: Plan exactly how you will deal with any unforeseen public knowledge of your negotiations. What will you say? In what media? Who will speak for you? What image do you want to project if the worst happens and you are negotiating in the public spotlight? Choose your strategies long before you need to fall back on them.

WHEN TO USE OUTSIDE CONTACTS

WHY AN OPPONENT MAY HESITATE TO NEGOTIATE WITH YOU

Your opponent seems to be taking your stated desire to negotiate very lightly. This could be for any number of reasons, including—

- Lack of understanding about how serious you are.
- Absence of awareness of how strong you are.
- Inadequate knowledge about how nice you are.
- Distorted perspectives about how reasonable you can be.
- Blindness to who you know.
- Ignorance of your competitive alternatives.

Find specific ways to have outside parties tell your opponents what you want them to know, and nothing more. Thus, you arrange to have your banker tell your opponent's banker, "She's the fairest kind of person." Or, you arrange to have your college roommate, who knows your opponent, say, "He knows all the people we know."

HOW TO DEAL WITH A CONFUSED OPPONENT

Your opponent seems honestly confused about some part of your negotiating proposals. Often, an opponent does not understand something that will help your case, such as—

- The numbers.
- The beneficial imagery.
- The potential long-term benefits.
- The technical information.
- Some reality, such as competition closing in, banks getting tougher, or people getting restless.

Arrange to have a truly neutral third party present the information for you. Select someone your opponent will listen to because he or she is neutral.

Thus, you say, "I insist you check these numbers with your accountant." Or, "Why not check this out with your old banker friend?" "The engineers in your trade organization can explain the technical details." Or, "Ask your good friend, Sally, about what she sees in the future concerning this idea."

KEY TACTIC: When to Call in a Third Party

Never invite your opponent to invite a neutral third party into your negotiating situation unless your case in a specific area is so strong that you know the third party's reaction in advance. If you have any doubt, forget it.

HELPFUL HINTS FOR KEEPING UNINVITED PROFESSIONALS AT BAY

Unlike outsiders you ask to join a negotiation, some professionals arrive without invitation. This section explains how to deal with them.

A SUREFIRE RESPONSE TO UNSOLICITED ADVICE

A professional friend of someone connected to the negotiations offers unsolicited opinions. When this happens, stop everything and tell your opponent that both of you must review the security aspects of the negotiation. How exactly did the friend learn about your negotiation? How much does he or she know? How can we prevent a similar occurrence? How can we assure one another, right now, that this wasn't deliberately planned to exert pressure? "Unless we can clear all of this up," you say, "the negotiations can't resume, because they are in danger of further influence from outsiders."

HOW TO REACT TO A PROFESSIONAL WHO SHOWS FAVORITISM

People on both sides invite a professional they regard as neutral. For example, you may ask a town clerk to bring records. Problems result when the professional turns out to be unwilling to watch and instead starts to voice ideas about the negotiation. At the first sign of this busybody behavior, stop everything until the busybody leaves. If necessary, you can always arrange to have this person come back for one specific purpose, and then leave immediately.

In another example, an independent banker, appraiser, broker, or commission or fee agent who is not part of your negotiations starts to ask questions, imposes opinions, or both. For example, a banker who was asked to hold escrow funds wants to know about all parts of the negotiation related to the funds. Such questions threaten to reopen negotiations if they make the other party nervous about what has been decided.

Tell independent people exactly what negotiators want and don't want. A good excuse is, "We've decided not to discuss what we agreed or why. Therefore, will you simply do this for us?"

WHAT TO DO WHEN PROFESSIONALS TRY TO TAKE OVER YOUR GAME

Before you invite your lawyer, banker, accountant, or consultant into your negotiations, you always take steps to have them understand—

1. Your goals.
2. Your feelings.
3. The specific contribution your professional is to make to your negotiations.

When you do this, most professionals will support you 100 percent.

Sometimes, however, professionals get carried away by the negotiations and try to extend their authority and influence. A professional who really likes to hear himself or herself talk may try to become the leader of your negotiations. If professionals on your team start to overreach themselves, seek a postponement or a break in your negotiations. Straighten the situation out with your professional in a private discussion. If this doesn't work, get a replacement!

WHAT TO DO WITH THE OTHER SIDE'S PROFESSIONALS

If your opponent's lawyer, accountant, consultant, banker, or other expert starts to talk to you as if it were his or her negotiation, say with a smile, "Hold it! We seem to be confusing what's happening here. It is my understanding that I'm negotiating with your client, not with you. At least, that's what I agreed to. If I'm wrong, I think your client should tell me so now, so we can be clear on the rules of the game."

Your real negotiating opponent will react in one of two ways:

1. Reaffirm that what the professional said is his or her position and that it was said at your opponent's instruction.
2. Reveal that he or she is weak for some reason related to this professional.

If you sense that your opponent's professional is controlling your opponent, cancel or postpone negotiations until you can get a matching professional at your side, or begin to negotiate with the professional in an official capacity.

The key is to clear the air for yourself, so that you are not being double-teamed and outnumbered. You must negotiate with one person at a time, and you must let others know that this is your requirement.

TIPS FOR DEALING WITH OTHER THIRD PARTIES

The same rules that apply to professionals apply to any other people who try to take over a negotiation. Husbands and wives may try to double-team you. Don't let it happen. Two friends may try to double-team you, so don't let that happen either. And, if your spouse or friend starts to take over your leadership role in a negotiation, privately straighten the matter out or arrange to have this person leave.

WHAT TO DO WHEN A GROUP CONFRONTS YOU

A special situation occurs when a group suddenly confronts you and everyone in the group begins making demands of you. Never respond to any individual demands until you have insisted on having one spokesperson. Then, each time someone in the group makes a demand or states a position, do not directly answer that person. Instead, turn to the elected spokesperson and say, "Is that the group's position?"

If the answer is no, then you have them quarreling among themselves, which buys you time and information. If the answer is yes, respond to the designated group leader, not to any other individual. Don't be rude to anyone. Do everything very reasonably and politely.

HOW TO HANDLE THE BUYER-SELLER-AGENT TRIANGLE

In some cultures around the world, the marriage contract involves three people: the husband, the wife, and a third party who receives a fee for helping negotiate the contract. No pay, no marriage.

Unfortunately, today's negotiating world is often less black and white about who gets paid what, if anything, when a third party arranges or contributes to a contract between two other people. Many merging companies fail to reward the third parties who put them in touch with one another, and this can cause problems. When two parties to a negotiation forget to reward a third-party contribution, their forgetfulness may be—

- An oversight.
- A deliberate attempt to cheat someone out of money, power, or reputation.

A deliberate attempt to cheat someone out occurs because—

- Both parties to the negotiation are cheating, or
- One party is cheating and the other party doesn't know about it.

WHY PEOPLE FORGET A THIRD-PARTY'S CONTRIBUTION

People who do not intend to cheat may forget a contribution for several reasons:

- The third party may have made his or her contribution a long time ago. Thus, a real estate broker introduces two people one year, and they complete their deal one or two years later. By this time, both buyer and seller really have forgotten how they met. Time causes loss of money.
- The third party allows his or her role to be confused. Thus,

two negotiating people forget the third-party's contribution because the rules of the game were so blurred. Confusion causes loss of memory, especially if the confusion includes earlier friendship with a third party. For example, if a third party puts two people together on the golf course during a friendly game, the two people who make the deal may forget the business part of the outing.

- The third party loses contact with the two people he or she brought together. Out of sight, out of mind. Sometimes the third party may have died or become ill.

- The third party gains some obvious benefit from a transaction between two other people. This tangential benefit leads the parties who negotiate to forget that more is due. For example, a consultant brings two people together for an expected fee. One of these people refers the consultant to yet another situation which results in a lucrative new client for the consultant. The person making the referral may feel that he or she has done the consultant a big favor which overshadows the original fee. This is not a real trade off, but as an honest case of forgetting that more is due.

  This is often the case with powerful people who know their power is helping other people. They feel so good about it that it never occurs to them that they may be overlooking an earlier promise to someone about something else. The bigger a person's ego, the easier it is to forget a detail such as a fee that's due.

THREE RULES FOR POLICING A THIRD-PARTY FEE TRIANGLE

Rule 1: Whether you are a party to a negotiation or a third party who expects to earn a fee from assisting in a negotiation, get the specifics in writing. Ask your lawyer to guide you.

- It's no fun to be sued after a negotiation by a third party to whom your opponent may have made a promise that you knew nothing about. So, ask your opponent to go on record, in writing, about what is or is not owing to third parties.

- Having a third party telling other people that you welched does your reputation no good. This is especially unfair if you forget your responsibility without intending to do so. So, have a written record to prove your position and to remind you of your responsibility.

- A verbal agreement with a third party is rarely fair and always legally risky. Without a written record, the third party may inflate the agreement. This may be deliberate or an honest misunderstanding. Be very specific, never general, in any written agreement. Ask your lawyer for help.

Rule 2: Find a way to get your fee or commission written agreement recorded somewhere. If you can't have it recorded, have someone keep track of it. This someone could be your lawyer, banker, family member, or friend. This protects you over a lengthy period of time in the event of death, illness, or your own forgetfulness.

Rule 3: Keep time on your side if you are the third party earning a fee or commission. People who need you today often forget this fact tomorrow after you solve a problem for them. The dentist who pulls your aching tooth today may ask $100 before the tooth comes out, and you'll happily agree. But if the dentist doesn't ask when you're in pain, paying the $100 later may seem outrageous.

Even if the dentist asks beforehand and you agree, you may resent the dentist's bill when it comes in a month later. Time blurs your memory about how badly you originally needed to have the tooth pulled.

These tips will help protect your fee or commission:

- Police yourself about when best to establish your fee or commission, but always do this before performance.

- Police yourself about how soon you are to be paid after you do your work, but aim for payment as soon as possible.

- Police yourself to get advance legal advice about the written record that you have all of the other parties sign.

If you are a salesperson, police the records upon which your commissions are based, and do so in a timely fashion. Sometimes, one or more of your sales may be misapplied or overlooked by someone who makes a clerical error.

HOW TO THWART INTRUSIONS FROM FAMILY AND FRIENDS

By now you may expect outsiders to try to influence negotiations. You may not be as clear for the ways your own family members and friends can affect your deals. Families and family friends may form an effective negotiating team, but more often the combination produces a negotiating failure.

SITUATIONS WHERE FAMILY AND FRIENDS MAY TRY TO HELP

- Family and friends who try to resolve a serious marital dispute or divorce are usually guilty of confusing the issues with their own feelings, emotions, and opinions. Too often, the helper's feelings don't reflect the way the two people directly involved feel.
- In purchasing a car, home, or any costly product, family members and friends often recite information and opinions based on their feelings. Their input is seldom related to how the people making the purchase feel.
- Fellow workers can provide the worst advice about career choices and career negotiations. Colleagues often base advice on their work experiences and abilities, which usually have nothing to do with the person they are advising.
- Well-meaning people often assume they can help in your investment decisions, when in fact they know little about your personal financial situation and goals.

A WORD OF CAUTION ABOUT ACCEPTING ADVICE

Negotiation is such an important part of all of our lives that we must be alert to the dangers of acting on other people's opinions rather than our own instincts. In any important negotiation, we must be our own negotiating captain. This does not mean we should not listen to well-meant advice—we should. But we must go one step further and ask ourselves, "Am I being confused in ways that are corrupting my ability to be my own negotiator?"

Because we are so close to family and friends, we are easily influenced by them at times when we should rely on our own logic.

WHY OTHER PEOPLE'S PERCEPTION OF YOUR NEGOTIATIONS ARE CRUCIAL

Most societies place a high value on fairness. Even primitive cultures have ways to give an outnumbered enemy a fair public contest to save his or her life. Our legal principles are built on the public's concept of fairness.

Negotiations take place in front of social organizations: the family, the office, the plant, the neighborhood, the community, the nation, or the world. Some public is always watching your negotiations, even though it may be a very small public.

THE DIFFERENCE BETWEEN LOOKING FAIR AND BEING FAIR

Whether or not your negotiations appear to be fair becomes a critical factor. The public knows many negotiations are not fair, and people can live with this reality, as long as the situation appears fair. Consider these examples:

- Lobbyists have long been a fact of political life. Thousands of lobbyists unfairly influence governmental negotiations all of the time. But if they do it quietly and discreetly, the system still appears fair. However, if lobbyists are careless about their public image, they stand to lose the image of fair play, and this would greatly hinder their ability to negotiate successfully.

- In human rights, fairness goes hand-in-hand with morality. If a group rallying around a moral cause uses unfair tactics, the original moral issue which the group was trying to negotiate gets blurred, if not lost.

WHAT THE ARMS-LENGTH METHOD HAS TO DO WITH FAIRNESS

When two people agree to do something which might appear to be a conspiracy, they can often avoid the label of "unfair" if they invite an outsider to help them agree to what they already want. This tactic is manifested in negotiations as—

- A consultant making an arms-length judgment.
- A lawyer making a legal finding.
- An accountant quoting a tax code.
- A boss adjudicating an argument among three departments.

The trick of arms-length tactics is to create an image that decisions were reached through fair, logical discussion of parties in a triangular relationship. The third-party component of the triangle can be one of three types: a third-party expert, such as a consultant, accountant, or appraiser; a third-party reality, such as a law, regulation, or economic contract; or a third-party moral force, such as a boss, counselor, church leader, esteemed public figure, or even an attitude or opinion.

The two negotiating parties and the apparently impartial third party always maintain distance from one another. The third party is always perceived as telling the truth, being neutral, and being worthy of respect. The possibility that the third party is in one or both of the other party's pocket is never revealed. Often, the negotiator has not even discussed a "fix" with this third party. For example, if a board chairman who wants board agreement on something has already made a decision, the chairman can hire an outside consultant without ever saying that this person should vote a certain way. A smart consultant knows where the money for his or her fee is coming from and how the chairman really feels, despite instructions to "Call it like you see it."

If the impartial third party is a law, regulation, or moral attitude, it surfaces in the negotiation to serve a purpose. Laws, regulations, and moral attitudes which contradict the one being cited are carefully avoided because they might upset what has already been agreed.

The old lyrics, "It ain't what you do; it's the way that you do it," fit many negotiating situations. The best way to do it is in a manner that the public perceives to be at arms length. For example, sports fans may know that many fights are fixed, but not this fight, they reason. And so, neutral third parties often save the day for negotiations. The fight wasn't fixed after all, or so it appears.

SECTION 4

TECHNIQUES FOR SIZING UP AN OPPONENT

TECHNIQUES FOR SIZING UP AN OPPONENT

Just who is this person sitting across the table from you? What have other people told you about your opponent? What do your instincts tell you?

While our opponents seldom fall into completely predictable behavior patterns, they all send signals about their mood, their goals, their character, and much more. A key aspect of being a negotiator is learning to read these signals.

This section describes 15 situations that deal with the need to understand your opponent, and the section explains what you do to win in each instance. By looking at body language, by staying alert to unspoken motives, and by rationally assessing your opponent's demeanor, you will begin to gather information that can steer you through a successful negotiation with this person.

WHEN ARE TRUST AND A HANDSHAKE NOT ENOUGH?

We would never recommend eliminating handshakes and trust from the negotiating scene. But we do suggest asking yourself whose hand it is that you are shaking and how much you can trust this person.

As a rule, you will thoroughly check out your opponent's past, paying attention to the length of his or her relationships and with whom these relationships still exist. The old adage, "You are judged by the company you keep," is still valid. More and more, though, it is becoming difficult to learn who is keeping company with whom. Read the newspapers. The federal government threatens to give lie-detector tests to its own people, and a top company secretly hires investigators to work alongside employees to learn who is guilty of in-plant drug use and thievery.

No matter how extensive your background checks, ultimately you must rely on your judgment. What would the worst consequence be to you if your reliance on trust or a handshake proved wrong? Most people would agree that Chamberlain gambled too much on trust when he took Hitler at his word. In really important matters, demand more than a handshake and a promise!

Regard handshakes, promises, and trust as perishable commodities to be carefully monitored. Today our trust may be well founded, but we must remember that people change. Get legally binding contracts in writing, and include penalties for nonperformance.

HOW TO DECIPHER A PRETENTIOUS OPPONENT'S MESSAGE

An old saying goes, "Show me someone who toots his (or her) own horn, and I'll show you someone who has run over a lot of people." Unfortunately, many negotiators still get taken in by the righteous approach. This approach can range from an opponent who puffs up and says, "Do you doubt my word?", to one who inundates you with written evidence of his or her reliability, such as credit reports, magazine articles, bank statements, and memberships in prestigious academies, clubs, or philanthropies.

Whatever the form of an opponent's holier-than-thou approach, beware! The truth may be as the person represents it, but more likely the presentation is a smokescreen to impress you enough to stop you from digging further.

Here is one very successful negotiator's opinion of holier-than-thou negotiating types, "They're exactly like 99 percent of our prison population, all of whom blame their incarceration on someone else or on some unfortunate circumstance. They're always clean in their own eyes."

The very things that holier-than-thou opponents tell you they are proudest of are what you should investigate most carefully, and until you are proved wrong, discount.

A holier-than-thou opponent is not to be confused with a boaster, who is obvious and therefore less dangerous. The holier-than-thou type is often smoothly confident in approach, low key in manner, and constantly uttering pronouncements of piety, purity, and concern for you. Never let a holier-than-thou opponent sense your skepticism. Make it appear that you are basing your negotiating strategies and agreements on your opponent's good reputation. Meanwhile, keep upping your legal, financial, and performance requirements. Smile as you increase your demands, and your holier-than-thou opponent will never connect your demands with your disbelief of his or her story. The reason for this is that the holier-than-thou type believes most of what he or she is saying. The size of this person's ego is equal only to the size of your opportunity in this situation.

DISCOVERING WHO COUNTS TO AN OPPONENT

Ask yourself *who* is important to your opponent. This question, of course, often goes hand-in-hand with knowing what issues are most important to your opponent. If you find the *what*, it is often easy to find the *who*. On the other hand, you may discover the *who* first, and may never fully understand the issues which explain why that person is so important to your opponent. Nonetheless, even without knowing *why* a person is important, you can still look for ways to have this third-party precondition your opponent.

11 CLUES FOR FINDING THE PEOPLE WHO MATTER TO AN OPPONENT

- Where did he or she go to school?
- If married, to whom? If unmarried, who is in your opponent's intimate circle?
- With whom has your opponent worked in previous jobs? Do these people now figure in his or her life?
- Who considers your opponent their client? Which bankers, lawyers, accountants, doctors, and consultants?
- Who can you discreetly reach in his or her organization who might reveal clues? A secretary? A flunky? A disgruntled employee? A retiree? Any contact may want to gossip about your opponent.
- With what public activities is your opponent associated? Philanthropies? Civic offices? Honorary posts? Public boards?
- To what business associations does your opponent devote significant time? Trade associations? Boards of directors? Professional clubs or associations?
- What social activities and friends appear to be important to your opponent? Theater? Bridge? Clubs? Family? Church?

- What income sources are important to your opponent? Who affects those incomes? Superiors in his or her organization? His or her brokers? Publishers? Lawyers? Bankers? Associates in a second business?
- What sports, hobbies, or recreational activities are important to your opponent? Who spends time doing these pastimes with your opponent?
- Who are your opponent's mentors?

HOW ANOTHER PERSON CAN HELP SET UP A THREE-WAY LINK WITH YOUR OPPONENT

Sometimes it can be so easy, so natural to use a triangular approach to influencing your negotiations in a positive way. Of course, you must first learn who counts to your opponent. Among these people, there may be only one or two with whom you can logically, conveniently, and rapidly make contact. This example illustrates how the principle works.

The owner of a fairly large business in a small town contacted someone in a related business in a nearby town. The two had never met.

The person who received the owner's phone call remembers, "Suddenly, I hear from this owner who has decided to sell his business quickly. He asked if I would be interested.

"Of course, I agreed to talk. I knew our first meeting could turn out to be a serious negotiating session. But I knew absolutely nothing about the owner.

"I have a golfing buddy who is a lawyer in this guy's town. So, I called the lawyer to ask about the business owner. My friend didn't know the guy personally but had heard he was quite wealthy and had quite a temper.

"At least I had that much to go on when I met the guy. He was a difficult person to read. Very autocratic, opinionated, and impatient. He described his operations, though, and I was very impressed. In fact, I decided at that first meeting that I wanted the company. The owner said the seven-digit price was not negotiable. He was selling for health problems which he did not want to discuss.

"I took every record that I needed with me, and the more I saw of the business the more I wanted it. The price was within range, and based on what I had seen and learned about my opponent, I decided that price was nothing I could haggle about. Any effort to reduce the price might blow the whole deal. The owner had given me a ten-day verbal option. The next move was up to me.

"I was tempted to close the deal within a few days. Why wait, I thought, there's nothing to negotiate. But on the fourth day after our meeting, I decided to try to find out a little more about the owner. After all, I still had six days to play with.

"I called a number of friends on the chance that one of them knew the man. None did. So, I drove over to his town and stopped in at the local bank on the pretense of opening a personal checking account. While I was picking up the forms, I talked to a young loan officer at the customer desk. Without explaining my interest, I asked if she knew the owner. I said I'd recently met him for the first time. The young woman perked up when I asked the question. She didn't know him well, but she said he had a fine business and had been a bank customer for years. Everything seemed normal in the loan officer's reaction until she happened to say, 'Wasn't that a shame that he lost that automobile lawsuit. After all, it was dark, and the victim was wearing a black raincoat.

"I nodded in agreement and left the bank as fast as I could to go to my friend's law office. 'Why didn't you tell me about the accident?, I blurted out. My friend had no idea why I was there, but half an hour later we had all of the details about the accident, including the seven-figure judgment levied against the business owner.

"The next day, I visited the owner. 'No wonder you didn't want to discuss your health problems. I'd be sick too if I had your situation,' I said.

"Now we had a negotiation going because he could no longer pretend he didn't have a serious financial problem."

The person telling this story did buy the man's business, but saved about $350,000 off the purchase price by taking the time to develop a triangle. The buyer found a third party who counted to the buyer. The third party also happened to count to both parties because the third party had information about the judgment.

Lesson: No matter how sure you are about any agreement you are about to make, pause and try to put together a triangle. This can help you precondition an opponent in your favor and learn more about your opponent's motivation.

REASONS TO REMEMBER BODY LANGUAGE

Most of us can read other people's body language and send appropriate signals if we pay attention all of the time. Many negotiators, however, get so caught up in the words, numbers, and reports surrounding a negotiation that they forget all about body language. Top negotiators never do, though. After all, body language is one of the easiest codes to break if you pay attention.

BODY LANGUAGE: COMMUNICATION THAT PREDATES SPEECH

Some people speculate that there were no early societies until prehistoric humans learned to smile. With no other communication tools, they came to rely on the smile as a way of signaling peaceful intentions.

Millions of years later, the symbolic dialect of body language has been highly refined. Many trial lawyers regularly employ psychologists to read the body language of prospective jurors. How they fold their legs and arms, rub their noses, and place their arms behind their head are supposedly clues to finding jurors with the desired attitude. Open arms and legs and steepled fingers, for example, may be signs of flexibility in thinking and personality; whereas, folded legs or arms may reveal inner rigidity.

WHY BODY LANGUAGE MATTERS TO NEGOTIATORS

Since the days we first learned to communicate with our smiles, people have been discovering the nuances of body language on more and more sophisticated levels. In the Western world, people have used the thumbs-up, thumbs-down signals since the days of Roman gladiators. Today we all send and receive numerous messages through body language, but many people ignore important nonverbal signals, to their detriment.

For example, if you have had a physically difficult business trip and return to the office frowning, many people will misunderstand your expression. To them, it will convey either a business problem or displeasure with them. Unless you realize that your nonverbal communication might be misunderstood, you will fail to offer an explanation. Without knowing why you look upset, your people may get concerned.

Looking at your watch is often another troublesome form of body language. Some people are offended when, during a meeting that they consider important, other people glance at their watches. Looking at your watch may have been necessary to continue the meetings, but unless you explain this, the other people are likely to misinterpret your gesture.

HOW TO UNCOVER YOUR OPPONENT'S MOTIVES

Basically, there are two types of negotiations, those intended to avoid problems and those set up solely to cause you problems. So, how do you know if your opponent needs your help or your scalp? Everyone understands negotiation intended to avoid problems. Both parties want to reach an agreement on something, and each person maneuvers to remove the barriers that are in the way of an agreement. Oddly, very few people realize that the second type of negotiation, the kind meant to cause problems, even exists, much less that it has nothing to do with really seeking a final agreement.

EXAMPLES OF NEGOTIATIONS BASED ON HIDDEN MOTIVES

- A seller arouses your interest in purchasing something solely to use you for leverage against a more promising prospective buyer.

- An employer wants to get rid of a key manager but doesn't want to reveal this objective to company executives. The employer puts the unsuspecting manager into a negotiation with the company bank about an impossible interest reduction. When the manager fails to achieve a goal that was unattainable in the first place, the employer fires the manager. The negotiation failure is excuse enough for the executives because the employer led them to believe the negotiation would be "a piece of cake."

- A key employee plans to retire in 18 months, but the company president is pushing hard to convince the employee to start another operation in a distant city. This would mean extensive time away from home and increased stress related to travel. The employee starts negotiations with real estate groups, unions, and machinery manufacturers to buy time until retirement.

- A buyer gets you to start price negotiations for the sole purpose of using you as a lever to get a price cut from present suppliers.

The buyer never orders anything from you and never intended to do so.

- A union agent suddenly confronts you with wild accusations and demands. This unexpected, forced negotiation is aimed at making you lose your cool. The union agent can use any display of temper to cast you in a bad light. The agent does not expect you to agree to the demands, but the confrontation will remind union members how much they need their agent to fight for them.

- A vice president hoping to beat out a colleague for the soon-to-be-vacant executive vice president's job devises a conflict with the other candidate. The company president is forced to step in to negotiate for the two vice presidents solely because the instigator wants to use the negotiating session to impress the president. The instigator knows that the other vice president will probably lose control in front of the president, and that the president expects employees to stay calm.

A CHECKLIST FOR SPOTTING ATTEMPTS TO USE OR ABUSE YOU

- Avoid becoming a seller's shill, that is, someone to whom the seller never really plans to sell.

- Avoid helping someone maneuver your negotiations into an impasse that serves your opponent's ulterior motives.

- Avoid participating in any negotiation which you know cannot succeed, but for which you could be blamed.

- Always ask yourself, "Are these negotiations real, or is someone simply buying time for some unknown reason?"

- Never lose your cool when someone tries to force you into an unexpected confrontation. This is not negotiation; it is an attack. You can buffer such an attack by smiling and walking away from whatever audience your opponent has arranged to be present.

- Never let competitive people who are your equals force you into negotiations designed solely to make them look good in front of your boss.

TECHNIQUES FOR READING AN OPPONENT'S POSTURING AND THEATRICS

Every negotiation is a play whose conclusion has not been written. Remember that there are two writers vying to determine the outcome, and you are one of them. The key is not to become spellbound by a clever script. Many sharp negotiators seek to make you more of a spectator than a participant. Avoid this by recognizing their tricks.

TRICKS THAT CAN MESMERIZE UNSUSPECTING NEGOTIATORS

- Control by tone of voice.
- Manipulation by appeals of togetherness.
- Use of body language that signals comradery.
- Domination by intellectual superiority.
- Appeals to curiosity.
- Intimidation by starkness of emotion.
- Trading perceptions for realities.

EXAMPLES OF USING THEATRICS AND POSTURING AS CONTROL TACTICS

- *A Courtroom Example Using Mesmerizing Tactics*: The trial lawyer was negotiating with the jury for his client's life. The defendant was a beautiful young woman accused of killing her husband one night when he came home in a drunken rage and, according to the defendant, threatened her. The defense attorney's summation was a plea for the jury to believe that the defendant was telling the truth. The attorney used body language, theatrical facial expressions, voice tone, and starkness of emotion to convey the message.

The lawyer walked back and forth, close to the jury box, as he delivered the summation. As he moved, he glanced at the defendant with every other sentence. Every time he looked toward her, the jurors' eyes followed his to the young woman, then focused on him. The jurors seemed hypnotized by his stalking.

As the lawyer unfolded the story of the defendant's arrival home on the night her husband was killed, the lawyer became the drunken husband. He raised his voice ever higher to a shout. His voice portrayed the husband's emotions, and his grimacing face showed the rage of a man gone wild with emotion. At one point as he stalked, he stumbled, very much as a drunk might stumble. Through it all, he kept turning to look at the young woman, who herself now had a look of terror on her face.

Did the jury believe the young woman's account of the night's events? Of course they did, because the attorney convinced them that they had been there.

- *A Big Ticket Sales Example of The Wonders of Acting*: The sales manager was negotiating with the school board's purchasing committee about millions of dollars worth of student teaching materials. Her posturing and theatrics consisted of intellectual awe and feelings of togetherness.

The negotiation began with a monolog from the sales manager. She stood as she spoke and produced a barrage of facts, figures, and case examples. Her delivery was rapid with an emotionless, intellectual tone. She continued for ten minutes and hardly seemed to pause for breath. She painted an impartial, statistically based picture of the trouble the nation's students were in. The volume and brilliance of her argument left committee members in awe of her intellectual capability. They felt like college students with a new, interesting lecturer.

The sales manager invited questions about her products and prices. As she did this, she pulled a chair over close to the committee members, sat down, and gave each a welcoming smile. She made it easy to ask questions. As she fielded their questions, she was no longer the lecturer. She seemed to be more like a close friend whom they might call to their living room to solve an emergency with one of their own children. Her smile, her tone, and facial expressions personified compassion. She was there helping in their time of need. And, how was she helping? With her products, of course. She was 100 percent believable. She didn't seem to be selling products; she was offering compassion and help for their children.

This woman was a spellbinder. Her mix of intellectual awe and togetherness convinced the committee that what they bought from her wasn't products, but magic. This, by the way, is why she is the highest-paid executive in her company.

- *An Example of Perception over Reality*: One executive used an expensive tan attaché case to control negotiating opponents during a two-hour speech about why two companies should merge. He based his approach on audience curiosity and audience willingness to accept *his* perceptions of *their* reality.

The head of one company wanted the merger and knew that the other side had many strong doubts about it. The president in favor of the merger had many convincing arguments, but explained, "There were so many detailed reasons to cover that I knew one of two things would happen. I would be interrupted and hung up on long discussions on one or another reason. This would use my time. The other possibility was that they would become bored with my lengthy details and would, in effect, go to sleep on me.

"So, I decided to stand up as I talked," the president told us. "As I stood up, I ostentatiously put my large tan attaché case in the middle of the table, so that I had to lean forward to reach it.

" 'The answer to all of your questions,' I began, 'is in here.' As I said the words, I slapped my palm with some force on top of the attaché, which was lying flat on the table.

"Then, for the next two hours I didn't present one fact. Instead, I dished out romantic generalities about why we should merge. I said, 'Do we want our combined sales to steadily pull each other up to new records?' Then I slapped the briefcase again and said, 'Of course we do, and the facts are in here.' All of them looked at the briefcase. I went on and on. I said, 'The incredible cost benefits of combining our operations surprised even me.' Again, I slapped the case and said, 'And the proof is in here!

"This went on for almost two hours, and I assure you no one went to sleep. Everyone heard all of the exciting generalities about what the merger would mean. It was a pep talk, nothing more. But it sounded factual because the facts were in the bag.

"At the end of the meeting, I suggested we adjourn overnight 'to study the facts' I had just presented. I opened the case and gave everyone a thick bound copy of the report I'd based my presentation on. It was thick and overflowing with details."

The ominous-looking reports that had been in the attaché presented charts, graphs, tables, and a mound of details that few people would want to plow through. Even if the executive's opponents had wanted to read the report, one night would not have been enough time, and this is exactly why the executive used this tactic. He knew that no one would read the materials before the next day's meeting. Just to make sure he planned an elaborate dinner followed by entertainment that evening.

The next day they voted for the merger. They all believed they were voting on facts, although none of them stayed up to read the report.

NOTE: A variation on this tactic has been seen in recent Congressional Annual Budget legislation based on reams of information presented *just hours before* the key vote is taken. Time available to read is never adequate before the final vote is required, but the pile of supporting paper adds credibility to the total dollars voted.

WHAT TO DO WHEN YOU MEET AN IMPORTANT OPPONENT

Really important people may get into the habit of intimidating you by demanding your trust, tacitly asking you to accept their positions, and expecting you to become an awed spectator of their posturing and theatrics. Rereading three sections of this book will help you begin to develop strategies for dealing with the big shots. These sections are 4–1, "When Are Trust and a Handshake Not Enough?"; 4–2, "How to Decipher a Pretentious Opponent's Message"; and 4–6, "Techniques for Reading an Opponent's Posturing and Theatrics."

Remember, really important people should never be confronted head on. Since they count on intimidating you, let them think they are succeeding until the very last moment. This will make them careless in their negotiations. At the same time, you double your effort to discover their true needs and motivations and their real interest in you.

Try to learn how your opponent achieved such an esteemed position:

- By inheritance?
- By ability?
- A combination of both?
- Luck?
- Patronage?
- Politicking?
- False myths about the person?

Some people who appear to be big shots will come up short on real ability. In such cases, you have every reason to expect to win at the negotiating table simply by outthinking your opponent. Even when ability is clearly a key to your opponent's success, you still may have the advantage. You may be hungry, and your esteemed opponent may be going soft as a result of success.

Important people want to continue to look good. All of your negotiating tactics must revolve around this fact. Consider these tendencies:

- Sometimes important people will agree with your demands because they think it will enhance their reputations.

- Sometimes they will agree with your demands because they fear that to do otherwise will hurt their reputations.

- Sometimes they will agree with your demands because you have convinced them that you are another of their admirers. These people will give you what you want to keep you from becoming disenchanted with them.

Remember, winning with important people is usually easy.

WHAT TO DO WHEN ONLY NUMBERS MATTER TO YOUR OPPONENT

A top negotiator once remarked, "Show me a person who only wants to talk numbers during a negotiation, and I'll show you a loser every time because there are few things that numbers can really describe. And few numbers I can't come up with."

Numbers cannot accurately describe many things, such as—

- Future productivity potential.
- Future morale.
- Future market demands.
- Future economic trends.
- Future competition.
- Future loyalty.
- Future innovations.
- Future technologies.

EXAMPLES OF HOW NUMBERS-ONLY PEOPLE GET OUTMANEUVERED

- The sellers of residential real estate based their price on historical numbers added to orderly future projections. They learned after the sale that their old neighborhood had been rezoned as commercial property. Its value had skyrocketed before they sold it.

- A boss, though grateful for a key executive's 15 years of loyal service, kept giving the employee routine historical salary increases. The executive left to join a competitor for twice the old salary.

- A company sold a money-losing division at a better price than expected, only to learn that the division's research had three breakthrough processes. These discoveries had not shown up in the seller's numbers, but they made the new owners very rich very quickly.

- The buyers of the largest wagon manufacturer in the United States ignored an upstart named Ford.

TIPS FOR DETECTING NUMBERS-ONLY PEOPLE

Tip 1: Ask yourself if the numbers-only opponent is blind to hidden values or potential. If so, never call attention to hidden assets.

Tip 2: Switch the roles in Tip 1 and ask yourself if your numbers-only opponent is using numbers to hide some present weakness or feared future development. Do the numbers seem too good to be true?

Tip 3: Don't be afraid to float meaningless number projections on numbers-only opponents. Do this to test their preoccupation with numbers. Some numbers-only people will accept the wildest projections simply because you present them in numerical terms. Because they believe numbers, such people may not challenge the assumptions underlying your projections.

If a numbers-only person sees through your wild projections, smile and use flattery by saying something such as, "I should have known better than to try to work with numbers when I'm up against an expert." Try again in another area. Most numbers-only people are not good at seeing through future numbers.

Tip 4: Let the numbers-only people think you are putting all of your numbers on the table, but don't. Thus, if your company has a high employment history in eight out of ten years, use an average high employment figure so you don't have to explain the two problem years.

Tip 5: Most numbers-only people are really poor at numbers. To protect themselves, they rely on a few benchmarks, a few ratios that they think matter, and an often limited grasp of balance sheets. For example, they may be unaware of how inventories and accounts payable can be complete myths, depending on who is counting what in what time period.

Tip 6: Always let numbers-only people think they have an advantage because of your lesser number skills. This way, when they ask you for certain figures, they will be less concerned about any slant you may put into your numbers.

KEY TACTIC: Do Rely on a Numbers Expert

To break the numbers-only code, be sure you or a close associate is a real numbers expert. Then, act as if you are weak in numbers to check to see if your opponent sees through what you are doing. Remember that most numbers-only people, especially bankers, are poor with numbers. So, float wild numbers in their direction to see exactly how sharp they are. You can rely on your guise of limited expertise with numbers. Also, never tell your opponent about the hidden values that numbers cannot show. You, on the other hand, dig like the devil to discover nonnumeric values that affect your interests.

HOW TO TURN THE TABLES ON A LYING OPPONENT

Who wouldn't feel rebuked and falsely accused if you openly called the person a con artist? Most people do not deserve the label most of the time. Unfortunately, circumstance sometimes leads a person to conjure up one big lie. Often when this happens, it is not because the person planned it. It may result from too many pressures. Here are some examples of how otherwise trustworthy people went astray.

EXAMPLES OF HOW PEOPLE NOT PRONE TO CHEAT COME TO TELL ONE BIG LIE

- Four-medal Olympic track star Jesse Owens ultimately received the nation's highest civilian medal from the President of the United States for a lifetime of service to others. Yet for a time in the middle of his career, he failed to file any federal income tax returns. He was tried and received a modest sentence because his behavior slip was obviously out of character.

- One of the nation's largest, most respectable trucking lines received a multimillion dollar loan from one of the nation's largest banks. Shortly thereafter, the trucking firm went bankrupt, and the bankers found that they had been deceived, as were the company's prestigious auditors. Thousands of accounts payable invoices had been hidden from the auditors. This was one big lie that cost millions of dollars and was 100 percent out of character for the company's management.

Lesson: A con artist's threat is rarely obvious. Expect it, allow for it, and even enjoy the extremes to which your opponent will go with the con. Be especially alert for the people who have not often strayed from the truth because they can catch you off guard if you happen to be the person upon whom they pull their one big lie.

HOW TO SPOT THE LIES THAT CAN HURT THE MOST

Unfortunately, you must learn to rely on a kind of controlled paranoia about every significant negotiation you enter. Assume the worst possible scenario, and say to yourself, "Just in case."

Start with the most significant facts or positions in your opponent's presentation. Choose issues about which you have little doubt, and re-examine them on the assumption that one or more of them may be your opponent's once-in-a-lifetime big lie. Take special care with points that your opponent knows are most important to you. Here are some examples.

- Suppose you are a banker. Your opponent knows how important financial strength is to you. Be skeptical of your opponent's reports about his or her greatest financial strengths.

- If you are a buyer, your opponent knows which product or service features and terms mean most to you. Question the representations and claims which are closest to your heart. After all, a seller who would tell one big lie wants to be sure it is about something that will make you want the deal.

- If you are a lender or seller, watch out for the buyer's ability to live up to his or her payment agreements. Most big lies from buyers concern their ability to pay. Sometimes the seller may catch a lie years later when a buyer who was performing on schedule fails to make a balloon payment.

Arrange outside guarantees on any area where a big lie could seriously damage you. If you are a banker, tie up personal assets of all family members if something goes wrong. If you are a seller, tie up collateral beyond the basic deal if payment is not made. If you are a buyer, tie up funds, possibly in escrow, until all that has been promised is received, proved, and tested.

Whenever possible, have your lawyers arrange automatic protection for you. Do not rely on years of litigation to receive recompense. A person's legal obligation to pay may be hollow assurance if there is no money left. Expect the worst in every important money negotiation, even with loved ones. Then, protect yourself with a whopper of your own.

"I know that nothing could ever go wrong with our arrangements. But as a routine recommended by my professional advisors, we will have to build in the following guarantees to our agreement, much as I hate to do it."

HOW TO REACT TO PEOPLE WHO TEST YOU ON EVERYTHING

The plant manager explained a daily negotiating problem. "I have this one top flight person who can dance rings around the other toolmakers. Whenever I have a challenge that no one else can solve, I know he'll be able to do it.

"But, because he's so good, he's a special kind of prima donna. He has the habit of saying no to everything several times before he finally agrees to do what I need. If he weren't so essential, I'd have kicked him out of here years ago!"

Whether you are in a very special negotiation or a routine one, an opponent who knows that he or she has what you need may develop a habit of testing what you're willing to pay every step of the way. What you are expected to pay usually involves much more than money. Frequently, you are supposed to sacrifice patience, ego, authority, and reputation.

TWO RULES FOR TURNING THE TABLES ON PEOPLE WHO ALWAYS TEST YOU

Rule 1: Find ways to appear not to need what your opponent thinks you have to have. An opponent who habitually tests you is getting a psychic kick from playing with you. If you refuse to play, you take away the other person's fun. When you do this, your opponent will miss the old kicks and will often do anything to get you back to the playing table.

Rule 2: Find ways to hide the fact that your opponent is getting to you. Don't lose your patience. Don't lose face. Don't let the game time run too long. If necessary, excuse yourself for something that suddenly comes up.

Remember, people who develop a habit of testing you are enjoying themselves. Take away their enjoyment, and they may give up the habit.

HOW ONE NEGOTIATOR TAMED A DIFFICULT BUYER

A particularly difficult buyer for a large chain of stores had the habit of absolutely humiliating sales people before finally granting a big order. Here is a sampling of this buyer's tactics:

- Keeping people waiting for hours.
- Keeping people standing during the first several minutes of a meeting in his office.
- Interrupting negotiations by making phone calls during negotiations with a sales person.
- Suddenly leaving the office in the middle of negotiations without an apology or explanation.
- Waving a piece of paper on which, supposedly, is a ridiculously low competitive bid.
- Threatening to call the sales person's boss to complain about a lack of cooperation.
- Throwing a signed order across and off the desk, thus forcing the salesperson to pick it up off the floor.

A very successful sales person told us about this buyer's legendary behavior. "That buyer's been getting away with it for years, and he's still getting away with it. But not with me anymore; I guarantee you that.

"I reversed everything. When he kept me waiting in the outer office, I took along a novel. Then when he finally asked me to come in, I deliberately read one more page and said I always enjoyed waiting at his place because I love to read. I could see his face drop. Then I brought the book into the meeting, and every time he left the room or started to use the phone I grabbed the book and made sure that he could see that I was enjoying myself with my reading, as if I welcomed the chance to get back to the novel.

"And when he kept me standing in front of his desk and then finally told me to sit down, I refused. I laughed and told him I really preferred standing up because I did so much driving that it felt good to stand. I could see this really bothered him.

"On my second visit, I did the same things. On my third visit, he was able to see me immediately. He practically begged me to sit down as soon as I was in his office. He didn't leave the room or pick up the telephone once. And when he finally signed the order, he carefully handed it to me instead of throwing it across the desk.

"Funny," the sales person chuckled, "he's really a nice guy who shaped up in a hurry when I refused to play his little games by pretending to enjoy what he was doing to me. I guess the fun went out of it for him. Plus, I think he respects me much more now. At least his orders suggest that this is the case."

WHY ANXIOUS BUYERS HIDE BEHIND CASUAL AIRS

Almost everyone at some point has said to a friend, "Act disinterested when I ask the price." Usually, the disinterested parties playing this game are secretly most anxious to buy. Most sellers have long come to expect the couldn't-care-less approach. Often, their response is to turn the game around and act as if they aren't anxious to sell when in fact they may be most anxious.

WHY NEGOTIATORS MUST WEIGH THE PROBABILITIES AND CREATE CONTINGENCY PLANS

Years ago the economics theorist Henry Morgenstern illustrated a lecture with an example of a train leaving London with an escaping fugitive aboard. Scotland Yard detectives missed the train but decided to pick the fugitive up when he got off of it. But where would that be? There were three stops before the train reached its final destination.

"He'll expect us to expect him to get off at the first stop," a detective reasoned, but then added, "Well, then again, he'll probably guess that we don't think that he'll get off, so he may get off after all."

"But," another detective speculated, "if he thinks we think he thinks we think, then maybe he will not get off."

A long silence came over the detectives. They realized that this intricate "we think he thinks we think he thinks" process would be complicated further, because there were four possible departure points. What quickly became apparent was that the detectives were over their heads in this probability game. So, what did they do? They put four plans into effect, which required four times as many people to cover all four stations.

Lesson: When negotiating a serious matter with a capable, serious opponent, we are never quite sure at which station the person will get off. Our guessing about the opponent's guessing must always be backed up by contingency plans just in case we are wrong.

HOW THE CASUAL GAME CAN FOOL YOU

A seller may out-think you when you act as if you are indifferent about a price. The seller may deliberately seem very anxious to sell. At this point, you may think you have it made. Meantime, the seller may have quietly raised the price because he or she recognized your casual clue and because, by acting anxious to sell, the seller may have lulled you into thinking that you are winning. You may not even bother to notice the price hike!

HOW TO TELL WHO IS GETTING OFF AT WHICH NEGOTIATING STOP

If your opponent picks up your casual clue and pretends to be anxious as a way to slip you a much higher price, why not try to take things one step further? Begin by deciding to appear anxious instead of casual. This way, your opponent may not spot your tactic so easily and may not realize that you are playing the game. When this happens, you're ahead. Now when your opponent shoots a higher price at you, immediately act very dejected and say, "Gosh, I really wanted that but. . . ."

At this point, the seller is in a much less secure bargaining position than had you started out acting casual and gotten caught. Your opponent still has not caught on that you are playing the casual game in reverse. You are using your strategies, but your opponent is not even planning to out-think you in the casual game.

A FOUR-STEP STRATEGY FOR WINNING THE ANXIETY GAME

Step 1: When you spot a casual, couldn't-care-less clue, most times you can then out-think your opponent by not being casual in return. This is not what your opponent really expects. Appear anxious to sell because your opponent was expecting a tough negotiation.

Step 2: Try a higher price than you might normally exact to see if your apparent anxiety is paying off. Usually, you'll get away with it because your opponent thinks the indifferent approach has worked. Considering your anxiety, your opponent does not imagine that you would raise your price.

Step 3: Have a fallback position if your casual opponent is sharper than you anticipated. Thus, suppose you acted anxious to sell and quietly raised your price. Your casual opponent rejects the price. Immediately, you switch from anxious to casual by saying something like, "Oh well, I was hoping to sell you, but I should have known better."

At this point, an opponent who assumed he or she had out-thought you is not quite so sure. Your opponent expected you to lower your price either because of your anxiety to sell or because the price may not have been the lowest one you could offer. You have not played the game, and now you are walking away. Maybe your opponent thinks it was your lowest price.

Step 4: Let the buyer make the next move. Often, it will be to accept your price.

Lesson: When you suspect that someone is playing the casual game, reverse the rules.

WHAT TO REMEMBER ABOUT NICE GUYS AND RESPONSIBLE PEOPLE

When a union negotiator and the new owner of a company met for the first time, the company owner said, "What a responsible person." The union person was a much sharper, more experienced negotiator than the company's new owner, however. The union person knew better than to make such a judgment about the new owner and decided to let some time pass before assessing the owner in any meaningful way.

WHY EXPECTING THE WORST CAN LEAD TO THE BEST RESULTS

When the next union contract came up for negotiation, the company owner entered into negotiations in an amiable frame of mind. "After all," the owner reasoned, "my opponent is a very responsible person."

On the other hand, the experienced union leader assumed the worst, that the owner who was so nice in social circumstances might be quite a different person under pressure. Of course, the union leader always provided opponents with many hard times during negotiations.

As it turned out, the company owner handled the pressure well, without losing composure or becoming illogical. Even so, the owner lost some negotiating ground by not exerting the same pressure on the union negotiator that he experienced. Thus, when negotiations were complete, the union representative said, "The owner is the kind of person you can count on." The now more experienced company owner, however, no longer regarded the union representative as a very responsible person. Instead, the company owner confided to a friend, "That jerk kept testing me, and I wasn't ready to return the play. Next year I'll see what this person is really like under real pressure." Meanwhile, the company owner had to wait another year to try to regain the ground lost by not exerting pressure on the union leader. The owner had violated the first rule of negotiating: never take anyone for granted.

SIX RULES FOR NEGOTIATING WITH NICE GUYS

Rule 1: People can change under pressure. Remember that 50 percent of the U.S. population get divorced from nice people.

Rule 2: What counts is not how nice a person is, but what he or she counts for.

Rule 3: Any nice guy should be tested during negotiations, just as you would test someone you know to be difficult.

Rule 4: Nice guys who are experienced negotiators never check their guns at the negotiating door. They are always ready and expect you to be ready, too.

Rule 5: Manners, mannerisms, personalities, and reputations have little to do with negotiating realities. Many inexperienced negotiators are so busy shaking hands with the nice guy opponents that they do not notice that their pockets are being picked.

Rule 6: Every sharp negotiator will take pains after a negotiating session to make you feel good about what has been agreed. Nice guys are especially good at making you feel good.

WHAT PERCEPTIONS HAVE TO DO WITH NEGOTIATING

Brilliant trial lawyers rely on stereotypes to select jury members whose gut reactions to issues in a case are likely to favor the lawyer's client. Brilliant negotiators rely on stereotypes to lead their opponents' favorable feelings about themselves and their motives.

USING STEREOTYPES TO CLOSE A SALE

A real estate agent negotiating the sale of a country property sensed she was close to a deal but also sensed that the buyers were still not quite sure. She needed something to put them over the edge.

"Let me tell you about the lady who lived here before," she confided to the buyers. "She was 99 years old when she died and had never been sick a day in her life. She always claimed it was the water in the well on the property. It is the clearest water in the country." The agent chuckled and continued, "Of course, I don't think we can be sure it was the water. I'm more inclined to think it's the property's location, high up on that hill in the clear mountain air.

"Or, it might have been exercise. I've never seen a more beautiful piece of land for taking walks. There are all of those pretty paths and that steep mountain to climb.

"Anyway," the agent smiled, "she lived to be 99."

The buyers closed the deal quickly. "This is perfect," one of them said, "for a long, healthy retirement. It is a healthful spot that anyone would be lucky to get, and maybe there is something to the clear water in the well."

The agent created a perception of health, long life, goodness, clean water, fresh air, and exercise based on stereotypes. It was not essential that the agent tell all. There was no need, for example, to mention the 99-year-old woman's parents in another state who lived into their 100s. There was no need to mention that the property owner favored bourbon over well water, or that a hired hand died of a heart attack as he climbed the steep mountain.

SEVEN KEY STEREOTYPES

- *The caring individual.* Here your negotiating opponent makes such remarks as, "If I didn't really care about you, I'd never agree to this." The issue could be price, an organization chart, a purchase, or any point of negotiation. Many opponents may try to convince you that they care when this is far from the truth.

- *The reluctant seller.* Such a negotiating opponent says, "If I had my way, I wouldn't sell, especially at this price. But I've got to face reality. If I have to sell, this way at least I'm pleased it's to a person such as you. But it still hurts!" This type of opponent almost makes you feel guilty about your good luck at his or her misfortune.

- *The reluctant buyer.* This stereotype involves your opponent's protests about his or her buying problems. "I really shouldn't be doing this, especially at this time and this way. I promised myself that I wouldn't make such a move, but here I am breaking my promise to myself." Unless you are careful, this kind of person will convince you that you are corrupting him or her by selling something.

- *The loyalty stereotype.* Here your negotiating opponent convinces you that he or she is agreeing because, "It's the only thing I can do out of loyalty to you and to the things you stand for. You're my kind of person. If people like us don't work things out, then there's little hope for the world."

  This tactic is especially effective when someone is taking you to the cleaners and wants you to feel good anyway. Consider the car dealer who sold the oldest customer the most expensive model because, "It's in short supply, and I'd rather have my old friends get it than some stranger who just happens to walk in here with a pocketful of money. You deserve to have it."

- *The excellence stereotype.* In this case, your opponent would have you believe his or her standards are unmatched anywhere. Thus, you are persuaded to agree to such arguments as, "This can only happen because I feel good about it. It fits my standards, and I put them above anything else. Our arrangement lives up to what I stand for and believe in, which is why I feel so good about it!"

- *The love stereotype.* Logic is supposed to have given way to love in this instance. "This could never be worked out this way if I didn't feel this way about you," an opponent might say. Love is a form of flattery, and many people can't believe that people shouldn't love them, which means that, despite themselves, they buy this stereotype most of the time.

- *The "it's perfect" stereotype.* Your opponent appears absolutely astounded at how precisely right something is for you.

  For example, a real estate agent practically cries with joy and says, "It's you. It fits you. It's right for you!"

  A financial planner sells you by saying, "It's made to order with you in mind. Are we ever fortunate to have found this for you!"

  The boss says, "Have I got the job for you!"

Always be skeptical of the other person's best wishes and excitement about your situation. It pays to question opponents' perception of you, and your perception of them.

WHAT EGO MEANS IN NEGOTIATION

When two individuals or two teams of individuals sit down at a negotiating table, they begin to interact on two levels. On the thinking, rational level, logic strongly influences negotiating agreements. On the emotional level, gut feelings unrelated to logic emerge as strong influences.

TEN WAYS THAT EGOS INFLUENCE NEGOTIATIONS

Everyone has a self-image. An individual's ego strength depends on how the person resolves emotional drives and needs. One person may see survival as the dominant ego need. Someone else may see pleasure as the reason to get up in the morning. For another individual, the pursuit of excellence may be at the core of how he or she approaches life.

There are ten primary emotional drives which shape out ego needs in varying ways.

1. *Survival.* This is the most important motivation, and it readily transfers to an ego need to stay alive in a business and social sense. Thus, negotiations that threaten this need are in trouble for ego, rather than monetary, reasons.

2. *Hunger.* A negotiator with this emotional need may not fear for his or her survival, but may be plagued with a hunger for something that pleases and satisfies. This person may have a need for ego food that is as strong as another person's drive for food to nourish the body. Thus, negotiations with a hungry person often break down for reasons having little to do with the desire for money.

3. *Excellence.* The basic drive here is to excel in our work and to have those around us know about the things we do well. Our egos need to be told that we are an excellent typist, an excellent engineer, an excellent surgeon. Some negotiations founder because someone's sense of excellence is being challenged.

4. *Dedication.* All people seem to need to be dedicated to one or more ideas. A criminal is dedicated to not being a squealer; an executive may be dedicated to carrying on the family business; and a technician may be dedicated to protecting the boss. Some negotiations fail because someone's dedication is ignored.

5. *Ownership.* From childhood forward, human beings want to own things, to control material objects, even to control people. Some business owners feel they own their employees. Some acquisitions or mergers are based on ownership needs as much as financial logic. Many negotiations get off the track because some people feel they will lose control rather than money.

6. *Exploration.* Often the need to explore is not connected with any real need for economic gain. In business, however, economic gain is used as an excuse to explore. A top executive in the computer business estimates that 50 percent of new computer purchases are based largely on the need to explore new technology.

   When people eavesdrop to try to find out what's happening in another department, they are showing curiosity and a need to explore rather than a business motive. Some people explore with the use of their power. They will try to see how far they can go, and this can devastate negotiations.

7. *Sex.* Sex is involved in countless ways in emotional behavior. Many marketing people consider sex to be the basic underlying buying motive in most individuals. The automobile, for example, is a sex symbol for many people. Many books have related the changes in behavior patterns associated with sex to the aging process. Thus, people may change in their relationships with one another and themselves as the sex drive yields to another dominant ego need. A person's sexual contentment can have a bearing on negotiations.

8. *Status symbols.* Status symbols date back to tribal members of ancient times who wore symbols to proclaim victories. Today, status symbols take many forms, such as prestigious schools and sought-after social invitations. Status symbols fulfill a basic human need. Negotiations which cause people to lose face are often in deep trouble.

9. *Imitation.* This is the need to copy those standards of society set by both our peers and superiors. This is a social need which often has absolutely nothing to do with gaining business advantage, but it can affect business negotiations.

Some deals fall through because one of the parties feels his or her peers or superiors would not see the deal in a good light. The negotiator's job is to always put the deal in the best social light.

10. *Pleasure.* We tend to do what is not difficult for us in an emotional or physical sense. People avoid things that are mentally hard for them. Thus, your opponent may reject a brilliant negotiating plan solely because it is difficult to follow. Negotiations that are completely void of fun feelings, and this includes the feeling that everyone is winning something, are often doomed.

WHAT THE IDEAL NEGOTIATION CLIMATE SHOULD PROVIDE

Most negotiations, of course, revolve around money, but money is not the only necessary component.

- All parties should feel that their ego roles—as they see themselves—will survive or be enhanced.

- All parties should feel that whatever they hunger for, apart from food and money, will be preserved. Thus, if they hunger for status, let them know it will be preserved or enhanced.

- All parties should feel that others respect what they do best. This addresses people's need for excellence. No negotiation should threaten this need to be respected by outsiders. Equally, a sense of private self-respect must be protected.

- All parties should be careful not to contradict one another's feelings of dedication. You may think they are silly, but they are not silly to that person.

- Take care to be sure that all parties to a negotiation retain ownership feelings about the things they need to control. It may be a mistake in a business negotiation, for example, to suggest replacing a staff or even office equipment which people have come to see as theirs.

- Everyone likes to be curious, to explore. All negotiating sessions should allow people to ask questions, even when they seem to be unrelated to issues at hand. If you shut off a person's curiosity questions by saying, "That has nothing to do with what we're talking about," then the rebuked person will harbor resentment. Your negotiations may founder.

- Negotiations must provide continuity of a person's sex drives.

Thus, if a person wants to buy a car from you for romantic reasons, you'd be foolish to ask the buyer to read the engineering manual. Or, suppose a person is involved in a divorce during your negotiations. Never try to counsel. Just offer agreement about what he or she tells you regarding the problem.

The trick is to go with the flow of your negotiating opponents' attitudes and feelings related to sex and sexual objects. Never try to educate or change your opponents' sexual ego needs. Take great care not to interrupt the continuity of their feelings related to how they're handling their sex drives.

HOW TO SPOT THE CON ARTISTS IN YOUR MIDST

Any negotiator will admit, at least in his or her heart, that sometime, someplace, he or she used a little con in a negotiation. A negotiator may have allowed an opponent to assume something that was not necessarily the case. But this is quite different from people who live their entire lives deliberately misleading people.

True con artists use their tricks to get kicks as much as kickbacks. In other words, money is never enough because a con artist needs the power feelings that result from successful deception. A con artist has to prove that the other person is an idiot, or the kick is missing in a negotiation.

ADVANTAGES OF GOING ALONG WITH A CON

- Since you never can respect a con artist, you suffer no ego damage if you allow the con artist to see you as a sucker just long enough to make the deal backfire on this opponent.
- Con artists are easy to defeat in negotiations because once you appear to buy their line they get careless about watching for your strategies.
- Con artists will trade kicks for money or other negotiating concessions if you save your key strategy demands until they have convinced themselves that they are way ahead of you. Then, when you surprise them with your afterthought demands, they will often yield to preserve their con.

TWO EXAMPLES OF HOW TO CON THE CON ARTIST

- In any organization, some people will use false excuses to justify their demands. Thus, an employee asks, "May I take Friday off? My son's teacher wants to talk to me."

You have known for years that this person has been conning you, but have not let on that you know. So, when you are asked permission for Friday off, you agree. The employee is relishing in having fooled you again and in the prospects of a day off. As an apparent afterthought, you say, "I'll have to give you Friday's work to take home on the weekend, so we don't get behind."

The employee agrees to avoid upsetting a successful con. Your package of weekend work, of course, is enough to keep anyone busy for two days.

• You are one of four department heads. For years, you have considered one of your peers to be an obvious con artist. This person seems to fool the other two department heads regularly.

One day, your colleague speaks up during an interdepartmental meeting to suggest a surprise birthday party for the boss. "I know we all want to give this party, but it will take a lot of work and planning. I know none of you have time for this, so I volunteer to head up the details. After all, you helped me in the past."

You can see it now. The con artist will be sure to have the boss know who gave the party, whose idea it was, who put in all of the work, who cares most about the boss, and that the other three managers were all too busy to help. Although you see this coming, the other two executives take the con. You pretend to be taken in as well. Once again, your coworker feels the kick of successfully deceiving three idiots, of winning their agreement on something that will become a personal career boost.

You let the con artist put the entire event together, but without letting on that you are watching every move. At the very last moment on the afternoon of the surprise party, you call the boss's wife at home and invite her to the party. You know the con artist decided not to have spouses present. Not only do you invite the boss's wife, but you share with her all of the details that have gone into the party. You arrange a chauffeured car to pick her up and drive her to the party just before it begins. She'll be there before the surprise, but not long enough for the con artist to talk to her. You make sure of this in your instructions to the chauffeur.

Everything goes off as planned. You'll never forget the look on your con artist friend's face when you lead in the boss's wife just seconds before the boss arrives. Your pal pulls you aside to ask what's going on, and you smile your warmest smile and say, "I know how hard you've worked on this, and the least I could do was to be of help in this small way to make the party everything you wanted!"

The evening is a smash hit. The boss is thrilled and, driving home with his wife, he says, "How did you get there?" She, of course, explains how you arranged the entire thing behind the boss's back. "He's quite a guy to have taken all that time and effort on my behalf," your boss smiles.

KEY TACTIC: *Wait until the Last Minute to Turn a Con Around*

You can always find an easy way to turn a con artist's con around. The key is to let the person think you've taken the bait until the very last minute. Then, turn the very things the con artist planned to your advantage. This leaves the con artist with no time to counter your carefully timed strategy.

WHAT TO DO ABOUT PEOPLE WHO REGARD NEGOTIATION AS FLATTERY

No discussion about how to win more in your negotiations would be complete without mentioning a unique type of opponent who loves to play the negotiating game, but couldn't care less about winning. This type of opponent negotiates to win acceptance and to validate issues that only he or she selects. Though an individual may be gratified through this process, no real negotiation takes place.

FIVE KEY FACTS ABOUT ILLUSIONARY NEGOTIATION

- People do like to hear themselves talk. It's flattering.
- Where better to have a chance to talk than during a negotiation about anything.
- Letting people talk during a negotiation does not have to cost you anything.
- Many people who have been permitted to talk through a negotiation will permit you to call all of the important shots, but will feel sure that all the decisions agreed upon have been arrived at jointly.
- To cement the illusion of a negotiation, provide many little points that your opponents can always win. Do this only after you find ways to have your opponent talk a lot about these points.

EXAMPLES OF HOW ONE NEGOTIATOR'S DECISION CAN APPEAR TO BE A JOINT AGREEMENT

Skillful negotiators learn to cater to an opponent's need for flattery and validation. In return, they often get to make decisions alone, provided they encourage opponents to view the decision as a joint agreement. Here are some examples:

- A surgeon decides to remove an important organ from a very ill patient. The decision to operate is a serious one. Obviously, the surgeon can avoid many problems if family members think of it as their decision.

Without telling the family what he has already decided, the surgeon says, "I think we should call in a consultant to help us deliberate about what we should do." The family asks the surgeon to recommend a good consultant, so he calls an old roommate from medical school. This is the same physician who asks the family's surgeon to serve as his consultant when the situation is reversed. The family members know none of this background. They are grateful to have someone recommended as a top doctor available as a consultant on an emotional, difficult decision.

The surgeon organizes the meeting and says that everyone will decide what to do. The consultant has seen the patient and concurs with the surgeon's earlier concerns. Both doctors say they are leaning toward an organ removal. A two-hour meeting follows. The doctors brief family members on the medical issues, although family members do not really understand them. Instead, they talk, ask questions, cry, and talk some more.

After two hours, the surgeon moves toward a close, saying, "So, what have we decided?" The consultant jumps in to say, "We really have no choice, do we?" Both of these experts are asking the nonexperts what has been decided, and each family member agrees to the operation. Later that day, a family member calls an out-of-town relative to report, "We had a two-hour meeting, and we covered every possibility. When it was all over, we were all in 100 percent agreement that we needed to operate.

"But I feel so much better," the caller continues, "because we all reached the same decision on our own. There was no rigged jury."

- A company president and computer consultant used the physicians' negotiation scenario in a directors' meeting to determine whether the firm should pay $2.7 million for a new computer system. In this case, the assembled directors get briefed on computers rather than anatomy, and they respond with the usual laymen's questions. The board votes unanimously to pay the $2.7 million, thus formalizing a decision the company president made three months earlier. After the three-hour session, a director was heard to say, "What I like is that this president lets us decide all the big ones!"

- A company president invites the firm's department heads to a meeting to decide who will build a new plant and for how much. No one knows anything about construction, but the president brings in three outside consultants and recommends them as the best in the field.

In this case, deliberations stretch over three days. Finally, everyone has talked extensively, and the group votes democratically to pick the very contractor and price that the president wanted. In fact, those terms are already printed in a letter the president is sending to the directors. Of course, no one will know that the letter was written and prepared days before the meeting. After the vote, one department head says to another, "I really admired the fact that our leader refrained from voting so as not to influence our decision. That's what I call fair!"

What better way to flatter your associates than to say you will not even vote. They feel so good that they overlook the puppet election staged right before their eyes.

SECTION 5

WHAT TO SAY TO YOURSELF ABOUT A NEGOTIATION

WHAT TO SAY TO YOURSELF ABOUT A NEGOTIATION

What you say to yourself in a negotiation can influence your success more than what you say to your opponent. What you say to yourself controls your attitudes, and winning attitudes are the keys to success. You'll find many constructive messages in this section, and all of them can help put you in the right frame of mind to accomplish your negotiating goals.

An important note: you need not use the tactics in this section in your personal life outside of negotiations. Still, you increase your chances of winning when you consciously prepare yourself mentally and emotionally for a negotiation.

HOW TO OVERCOME FEELING AS IF YOU ARE ON THE ROPES

In negotiations, as in any other activity, you will have good and bad days. At times, you will feel up for a contest of wits; at other times, you will be physically and mentally fatigued from long negotiations. Occasionally, problems and responsibilities completely unrelated to your negotiations may get the better of you, causing your concentration to wane. In fact, many negotiators count on you to wear down. They try to exert mental and physical pressures on you by nit-picking, prolonging sessions, staging confrontations, changing agendas, contriving false crises, and asking for last-minute add-ons to your deal.

ARE YOU ON THE ROPES?

1. Do you feel physically ill in some way? A bad cold? The flu? A hangover? A general feeling of malaise?

2. Are you feeling emotionally undone? Is your objectivity dulled by feelings of outrage? Boredom?

3. Do you feel mentally exhausted, unable to focus in your normally sharp fashion? Are facts, figures, and strategies getting harder to grasp?

4. Do you feel physically spent? Tired?

5. Has your opponent psyched you out?

Anytime you notice a feeling of being on the ropes, try to buy time until you feel better.

WHAT BOXERS CAN TEACH NEGOTIATORS ABOUT BUYING TIME

A boxer on the ropes has four options:

1. *Go into a clinch.* This stops the action and buys protection and time.

2. *Go down.* Take a long count to buy time and to get away from the ropes.

3. *Dance away from the ropes.* This reduces an opponent's chance to take advantage of you.

4. *Gamble on a wild punch.* A wild punch, blindly thrown, might be the only chance to connect with an opponent.

APPLYING BOXERS' OPTIONS TO NEGOTIATIONS

1. A negotiator can "go into a clinch" over one detail on the agenda. Pick an item on which you have a strong position. Haggling over this detail lets you avoid other areas where you might not be as strong, and it is an attempt to tire your opponent.

2. Unexpectedly "go down" on one agenda item, and then say, "I have to stop with this one item now to see how it affects my other needs." Your objective is to focus on one point to get an adjournment without breaking off negotiations completely.

3. "Dance around" the specific agenda items by introducing extraneous questions or what-if subjects. Anything to buy time. When you sense you may be losing momentarily, move away from the basic negotiations.

4. Throw a "wild punch" if your other options have not worked. A wild punch can take the form of storming out of the meeting, going over your opponent's head, intimidation, pleading for mercy, and similar behavior. All of these tactics are poor negotiating strategies under normal conditions, but if you are losing anyway and have tried the first on-the-ropes tactics, you may have nothing to lose.

HOW ONE FIRM WON WITH "ON-THE-ROPES" TACTICS

The sixth day of negotiations about a proposed merger of two medium-sized companies was ending. Talks were at an impasse over the final valuation of each company. The owner of one company had been a sharp leader for his four-member team, but at 3 P.M. on the sixth day of negotiations, he felt empty.

"We had three more hours to go in our scheduled session. The other side seemed fresh as a daisy, but I was mentally exhausted. Of course, I didn't show it, but I was in real psychological trouble.

"This had happened to me before. I knew I needed to get through those next three hours without making another serious decision. I had to buy time to recoup my spirits and my mental sharpness. So, I tried the tactic of changing the subject. I asked the engineering guy on my team to explain the advances we had made in one part of our manufacturing operation. [Dancing around.]

"He did an excellent, detailed job. Between his talk and answering questions, it chewed up about an hour. But then, the other side got anxious to get back to serious negotiations. So, I went back to an earlier item we'd agreed upon, the location of our joint company headquarters."

"I said I had second thoughts on the subject. [A clinch.] This got us into a hassle with a lot of rehashing of what we had covered three days before. Of course, I yielded on my 'second thoughts' after an hour had gone by.

"Now, I had only one more hour to kill. So, I jumped ahead in the agenda to a small item that I sensed was dear to the other side. I quickly made it obvious that I might yield on that issue if I understood more about their position. Actually, I had already decided that I couldn't care less about that small issue, but I just made it appear that it was necessary to convince me. That's what they did for the next 45 minutes. Finally, I gave in, and I could see how pleased they were. [Going down for the count.] So, I stood up laughing, and said that the time scheduled for negotiations was about over for the day, so why not break now for a drink. After all, 15 minutes was not enough time to cover our price valuation viewpoints properly. And, because they were still feeling good from winning their last point, they amiably agreed."

The next day this president was once again sharp. He won the price he wanted for his company. "My juices were flowing again," he explains. "After a good night's sleep, and by killing off those three bad hours the previous day, I probably made myself $5 million."

HOW TO GUARD AGAINST BECOMING INTIMIDATED

When the President invites a senator to a private luncheon, it may be the President's way of saying, "You have a friend in power." Such a reminder may be a morale booster, an act of appreciation for the senator's loyalty, or a long-term negotiating effort to improve the senator's opinion of the President.

None of these reasons for a display of power implies intimidation. On the other hand, suppose the President phones the senator and threatens to campaign for his or her opponents unless the senator falls in line. This is blatant intimidation.

In most negotiations, however, the line between a show of power and intimidation gets blurred. We may find ourselves wondering, "Is that an attempt to intimidate, or is it simply a coincidence of that person's power? Is it a threat or an appropriate display of power?"

AN EXAMPLE OF A MISINTERPRETED DISPLAY OF POWER

The head of a large department, for example, was negotiating with three subordinate managers concerning their requirements for new people over the next six months. One manager came up with a number that startled the department head, who blurted out, "You've got to be kidding."

Was this an intimidating threat or merely a powerful person showing surprise? We observed this case at close range. The other two managers assumed it was a threat and became intimidated. Each requested no new people for the next six months. On the other hand, the manager who had come up with the surprising new number of people stuck to his guns and received approval on the spot, to the amazement of the other managers.

Later, the department head told us, "Too many of our managers try to outguess me. They try to please me when I don't want to be pleased. I only want to be told what they need and why, as they see it."

The two timid managers were guilty of being intimidated by power that was not intended to intimidate. Equally quilty was the department head who acted in a way that confused some of the managers.

QUESTIONS TO ASK YOURSELF ABOUT INTIMIDATING BEHAVIOR

Of course, powerful people who tread lightly may be doing you a disservice by denying their colleagues their true opinions of what their organizations may need most. If you can read your powerful superiors correctly while your competitors cannot, you will gain more than they do in negotiations with these superiors. Ask yourself two questions:

- Am I being intimidated?
- Is this just a habitual response from a powerful person?

Even a casual study of your negotiating opponent's habits will go a long way to help you understand what a powerful person is really saying. You may also learn to recognize when that person is attempting to intimidate. Here are some quick tips for dealing with intimidation:

1. Don't read power habits as intimidation.
2. Don't use power habits that falsely imply you intend to intimidate someone else.
3. If you are really being intimidated, go on record with whatever you feel strongly about and wait to see what happens. Unless you do this, you aren't negotiating; you're just following directions.

WHY REPACKAGING OLD VALUES CAN ENHANCE YOUR POSITION

Note: This tactic is not related to repackaging price. In that instance, you use add-ons to raise or lower a firm price. What you do depends on whether you are a buyer trying to get free add-ons or a seller trying to charge more through high profit add-ons.

The climate of each negotiation is different and is influenced by each opponent and the world from which he or she comes. These worlds include social, economic, political, and educational backgrounds. Successful negotiations between people from vastly different backgrounds are often possible. Likewise, some people whose life experiences match very closely may be unable to negotiate anything.

To understand this paradox, consider the language of old values and how each party to a negotiation is able to talk the language of old values. People from vastly different worlds may negotiate successfully because they have each learned to speak the same language of old values to one another.

People whose worlds match closely may fail to reach one another on anything because one or both of them forgot to use the language of old values.

UNDERSTANDING THE LANGUAGE OF OLD VALUES

This partial list of old values reminds us of the common language many top negotiators rely upon to hold things together:

- *Loyalty* to something.
- *Pride* in something.
- *Honesty* about something.
- *Manners* in some things.
- *Patience* about some things.
- *Love* of something.

- *Dedication* to something.
- *Consistency* in some things.
- *Discipline* in some things.
- *Moderation* in most things.
- *Quality,* an appreciation of.
- *Ethics* concerning something.

USING LANGUAGE OF OLD VALUES TO TEST AN OPPONENT'S RELIABILITY

In advertising jargon, an "empty suit" is a derogatory expression for a person whose substance and purpose have been drained. In effect, what is left is a person who stands for nothing and who therefore cannot be relied upon to count for anything. Such a person still says the right things, maintains a prosperous front, and mixes with the right people. Yet this person operates with numbness. Nothing makes a sharp negotiator more wary than sitting across the negotiating table from an empty suit.

HOW AN "EMPTY SUIT" CAN SPOIL THE DAY FOR NEGOTIATORS: AN EXAMPLE

"I was an old friend of his father," the company president told us, "until that plane crash took my old friend.

"Now I have to deal with a son who stands for absolutely nothing. The kid is a marshmallow, the product of a no-pain existence for almost 40 years. It's not simply a question of a spoiled brat. I've known plenty of those, but this guy is a complete nothing. He just exists and goes through the motions."

As it turned out, the president's frustrations were justified. For years, his financial firm had been a driving force behind the prosperous conglomerate which the son inherited.

"His word counts for absolutely nothing," the president continued, "but worst of all, he counts for nothing. When his father died, we were right in the middle of three negotiations with three responsible companies. In two of the three cases, preliminary papers had been signed. In the third case, we had almost wrapped things up.

"So there we were, with three big deals all but concluded with three of the finest groups you could ever find. Of course, immediately after the accident, all of these people felt a responsibility to move forward to complete the transactions. They felt they owed it to the guy who was killed. Some people might have said, 'Hold it.' But not these people.

They felt ethically compelled to go forward because they had given their word.

"The son had been present at all of the earlier meetings with these people. He looked okay and said the usual generalities during social sessions. But he never opened his mouth during negotiating sessions. He never asked a question, and never had an opinion on anything. At the time, we all thought this was one sharp guy. He was willing to learn from his father by keeping his mouth shut until his turn came.

"Well, when his turn came, it was a disaster. In each of our meetings after the crash, the guy still kept his mouth shut. It quickly became apparent to everyone that it wasn't the 'smarts'; it was a case of nothing inside.

"I watched these people try to reach this guy. They were patient, and they tried everything.

"First, they all noticed that he did not have any patience or discipline. Whenever the meetings got into real work sessions, he looked at his watch or out the window. Once he worked a crossword puzzle. How's that for manners around people who are the best in their fields?

"When they tried to reach him through conversations about his college, family, and friends, there was nothing. No pride or loyalty or even love. Nothing!

"One of the executives finally asked this guy what his hopes were for the successful operations he headed. He smiled sweetly and said, 'I haven't given it much thought, really.' Within an hour, everyone in the three groups knew about this answer. Within 24 hours, all three deals were cancelled.

"It was scary," the financial company president told us. "The guy stood for nothing."

By revealing himself during negotiations, the son single-handedly blew the opportunity of a lifetime for his company. The three deals went down the drain because he failed to speak the common language of old values. He was tested with questions about his social, economic, political, and educational values, and he showed himself unable to speak the common language related to any of these types of values. He was an empty suit, the kind of negotiator capable negotiators dread, because nothing agreed upon can be counted upon.

TECHNIQUES TO TEST AN OPPONENT'S OLD VALUES

Concentrate on four types of values. During any important negotiation, always arrange for some apparently idle conversation about four areas of your opponent's life:

- His or her earlier educational experiences.

- His or her political feelings. (Reserve this topic for very important negotiations.)
- His or her social worlds: sports, interests, friends, and habits.
- His or her economic and business views and philosophies.

Use your opponent's vocabulary to discuss values. Never come right out and ask, "How do you feel about loyalty, pride, honesty, manners, patience, love, dedication, consistency, discipline, moderation, quality, and ethics?"

Instead, repackage such questions. This will give you the answers you need without having to pose formal questions. For example, by the time you get an opponent to talk casually about where he or she went to school and related experiences and friendships, plus his or her political feelings, social activities, and economic and business attitudes, you will have the answers to your "old values" questions. What's more, you never looked as if you were asking, yet you learned what kind of person is sitting across the table.

USING AUTHORITY SYMBOLS TO YOUR ADVANTAGE

Authority symbols include such things as—

- Numbers.
- Experts and consultants.
- Legal opinions.
- Policy manuals.
- Personality and dress.
- Third-party references.
- Physical environments and objects.

In planning, you will concentrate on which authority symbols best fit the parties and topics of a given negotiation.

A BASIC RULE FOR USING AUTHORITY SYMBOLS

A basic rule about authority symbols is that you always seek to have your symbols accepted while neutralizing or diplomatically casting doubt upon those of your opponent. For example, a car sales person reaches for an authority symbol, the small book that lists the trade-in value for your car. You listen to the valuation that the sales person gives you, and then you smile and say, "Why do you sales people use that book differently? It seems that everywhere I go, a different number pops out."

You are diplomatically placing the sales person's authority symbol in doubt. You never say that you disagree, but rather you suggest that other competitive sales people seem to disagree. Having reduced the effectiveness of the authority symbol, you produce a piece of paper from your pocket on which is written a price. The price has been initialed, and this becomes your authority symbol. You then say, "Here's a firm offer on my car which, as you can see, is a little better than your book shows." In fact, it is much better, but you play down the difference to make it easier for the sales person to save face in the event that he or she wants to match your authority.

In this example, we dealt with three different authority symbols:

1. *Policy manuals*, such as the little book the sales person used to quote a price.

2. *Numbers*, which in this case dealt with both the sales person's numbers and your numbers.

3. *Experts and consultants*, which in this case took the form of the person who initialed your price quote on the paper you carried into this showroom.

IDEAS TO BLUNT THE IMPACT OF YOUR OPPONENT'S AUTHORITY SYMBOLS

- A rich opponent seeks to intimidate you by arranging to have the negotiating sessions at his posh country club. (The club becomes an authority symbol.)

  You feel that for this negotiation you too must flaunt your financial strength. You arrive at his club in your private helicopter (which you chartered for this purpose). The helicopter becomes an authority symbol which connotes your affluence.

- In one negotiation your opponent shows up with a lawyer from a prestigious local law firm. You anticipated this use of a legal authority symbol, so you walk into the meeting with your lawyer from a prestigious big city firm. Now your authority symbol equals, if not exceeds, that of your opponent. Always try to better your opponents' authority symbols. At the very least, match them, because by matching you neutralize your opponent's advantage.

- Your opponent is a sharp negotiator. You are involved in a critical negotiation about the value of a piece of rental country property which you seek to buy. You know that she is a great numbers person and will come armed with statistics about everything in an attempt to value the property as high as possible. Her authority symbol will be numbers.

  In this case, say to yourself, "The heck with her numbers." You arrange for two previous tenants of the property to be waiting outside of the meeting. After your opponent produces her high price and backs it with the authority symbol of numbers, you introduce your authority symbols, the two previous tenants.

  "I thought we both might enjoy hearing from these people who have had actual experience with this property." You smile, and continue, "They tell me those neighboring properties make things miserable during the hot weather." At this point, your people outdo one another in their complaints about the sights and smells of a nearby pig farm. By the time they leave the meeting, your opponent knows her numbers have had it. Now, you can get down to realistic negotiation.

The two tenants were your third-party reference authority symbol.

The key to selecting and using authority symbols that equal or better those of your opponent is knowing that you need to do this. Many people accept their opponent's policy manuals, numbers, experts, or intimidation through name dropping, wealthy lifestyles, or displays of power. Many other people limit their use of authority symbols to the exact matching of their opponent's authority symbols. Such people always try to find a lawyer to match a lawyer, or numbers to match their opponents' numbers. If they can't exactly match in this way, they may say, "Oh no! My numbers won't stand up to theirs." If this feeling of inadequacy ever threatens your negotiating plans, remember how the numbers in our real estate example were matched—not by numbers, but by a pig farm.

WHAT TO REMEMBER IN NEGOTIATIONS BESIDES MONEY

In negotiations about price, never limit your strategy to money alone. If you are trying to negotiate greater productivity from production people, money is often the last issue you should mention. Factors such as pride, interdepartmental competitiveness, company survival, family feelings, and team or group opinions are often much more important than appeals based only on money.

If you are trying to hire a key executive, money may be much less important than intangibles such as recognition, excellence, security, challenge, exploration, or dedication. If you are negotiating to buy a company, a machine, or quantities of inventory, who are you and what you are doing may be as important to the seller as the monetary price under discussion.

MISUNDERSTANDING MONEY'S ROLE IN NEGOTIATION: AN EXAMPLE

A successful small business president believed that he could buy anything and anybody with money. In his middle age, the president suffered a massive heart attack. As he lay in the hospital fighting for his life under a plastic oxygen tent, he summoned his doctor to his side and said, "Get me through this, and I'll take care of you handsomely."

The next morning, the president died while the doctor was at home sleeping. "It was inevitable," the doctor said. The man's last negotiating appeal about money had failed!

Had the president been a close friend of the doctor, perhaps the doctor would have stayed at his side throughout the night. Could the doctor have pulled the patient through his seizure early that morning? We'll never know, of course, but we do know that money was the wrong negotiating tactic for the president to use.

WHY MONEY CAN BE LESS IMPORTANT THAN POWER

As we move through life, our daily negotiations with other people take a variety of forms. Often, money has nothing to do with our success or failure as a negotiator. When your assistant voluntarily misses the train to complete important letters, he or she is not making this personal sacrifice for monetary reasons. Earlier, you have negotiated with the assistant in nonmonetary terms.

When a team of doctors goes without sleep for 36 hours to save a President's life, they are responding to earlier negotiated, nonmonetary standards of behavior. If your right-hand employee voluntarily burns the midnight oil to get important work completed for you, this usually has nothing to do with motivation based on money. You have earlier negotiated a sense of responsibility toward yourself.

WHEN TO LEAVE MONEY OUT OF NEGOTIATIONS

The chairman of one of the nation's leading publishing firms was having lunch with a prominent senator. The senator told the chairman about a recent rebuff he suffered from a charming, white-haired octogenarian lady from whom he had tried to purchase several miles of beautiful sand dunes and ocean beach front for a vacation retreat.

"I know she needed the money," the senator explained, "but even when I doubled the price I knew she had in mind, she turned me down."

The chairman smiled at his luncheon guest, murmured a few words of compassionate understanding, and the conversation turned to other matters.

The following weekend, the chairman flew to the ocean front location which the senator had described. He fell in love with it immediately and determined to succeed where the senator had failed. But the chairman used a different approach in his negotiating plan. His strategy had nothing to do with price or money. Here's what he did:

1. He tried to learn who influenced the landowner. He looked for key people *at* her peer level, *below* her level, and people *above* her peer level, the people to whom she looked up.

2. As it turned out, the woman looked up to her daughter. She regarded a doctor as her equal and as her closest friend. She placed complete confidence in a caretaker for the protection and maintenance of her property; this person had served her for almost 40 years.

3. The chairman looked for key motivations in the lives of the

three people who influenced the woman. The daughter loved to sail. The doctor was raising funds for a new rural hospital. The caretaker spent all of his free time fishing on the beach, surfcasting.

4. Over the next several months, the chairman arranged to have the caretaker teach him to surfcast. The two men became very friendly. Then, through the caretaker, the chairman arranged to meet the doctor, and to have the doctor tell him of his new rural hospital plan. Of course, the chairman made a significant donation to the fund drive. And, through the doctor, the chairman first met the lady and her daughter. In the case of the daughter, the chairman arranged for her to crew one of his friend's sailboats in the next Bermuda race.

5. The chairman's actions drew the landowner's approval. After all, everyone she liked and respected now respected and liked him.

6. During all of this positioning, the chairman never raised the subject of the land purchase to anyone. He waited until he had captured the approval of the people under, over, and at the same level of the landowner.

7. Finally, he raised the subject to the doctor in a very off-handed way. He suggested that he would like to spend more time in the area if he could "find an attractive piece of land."

    To the caretaker, he said, "What's going to happen to your fishing beaches when she dies?"

    Then, to the daughter, he said, "I've just come into a small family inheritance, and I think I'd like to buy something down here, if it's not too expensive."

The chairman bought the land at 75 percent of the owner's original asking price. He not only got the land he wanted, but the chairman saved almost $1 million on the land the senator could not have for double the money.

THE SECRETS OF EFFECTIVE USE OF SILENCE IN NEGOTIATIONS

Many people oversimplify the use of silence as a tactic to intimidate others. For example, law enforcement officers believe that deadpan silence is the best demeanor in preliminary contacts with offenders. In fact, this posture becomes so habitual that when a police officer knocks on your door to ask whether your pet is licensed, you feel as though a neighbor just turned you in as a child molester. Such is our reaction to silence and deadpan expressions before we know someone's intention!

In case you doubt that the police officers are aware of this effect upon you, consider how even they have developed the corollary routine of good cop/bad cop for negotiations after the preliminary contact.

The need to have a good cop proves that even the police recognize that silence, accompanied by hard-nosed body language, goes only so far.

REASONS TO AVOID MAKING SILENCE A HABITUAL RESPONSE

Just as a police officer's stony, habitual silence can convey a misleading impression about the officer's purpose, many people habitually mislead others with their silence in negotiations. This happens when your habitual silence is not seen for what it really is, a habit. Instead, silence may upset negotiations in any number of ways, such as—

- Your silence is interpreted to be anger, and your opponent responds by getting angry.
- Your silence is interpreted to be disapproval, and your opponent puts his or her guard up.
- Your silence is interpreted as noncomprehension, and your opponent wonders how sharp you are.

WHY PROPERLY USED SILENCE CAN BE A PRIME NEGOTIATING TACTIC

Using silence as a listening tool can draw out your opponent's feelings. It pays to try to have your negotiating opponent reveal most, if not all, demands before you reveal what you want. Thus, silence can be a valuable tool if properly used. The key word is "properly." You may talk less to get your opponent to talk more. But never display complete, stony silence. Instead, smile or look attentive and say, "Tell me more about what you're thinking."

An opponent who knows you are listening will neither resent nor misinterpret your silence. In fact, the silence used in listening can be very flattering to the other person.

With practice, you can combine well-calculated silence with body language for effective results. For example, to show disapproval of your opponent's demands, you may stay silent while looking either confused or very stern. To encourage your opponent, stay silent, but let your facial expression reflect hope, anticipation, or intense interest. Lean forward in your chair to show you are awaiting every word with great expectation.

If you sense an impasse caused by your opponent's loss of emotional control, make up a diplomatic excuse to interrupt the negotiations. Through your absence, you are using silence.

Once you start to think about how to use silence and body language in clever ways, you will not be lacking ideas. The key, however, is to think about silence. Never let silence become habitual, or you will risk misunderstanding. Use your silence to be a good listener. Your opponents may find themselves thinking, "I can really talk to that person; I can really get through to that person."

HOW TO AVOID GETTING PARANOID

In negotiations, remember that the potential for undue paranoia is a two-way street. You must keep yourself from becoming unduly paranoid and be on guard for this possibility in your opponents. But don't forget, you should approach any negotiation with some fears about some aspects of the negotiation. By trying to anticipate trouble, you use controlled paranoia to stay sharp and alert. This is quite different from uncontrolled, undue paranoia.

SIX SIGNS OF UNCONTROLLED, UNDUE PARANOIA

1. You sweat, tremble, or feel ill.
2. You start to hate, resent, and despise the other side.
3. You have a gut-level fear of the other side. This is different from fear based on some logical reason.
4. You suddenly feel inadequate, spent, or undone for no logical reason.
5. You feel the need for flight, to run away, leave, get out!
6. You panic and can't be sure what you feel or what you should do. Your mind shuts down.

WHY A PARANOID OPPONENT IS ALWAYS A PROBLEM

Many wise-guy negotiators like to boast, "Hey, did I have them on the run!" When people say something like this, they are usually expressing victory feelings. These feelings are often based on the assumption that the opponents came apart at the seams in some way. Wise-guy negotiators may also boast, "I showed them who was in charge." But a person who thinks he or she won a negotiation through intimidation, through fear, or by causing undue emotional trauma may be in for some unexpected results.

Agreements based on fear or undue emotional trauma do not result from true negotiations; they are the products of power plays. People who are beaten by fear or trauma may return with a big brother at their side. In organizations, such people may seek revenge in other ways, such as—

- Lowering productivity.
- Confusing your delegation.
- Providing misinformation.
- Destroying your image.
- Aiding your competitors.
- Outright physical sabotage.

FIVE RULES FOR KEEPING HATE, FEAR, AND CONFUSION OUT OF NEGOTIATIONS

Rule: Never negotiate when fear rules. Your negotiation may be simple, such as negotiating with an employee to work late, or complicated, such as mergers, departmental reorganizations, or union contracts. Whatever the case, stop everything when you or your opponent shows undue paranoia.

Rule 2: After you have found a diplomatic excuse to interrupt negotiations, ask yourself who is getting paranoid. It may seem to be the other side, and maybe it is. Then again, it could be you.

Rule 3: Provide enough time for the feelings of paranoia to subside to controlled levels. For example, an opponent may still dislike you intellectually, but after a cooling off period, at least the person won't become enraged at the sight of you.

Rule 4: In every negotiation, give opponents a way to feel as if they won something, too.

Rule 5: Smile! A genuine smile will cure more paranoia in other people than all the pills and psychiatrists available. Smile across the table again, and keep doing it. Your smiles during even the most difficult negotiations will often turn out to be self-fulfilling prophecies.

IDEAS FOR USING THE REVERSE SELL

We all think we understand the reverse sell. After all, we may reason, "When you want to buy something and you hope to horse trade to make the deal, simply act as if you are not going to buy it. That will get you the lowest price possible."

Sometimes this works, but the problem with this approach to the reverse sell is, of course, that we all really do know it, including our opponents. Don't expect this tactic to be terribly effective in this simple form.

WHAT EDGAR ALLEN POE KNEW ABOUT THE REVERSE SELL

Think a few minutes about what Edgar Allen Poe called, "The imp of perverseness." This is the strange inner feeling we sometimes call "an urge to jump." Who has not looked off a high bridge, down an elevator shaft, or out of a plane and had the fleeting urge to take the plunge? The feeling is hard to define because our rational mind tells us, "Don't be ridiculous," at the very moment some other force is producing an urge to jump. Could this urge be our desire to experience the unknown?

THE ROLE OF CURIOSITY IN THE REVERSE SELL

Some people feel there must be an element of risk in what they do. This is certainly true with "the imp of perverseness." But another factor—curiosity—can be just as powerful a drive as "the imp," but without the risk. For example, suppose that, as you stand at the plane door toying with the idea of jumping, someone offers you a parachute. You may still jump, but the original urge, which was related to great risk or self-destruction is gone because the risk is gone from your jump.

HOW SOPHISTICATED USE OF THE REVERSE SELL COUPLES CURIOSITY AND "THE IMP"

- A stockbroker says to a wealthy client, "We could buy some of that, but you've had absolutely no experience in that area. The risk would be very great!"

  The rich client doesn't need more money, and the broker knows this. The broker arouses the client's curiosity with the phrase, "But you've had absolutely no experience with that." When the broker says, "The risk would be very great," the client feels the urge to jump.

  Unlike jumping from a high bridge, the broker knows the client will not lose everything if the stock loses money. The bridge isn't really that high. As a result, the client puts a large amount of money into a high risk, unfamiliar investment. The broker gets a heavy commission, because the higher the investment risk, the higher the commission.

- When parents bring home a new kind of food to a child who is traditionally a reluctant eater, one of them may say, "This is something very different. I'm not sure you'd even like it. Besides, it's not for you. It's for me. If you take any out of the refrigerator, I promise you you'll get a spanking."

  This child suddenly feels twin urges. Neither urge relates to physical hunger. The child's mental hunger relates to:

  1. Curiosity because the parent says, "I'm not sure you'd like it," and

  2. The urge to take risk by entering the refrigerator to sample the food and thereby risk a spanking. These parents know exactly what they are doing. For this reason, they unobtrusively stay near the refrigerator until the child opens the door. "Oh, alright, but just take one," the mother says. Of course, the child takes several. The parents carefully look the other way. To take only one would take away the child's risk.

Many sophisticated reverse sells utilize a form of, "You can't have it." This challenges a person to try, to risk. It also arouses the person's curiosity about new experiences.

EXAMPLES OF "YOU-CAN'T-HAVE-IT" REVERSE SELLS

- "Driving this car is like no other experience in the world, but I do understand it is too expensive for you. I wanted you to see it anyway."

- The employer says to the employee, "This job would probably be over your head, but I wanted you to look it over anyway."
- An interested buyer says to the seller, "You'd never be able to come down low enough so that I could swing it, but if you want to try me, go ahead. I'm listening."

The seller's feelings of risk and excitement in possibly cutting the price presents a challenge. The seller also faces the curiosity about what it would take to close the deal. When sellers apologize for showing you something they "know you can't afford," they add a third element to the risk and curiosity urges—competitive challenge. The reverse sell may have you telling yourself—

1. "I'll show them!"
2. "I'm going to be taking a risk if I buy it, but it would be exciting."
3. "I wonder what it would be like to own it."

WHEN TO CHALLENGE YOUR OPPONENT WITH REAL RISK

Failure and reward are two sides of the same coin; they are the two sides of risk. Normally in a negotiation, discussion of risk centers on ways to reduce the chances of failure. For example,

- "Do it this way, and you'll help your career."
- "This merger will make us unbeatable."
- "Give us this demand, and you'll avoid a strike."
- "Buy this product, and you'll never have a problem."
- "We have to move fast on this if we're going to move at all."

It always pays to suggest to your opponent that something be done because it presents "less risk of failure." But do not limit yourself to this method of using risk.

HOW TO USE RISK AS A CHALLENGE

Risk as a challenge is best applied to two situations:

- Where your opponent has a very strong ego, and
- Where your opponent feels that invincible resources are at his or her disposal.

A person with a strong ego may well be unaffected when you say that one option poses less risk than another. With such a person, the argument that agreement to do something will help his or her career may fall on deaf ears. The person with a strong ego sees no chance of failure and therefore no risk.

Negotiating opponents who feel they have invincible resources, such as money, loyalty, or skill will reject your argument for agreement that says, "Do this, and the roof won't fall on you." These people feel they have the resources to handle any problem. If the roof does fall in, they will simply buy or build another one. There are no risk feelings here!

IMAGINATIVE WAYS TO EXPAND THE REWARDS OF TAKING RISKS

In discussing the reverse sell, we considered how the urge to risk it all is not logical, but a desire for kicks. This idea was illustrated by the stockbroker who used this urge for excitement to lead a very rich investor to gamble big. We saw, too, that when you say to someone, "Of course, you couldn't afford to. . . ," then a person may feel the urge to take a risk and the urge to accept the challenge.

This reminds us to always explore our opponents to see how far they will go to experience the excitement of risk. Another way to expand the rewards of risk taking is to challenge an opponent to take the risk of excellence. Here is an example.

A surgeon who agrees to try an experimental surgical procedure can empathize with the patient's risk, but the surgeon faces another sort of risk, namely, the risk to a reputation of excellence. This risk applies to both the surgeon's reputation for excellence among other people and the surgeon's inner confidence.

The risk of excellence is a powerful negotiating tool for certain people, particularly people with large egos or seemingly endless resources. If you can determine what a person regards as his or her points of excellence, you can often base an irresistible challenge to risk excellence, as in this example.

A technical person knows that she is the highest paid specialist in the organization. She also knows no other organizations would match or better her compensation. This is true because of her excellent speed and accuracy on the word processor, and her expertise in your industry's technical vocabulary. She knows that everyone respects her abilities, even as she respects herself, and she works ten hours a day.

How can you get more work out of her? She already thinks she is at top speed, and you think she's at top dollar. To complicate matters, you cannot take her off any projects because all are high priority. But you have two important, highly urgent technical reports that only she could do. The reports require at least eight days of work, and they must be completed in one month.

If she were to work Saturdays and Sundays for four weeks, the work could be done. But to ask this of her would be ridiculous, you realize. To offer money would not be motivation enough because her earnings already far exceed her needs. She is already giving 100 percent. So, the only option left to try is the risk of excellence.

You call her in and explain the situation. You tell her that you know she is giving 100 percent and that she can't work four weekends in a row or more than 10 hours a day. You tell her that you know there is no other work that she can put aside because it's all equally important. Then, you hand her the materials on the two reports. You say nothing except, "Get these out of my sight. I know when we're licked."

For the next four weeks, you do not raise the subject of the reports. You carefully act as if your conversation never took place. At the end of four weeks, she walks into your office and puts the finished reports on your desk. You pick them up, smile, and say only four words, "Thank you very much." You limit your words because you know she did not do these reports for you. She did them for herself.

Four weeks earlier, you took great care to show her that you knew it was an impossible achievement for anyone. This is why she did the reports. Somehow, she raised her productivity to impossible levels. She did this not to impress you but to challenge herself and support her inner sense of excellence. We would guess that, when she first started to work on the two reports, she wasn't sure how they would come out, which is why you never asked her to try. This is why you stayed away from the subject during those four weeks. The key was to let her try the impossible on her own terms and find her own reasons for risking her opinion of her abilities.

HOW TO CONVINCE OPPONENTS THAT YOU'RE SERIOUS

This tactic boils down to convincing your opponent that you really aren't kidding and that there is no mistake about what you said. What you are really doing is assuring opponents that discussion on this point is over.

Caution: Never use this tactic on any negotiating point that you consider even faintly negotiable. Reserve this maneuver for times when there is no further negotiating room on your side of the table.

GETTING THROUGH AN OPPONENT'S GRID

We use the word grid to refer to the insulation we all use to protect ourselves in different situations. This is why we do not hear every insect on a summer evening. To do so would be to lose our minds. Instead, with our grid in place, we tune out much noise.

In the same way, our mind provides us with a grid for each negotiating situation; different opponents have different grids. In a lengthy negotiation, we hear at best only 40 percent of our opponent's words. This is true for most verbal communication under the most ideal circumstances, and many negotiating circumstances are less than ideal.

On key "no-give" negotiating points, we cannot risk 60 percent communications failure. We must break through the grid to get 100 percent attention. We can't rely on normal communication for no-give messages; we must use new forms of communication, as in this imaginative example.

THE MESSAGE OF THE ADMIRAL'S CIGARETTE LIGHTER

We had just finished luncheon with a newly retired U.S. Navy admiral who had become an officer for a large defense contractor. We chose a relaxed atmosphere to discuss serious business. We were attempting to get the admiral's agreement on a number of issues related to his company, and he was very flexible in his thinking. He obviously considered each of our arguments carefully. We were sure we were in complete agreement on several issues. The luncheon session lingered for many hours. We covered a great many topics, although no one took notes.

As we were leaving, the admiral presented each of us with a handsome chrome cigarette lighter. The lighter was emblazoned with a blue flag connoting the admiral's rank. Beneath the flag were words to the effect of—

- "Thanks for the meal which is very much appreciated."

- "Please remember that anything we discussed during our repast should not be construed to be an agreement on anything."

Given the admiral's reputation and power, he was constantly being wooed by people who wanted something from him. To make sure that no one confused his willingness to listen with consent, the admiral created a keepsake to get across his grid-penetrating message.

CREATIVE APPROACHES TO GRID-PENETRATING MESSAGES

- One union negotiator always carried a black crayon and a blank 3″ × 6″ yellow card in his jacket pocket. In most negotiating sessions, he never took the card out of his pocket. But in some key sessions after a heated discussion, he would stop arguing, reach into his pocket, and place the yellow card on the table. Always careful to be sure everyone was watching, he printed on the card in forceful, dramatic strokes.

    What he wrote was never more than one word. He would hold the card up for opponents to see, and he always selected one word to fit the no-give situation. Here are some sample messages: Never, Impossible, Insulting, Ridiculous, Hopeless.

    After holding up the sign, the negotiator would wait silently until all the other participants' curiosity led them to await his next words. Then he would reiterate the exact point on which he refused to yield. This tactic conveyed his message 100 percent of the time.

- If people are shouting emotional demands at you, turn your back and walk away. Do not walk out. Merely take a few steps away. Keep your back to the group or person, so your face isn't visible. When things quiet down, turn around, smile, and state exactly what you will and will not yield on.

    Your body language will get everyone's attention as you

walk away. By not showing your face, you stir their curiosity, and your smile will be a surprise. Now they will hear you.

• If you are in a sedate, dignified negotiating session where good manners prevail, you might emphasize your no-give position by carefully and slowly packing your papers and other belongings such as your briefcase, reports, pencils, glasses, charts, and books. You make it obvious that you are no longer listening.

By the time your opponents notice that you are preparing to leave and that you are not paying attention, they will be primed to hear the next thing that you say with 100 percent attention.

The key to grid-penetrating tactics is surprise. Do something that is out of character to gain 100 percent attention. You must reaffirm your no-give point clearly. Suppose, for example that your opponents never knew you to swear. If they hear you softly say, "Damn," the impact will be greater than a shout because it is so out of character for you.

HOW TO RESPOND TO YOUR OPPONENTS' REAL STRENGTHS

One type of negotiation is always completely worthless. We call this the "if-only" negotiation. Whenever you find yourself saying or thinking "if-only," you are in deep trouble. Examples follow of if-only thoughts to avoid:

- If only they didn't have so much money in their corner.
- If only they weren't so sharp at numbers.
- If only they didn't have time on their side.
- If only they didn't have such a demand for their product.
- If only they didn't have all of that heavyweight talent.
- If only they could see what I see.
- If only they understood what makes me tick.
- If only they knew how important this is.

HOW IF-ONLY ATTITUDES CAN DESTROY NEGOTIATIONS

What you get out of a negotiation often depends on how many if-only's you put into it. This happens because the moment you say if-only, you shut your mind to the possibility that what appear to be your opponent's real strengths may be illusions.

Consider this costly example. If you want to buy a business from wealthy people, you may say, "If only they didn't have so much money." When you stop here and accept this apparent reality, you may pay a much higher price than necessary. You may have overlooked possible deeper, stronger realities, such as—

1. The sellers' money has made them careless about finances; they couldn't care less about haggling over price.
2. Their wealth may not be as great as it once was. Perhaps recent events, such as a divorce, lawsuit, or poor investment, have jeopardized their wealth.

3. A power struggle behind the scenes may make a sale at even a low price a good deal for an owner who wants out.

4. Any number of irrational reasons may have precipitated the sale, such as, "I want out, because I'm bored with this whole thing."

Never permit if-only estimates of their strengths to become your reality before you dig deeper. Learn your opponents' real strengths. Otherwise, you give away a tremendous advantage before negotiations start.

FOUR TIPS FOR OVERCOMING AN IF-ONLY PROBLEM

1. Opponents' real strengths are often not what they first appear to be. Remember this.

2. When you say if-only, you accept strengths at face value. You fail to take the time and effort to dig deeper to learn about possible weaknesses, problems, or information which would reveal the real story behind their apparent strengths.

3. When you say if-only, you are psychologically damaging your negotiating attitudes. You concede something that may not be real. Even if it is real, you are conceding that you can't find offsetting strengths in your position.

4. When you are certain you have determined their real strengths, avoid the if-only approach. Instead, ask yourself "Where else?" Where are they not so strong? Then ask, "How can I exploit this other reality about their relative lack of strength?"

Your outlook depends a lot on mental attitude. Is your glass half empty or half full before negotiations start? Concentrate on filling your glass.

REASONS TO SEARCH OUT HIDDEN AGENDAS

This tactic comes down to mistrust based not on a poor reputation but on an awareness that most people cannot trust themselves. Most people do not always know why they act a certain way. They may always tell themselves rational reasons for their actions, but sometimes these rational reasons conceal a hidden drive which even they cannot consciously recognize.

Here is an example. The chairman of the board of a large Midwest conglomerate had just received notice that his divorce was final. This timing made him seem to want to talk about surrounding events. "I was kidding myself for years," he confided.

"I was telling myself that I wanted to keep a relationship with my wife, but on my terms.

"Three years ago," the chairman continued, "I spent $1.5 million to buy a big vacation spread on Cape Cod. My wife loves to paint, so I figured here was an ideal location to keep her happy, but out of my hair. After all, the spot was not that easy to get to from the Midwest.

"What I didn't realize was that I didn't want to get away from her part of the time; I wanted to get away from her all of the time.

"It cost me an extra $1.5 million to kid myself. She got the Cape Cod property under the divorce settlement. Had I been honest with myself three years ago, I never would have bought the thing."

We provide this personal example because it involves a top negotiator, a person of proven decision-making ability. In this case, even this man failed to negotiate his real need to be rid of his wife. He fooled himself.

Under the right circumstances, even the best negotiators can fool themselves. It pays to question ourselves as well as our opponents before any important negotiation. If we fail to do this, we may win a negotiation that we later wish we had not even considered. It also pays to question ourselves during a negotiation to be sure that some hidden drive isn't causing us to rationalize our actions.

HOW WE KID OURSELVES ABOUT NEGOTIATING MOTIVES

- You make unreasonable demands which you have convinced yourself are justified. Your true motive is to hurt your opponent.

- To please your opponent, you agree to points you could have won. Is this person a member of the opposite sex? An important person? Someone you fear?

- You break off negotiations for no real reason or without having reached an impasse. Your real reason for starting the negotiations in the first place was so you could break them off. Was this for power reasons? A way of kidding yourself about wanting to achieve results when all you wanted was to buy time or delay something? Were you using negotiations to avoid really starting?

In these examples, if you know your real hidden agenda objectives, these tactics may be valid. Problems result when you fool yourself, as well as your opponent. You may realize your true motives, and see how costly your self-deception has been.

FIVE TIPS FOR FINDING AN OPPONENT'S HIDDEN AGENDAS

1. *Before and during negotiations look for new behavior patterns in your opponent.* Is a happy person suddenly grouchy? When you notice behavioral change, expect this to affect your negotiations in hidden ways.

2. *Look for new associates around your opponent.* Ask yourself, who are these people? What do they stand for? How might they be influencing your opponent?

3. *Check on health-related changes in your opponent.* A recent illness? A family member's health problem? A new drug habit? An old drug habit out of control? More and more, last night's high affects daily negotiations.

4. *Check competitors or professionals, such as bankers, who may know something about your opponent.* This is much more than a credit check; it's a gossip check.

5. *Check people in your opponent's organization or family to the extent possible.* If your opponent's family seems concerned about the opponent in any way, beware. This may provide a personality insight for predicting how your opponent will treat you. The way a person treats his or her family may indicate how this person will treat you.

Also, if your opponent's key employees are "yes" people or if they are browbeaten, angry, or illogical, your opponent may have caused the behaviors, and this may hint at your opponent's real drives and objectives.

SECTION 6

WHAT MYSTERY AND FLATTERY HAVE TO DO WITH NEGOTIATION: 14 TACTICS FOR HANDLING PIVOTAL SITUATIONS

SECTION 6

WHAT MYSTERY AND FLATTERY HAVE TO DO WITH NEGOTIATION: 14 TACTICS FOR HANDLING PIVOTAL SITUATIONS

Important negotiations are like championship games. You prepare; then you play wide open. This can be emotionally draining!

The strategies explained in this section will get you through negotiations in terrific form. But once you've concluded your sessions, set these strategies aside until your next important match. Otherwise, you'll go stale.

ROMANCE TACTICS THAT CAN DISTRACT YOUR NEGOTIATIONS

In discussing flattery in Section 4–16, we saw the need to discount flattery that is used as a weapon against us during negotiations. In like fashion, we must guard against another form of persuasion that is calculated to weaken our negotiating position. We refer to this tactic as romance.

Romance comes in many forms, all designed by our opponents to trap us into costly agreements in their favor. Simply stated, they use romance to sweep us forward on the wave of emotion. We experience feelings which just happen to fit their negotiating purposes.

HOW TO SPOT BANDWAGON EXCITEMENT—A TACTIC DESIGNED TO SWEEP YOU ALONG

- The person trying to persuade you toward his or her merger terms might say, "This is the popular new way to do it. Everyone is doing it this way; we'll be right out front with this plan; everyone will be talking about us!"

- A seller of a product or service might say, "Everyone's buying it; the problem, before long, will be a shortage of supply. So, if you want to be sure that you'll be in the avant-garde, better let me sign you up now."

- A department head is meeting with subordinates to sell them on the need for more output from each staff member. The manager might say, "In this company, we have to be sure that the parade doesn't pass us by. We want management to see that this department is way out in front as we charge across the finish line at year's end."

Bandwagon excitement appeals boil down to combinations of four elements calculated to gain our agreement:

1. They seek to muster our feelings of excitement to sweep us along.

2. They suggest that we had best join the parade before it passes us by.

3. They urge us to get in step because it is popular to do so.

4. They suggest a competitive advantage for us by our leadership role, and our role is whatever our opponent wants us to do!

PRIDE, EXCELLENCE, AND STATUS AS ROMANCE TACTICS

These tactics are often hard to resist because they play on our ego. Consider how powerful the following nonmonetary appeals can be.

- *An appeal to pride:* "Wait until your family learns about this arrangement; they'll be so proud to know you."

- *An appeal to status:* "I imagine this will pop open the eyes of a few of your friends."

- *An appeal to excellence:* "This meets your standards in every way, and others will again be reminded of what you stand for."

HOW SOMEONE CAN EXPLOIT YOUR CURIOSITY ABOUT ROADS NOT TAKEN

Here are some costly examples of people who bought this appeal and regretted it:

- An executive was doing very well with her large firm, but she jumped ship to go with a small, high risk company. "I lost my marbles," the woman said. "They persuaded me that the wild unknown was a romantic place to be. I gave up everything to satisfy my curiosity about small companies. How could I have been so dumb in the name of adventure? Some adventure! They went bankrupt ten months after I joined them."

- The purchaser of an expensive computer system told us, "I got taken, badly taken, just because I developed this curiosity about computers. When they sold me the system, I absolutely believed I would be breaking new ground. What a letdown when I found it was the same old stuff wrapped inside the fancy computer trimmings with no new frontiers whatsoever."

- The seller of a small business said, "They came in with all this razzle dazzle about how I'd be part of their new big conglomerate. They promised me opportunities I had never imagined. I decided that this was a whole new world that I had been missing and that this was the time to leave my old humdrum life behind. I was heading into the stratosphere."

Unfortunately, the executive had no golden parachute when the promising new conglomerate encountered serious financial trouble. He was fired; the value of stock he received as payment for his company declined 70 percent. The stock has not come back and its prospects are bleak.

WHY BEING CLOSE TO LEADERS SEEMS SO ENTICING

People often do strange things to please others whom they consider to be important leaders. When they try to please a leader, they do so for selfish reasons. They expect some of the leader's power, wealth, or reputation to rub off on them. This idea is not a problem, provided that you do not deceive yourself about how close you may be to a leader. This is especially true after you agree to whatever the leader wanted.

Often, top leaders drop into a negotiating situation, persuade others to agree with them, and then drop out of the lives of the people they romanced. The next two examples illustrate possible consequences of being taken in by a vanishing leader:

- A once highly successful marketing executive said, "I was personally interviewed by one of the richest men in the world. He wanted me to come to work for one of his companies. I gathered he was vitally involved with the company. I agreed to join him at little gain in income because I figured I could ride his coattails. Then, I never saw him again, not once in three years I was with the company. All of a sudden there were six layers of authority between me and him, and I couldn't break through. One day during the fourth year, I finally managed to be in a large luncheon meeting where he was present. You know, he didn't even remember my name."

  This executive left the fast track of a previous job and succumbed to the romance of a leader. The executive failed to consider the possibility of being forgotten and buried in the leader's labyrinthian organizational structure.

- The owner of a profitable small business says, "The governor persuaded me to move my entire operation to his state. What a treatment I got. He personally met me at the plane; his wife took my wife shopping; he took me all around the state capital, and even included us in his inaugural ball gala. Six months later, I couldn't even reach him on the phone or get in to see him. Oh, his people were polite about it all; they always had a good reason about the governor being tied up with other things. But the fact remains that I moved my factory and my family to this state because I thought I would be gaining access to someone with political clout. I was much better off before this spellbinder sold me a bill of goods."

When you negotiate with a leader whom you admire, be sure that this person will be around long enough to implement the promises he or she makes or implies. When you agree to negotiating terms to hitch yourself to a leader's star, be sure that the leader's star isn't about to leave your orbit.

HOW TO GO HEAD-TO-HEAD WITH A RINGER

Here are some red lights and strategies to overcome them:

- Before negotiations, if your opponents are not sure who will be on their negotiating team, be equally vague until you find out who they have in mind.
- If your opponents plan to have a top-flight ringer at their side, arrange to match or exceed the strategy by having equal, better, or more ringers with you. For example, if your opponents hire the top law firm in your town, you hire the top firm in the state, and possibly the leading firm in the field.
- If you suspect that your opponents will bring in a specialist as a surprise ringer, be prepared to stop negotiations when the ringer appears. Refuse to negotiate until you call in your people.

Talks may have to stop for hours, days, or weeks until you get your ringers at your side. Too bad, but that's the way it is!

HOW TO CONDITION YOURSELF NOT TO OVERRATE AN OPPONENT

"T'.e world puts on you the same value you place on yourself." A corollary to this old adage is, "If you overvalue an opponent, the opponent will overwhelm you."

When you overrate your negotiating opponent, you underrate yourself. As a result, the deal you negotiate will undervalue what you might have won. Preventing yourself from overvaluing someone has nothing to do with avoiding honest appraisal of your opponent's strength.

The art of negotiation is not to duck your awareness of an opponent's strengths while you concentrate on areas that are your strengths. In fact, it makes absolutely no sense to go into a negotiation all hopped up through self-hypnosis about winning, winning, winning! It makes no sense to replace intelligent appraisal of your opponent's strengths with positive thinking about everything. It makes great sense, however, to tell yourself, "Hey, I know where this person is strong, but he or she may have forgotten to notice where I'm strong."

The stronger your opponent, the greater the odds that he or she will be careless. This is true because strong people know what they have going for them. The moment that you realize how an opponent's strengths may sap his or her sharpness, then you will never again overrate an opponent. Instead, you will value the role of underdog as you plan a big upset win over people who may take your negotiation for granted.

The results of a person who anticipates the role of underdog are vastly different from the results of a person who enters negotiation in a hangdog mood.

Underdog, maybe; Hangdog, never!

HOW TO REACT TO FLATTERY

In everyday life, a little flattery will never hurt anyone. In fact, our tie, dress, or new car takes on a special meaning when someone compliments our selection. On the other hand, during important negotiations, even random remarks about little things must be viewed with suspicion. Is your opponent seeking negotiating benefit through flattery?

SIX FLATTERING STATEMENTS NEGOTIATORS MIGHT HEAR

- The seller says, "I wouldn't give this price to anyone else. But you're my friend, so why not."

- The buyer says, "I know your reputation for honesty. I won't quibble about the price, except we do have to talk a little more to see if we can't get closer together on this."

- The boss says, "I'm giving you this extra work load because, to tell the truth, there's no one else in the organization capable of handling it the way you will."

- The professional says, "I want you as my client, not really for the fee, but for the mental challenge you give me. It's very satisfying to work with you."

- The would-be merger partner says, "We admire you and your company so very much, not so much for the profits you generate, but for the values you represent."

- The lawyer says to the jury, "I would never suggest how much you should award my client in this case. I know you are all unselfish humanitarians who embody the spirit of this nation's founding fathers, the spirit that protects, the individual against selfish institutions." In this case, the lawyer cleverly pretends to assume that the jury will vote for his client. He uses flattery about the jury to shift the issue from who is right *to how much*. His flattery in effect says to the jury, "With such superior people as yourselves, your wisdom is obvious to me." At this point, many jurors will hate to act in a way that contradicts the lawyer's description.

A TOOL TO KEEP YOU ON THE LOOKOUT FOR FLATTERY

A very successful negotiator, now retired, revealed her approach to negotiating flattery of any kind, "I always remember what the letters in the word flattery stand for."

"F" reminds me of all the *friends* I once had when they wanted something from me.

"L" Reminds me of all the *love* that people offered me when I had something to give to them.

"A" reminds me of what happens *after* people get what they need.

"T" reminds me of the *temper* that often lies hidden beneath the nice words.

"T" also reminds me that many people *test* you through their flattery.

"E" reminds me that flattery during negotiations is usually *empty* of rewards for me.

"R" reminds me of the need to *renegotiate* with anyone who has successfully fooled me with flattering words.

"Y" reminds me of the *yearning* in everyone for friends, compliments, recognition, wealth, and power. These are the very yearnings that false flattery trades upon. And, these are the yearnings I police in myself every time sweet words of flattery come floating across the negotiating table.

WHY YOU CAN WIN THROUGH INDIRECT SUGGESTION

Suppose several employees in your office are asking you to invest in an expensive air-conditioning installation. Last year, some of these people threatened to quit if you didn't do something by this year. But you do not have the money this year, and now it is the first day of May. How do you control the ugly negotiating demands you see coming?

You decide to use indirect suggestion. You buy a dozen inexpensive, compact fans. You place the fans in conspicuous locations and attach long streamers of colored paper to the grills, so that the streamers are very visible when the fans are on. Everyone sees the streamers blowing like crazy, and they assume that it is cooler, plus they see the flashy fans and assume that you met their demands.

Had you tried to negotiate directly with your people to convince them that the fans would be the answer, they would have laughed at you. By implementing a solution without discussion, you have reached agreement with most people. After all, they can see how hard the streamers are blowing. This indirectly suggests to employees that the problem has been solved.

A FURTHER EXAMPLE OF INDIRECT SUGGESTION

You know that one of your key people is thinking of quitting because she feels she is not appreciated. You do not have the money to give her an adequate raise right now since the raise would have to be at least several thousand dollars to demonstrate your appreciation.

You do, however, have a bit more than $1,000 available. To offer this amount as a raise would be an insult. So, you spend it on new office furnishings for her. And, you use surprise. You don't tell her that over the weekend she'll be getting a new desk, a couch, carpet, plus new paint for her office.

When she comes to work Monday morning, she is overwhelmed. She can see that she is appreciated; she feels appreciated. And, her productivity hits even higher levels. You negotiated for this higher productivity by using indirect suggestion, and you postponed a normal salary negotiation until later when you will be more likely to find it affordable.

IDEAS FOR USING INDIRECT SUGGESTION

• When you want to signal appreciation, do something thoughtful that says more than money could.

• When you want to head off negotiations you know you can't win, indirectly suggest another solution.

• When you are a sales person who wants a buyer to see more in your product than just the product, casually say, "We're planning a special Super Bowl party next year for our customers."

    You may wonder if such indirect "bribery" is a valid negotiating tool. It is, provided that it is always artfully done in an indirect manner.

• When you are a buyer who wants a seller to feel that he or she is getting more than just the terms of a sale, say, "I hope we can do business again soon." Or, "I hope that we can put this deal together because you never know where our relationship may lead."

An indirect future promise is the negotiator's most potent invisible bargaining chip. If you can convince your opponent that there may be future hidden advantages in agreeing to your demands, then you motivate this person without officially committing to anything. You arrange to have your opponent read your indirect suggestion any way that helps your bargaining position.

KEY TACTIC: Learn a Lesson from Politicians

Successful U.S. President's often phone key members of Congress for support on pending legislation. At other times, Presidents go a step further. They invite members of Congress to the White House for a face-to-face meeting.

    An invitation to the White House thus becomes an open-ended indirect suggestion. It can be read to suggest indirectly future closeness to the President. Of course, the President never actually suggests any future benefits. The visitor simply reaches her or his own conclusions.

WHY POSSIBILITIES FOR INDIRECT SUGGESTION ARE EVERYWHERE

Think about all of the profitable places that you can make indirect suggestion work for you by simply supplying an object.

- Leave the lawn mower outside the house to suggest indirectly that someone might want to use it.

- Buy a new office file cabinet to suggest indirectly that certain people might want to clear their desks.

- Put a new broom in a warehouse to suggest indirectly that conditions are getting sloppy. Perhaps someone will pick up the broom and use it from time to time.

- Buy self-correcting typewriters for your people to suggest indirectly that you aspire to better letters.

- Supply private parking places for your key people. Their names carefully hand-lettered on their space to suggest indirectly how important they are to you.

- Leave a confidential report or money on your desk when you step out of a meeting in your office for a long break. The person who remains waiting in your office now knows you trust him or her.

- Install a coffee machine to suggest indirectly that it is a better solution than leaving the premises to go out for coffee.

- Install a round conference table to suggest indirectly that you want more democracy, less hierarchy in your meetings. No more maneuvering for status seating.

When an object succeeds in getting people to act or think in the way you desire, you have negotiated with them.

DECIDING HOW HIGH IS TOO HIGH TO MAKE DEMANDS

In all honesty, before a negotiation you can never be sure how high you can take your demands. This is true even when you think you have a price range bracketed. Unless you are selling a mass market product, such as lipstick or an automobile, you usually have neither the time nor the money to test market your wares in a controlled, accurate, and conclusive manner. So, depending on what you are selling, you will attempt to test the market in informal, nonconclusive ways. This will give you a reasonable price range. Still, you can't be sure.

Finding the right price for items that are not designed for the mass market, for nonunion wages, or nonprofessional executive services is like guessing which person would be willing to marry you. Until you ask, you just can't know. Even then, you might wonder if another buyer who might have given you more was just around the corner.

HOW TIMING INFLUENCES PRICE

Timing is an important aspect of price. The more time you have to shop around for buyers, the better your chance of getting a higher price. This means that not having to negotiate your sale in a hurry can pay off.

The best way to test your final price may be to carry on several negotiations simultaneously. You do not let a potential buyer get away until each one is bidding against the other. They may not realize this, however. Here again, you have the time to wait until you get more than one potential buyer interested.

Timing also influences price increases and decreases. Just when you may think you have narrowed down your price range, an outside influence often complicates the situation. For example, if you are a job seeker, a competitor suddenly appears. Or, if you are selling a high ticket item, interest rates suddenly rise. In another case, everything is in order, and then something unexpectedly happens to change the buyer's mood.

Now you see the dilemma we are often in. We need time to get our best price, but time can work against us if outside influences suddenly alter prices. There is no pat way to straddle both sides of the fence. Sorry!

PRICING TACTICS TO HELP YOU GET MORE IN NEGOTIATIONS

1. Try to gain agreement on everything else before handling the price issue.
2. From your negotiations on agenda items other than price, you will often come to understand the potential buyer's interests, mood, and character. After all, until you qualify a potential buyer's ability to pay, why worry about a price or anything else?
3. After determining that you have a qualified potential buyer with a reasonable amount of interest, and once you reach agreement on issues other than price, you are ready to take up this issue.
4. Start to talk price from the top down. It is easy to climb down the price mountain, but almost impossible to drag a potential buyer uphill once you have quoted a lower price.
5. If the potential buyer rejects a high price, make the buyer drag you down the price mountain. If you are willing to go down "x" percent, do it one percentage point at a time! Remember, as you drag your feet, the potential buyer gets tired and possibly impatient enough to settle higher than the "x" percent limit you have in mind.
6. If the potential buyer insists on a price below your limit, do not give up the ship. Instead, repackage the deal. Offer to give less for the same price, or ask for price add-ons that make up your dollar deficiency.

    When you attempt price add-ons, you are really trying to make the deal you would have given the buyer anyway appear to be something new which costs extra. Thus, the potential buyer says he or she will pay "x" thousand dollars. You know this is "y" dollars below your minimum. So, you ask, "In cash?" If the potential buyer asks for payment terms, you have a chance for an interest add-on.

KEY TACTIC: What to Do about a "Take It or Leave It" Price

When you meet a genuine "take it or leave it" price offer
from a potential buyer, the trick is to keep talking as you
probe for add-on possibilities.

HOW TO BE SURE YOUR OPPONENT WINS SOMETHING

A carefully negotiated agreement that comes apart at the seams can be very expensive in time, money, and lost opportunities. When this happens, it is often because the other party suddenly decides that the deal was really a lopsided victory for you.

WHAT HAPPENS WHEN PEOPLE FEEL THAT THEY'VE BEEN TAKEN

People who feel that an agreement is unfair will resort to a variety of tactics, including the following:

- Attempts to stop payments required under an agreement.
- Attempts to stop performance requirements under an agreement.
- New employees who quit soon after their hiring.
- Older employees who unexpectedly retire because of the new jobs you worked out with them.
- Employees who simply fail to carry out the tasks you delegated in negotiations with them.
- Products that are returned with claim for 100 percent refunds.
- Mergers that never go through.
- People who refuse to ever again do business with you.
- Horror stories for your competitors to use about you.

TEN KEYS FOR KEEPING YOUR OPPONENT HAPPY WITH A DEAL

1. *Never seem to rush an agreement with anxiety-laden people.* If you hurry such people, their anxiety increases about everything they agreed to do.

2. *Always take time to find ways to remind people that you are a warm*

human being. This calms anxieties and makes it difficult for people to feel they have been taken.

3. *The more you listen to people about anything, the more they will think the terms agreed to were based on their needs, even if this is not the case.* It costs little to listen.

4. *Never let negotiators feel that they have intimidated you into an agreement.* When this happens, they always wonder, "Could we have gotten more?"

5. *Try to make humor part of any negotiation.* This always creates good feelings even about tough negotiations with someone. Show your ability to laugh at yourself. This shows what a really nice person you are.

6. *Before finalizing an agreement, always ask, "Are there any other questions?"* This makes people feel the negotiation process has been fair.

7. *Try to find ways to show people that what has been agreed will make them look good to others: the opposite sex, their peers, their subordinates, and their superiors.* For example, you might get away with discretely cutting a person's authority while simultaneously increasing the importance of his or her title.

8. *Try to prevent fear from becoming an influence on the other person's agreement.* Most people ultimately crack under the continuing pressure of fear. When this happens, the person may ultimately say, "The heck with what I agreed."

9. *In any agreement, assure the other party of success in certain areas.* Here are two examples.

   • If your negotiation results in the other person's loss of authority, create little special assignments that give the illusion of an important job.

   • If you sell someone a product or service, find ways to be sure that the buyer feels some success. Have third parties tell the person what a good deal he or she got.

10. *Wherever possible, use indirect suggestion.* This means that if you want a person to feel good about an agreement, you never directly say, "You got a good deal." Instead, you might smile a weak smile and say, "I'm very satisfied." Then the other person will believe he or she has got a good deal because they think they see you convincing yourself.

    Or, you might fight on the smallest of points, even though you are easily willing to yield. When you nitpick and lose, the other person often thinks he or she has won the war. In reality, your tactic is a diversionary action, not war.

Winning can be an illusion which you create for the other person. As a rule, always keep your mouth shut, even to close friends, when you have won big. By your silence, you ensure that gossip will not destroy the illusions you have so carefully placed in your opponent's mind.

HOW TO KNOW WHO HAS DEAL-MAKING AUTHORITY

Except for simple, one-on-one negotiations involving cash and a product that you can immediately take possession of or transfer legal title to, expect the authority to make deals to be split among several people. Such authority may often be informal, as these examples reveal.

EXAMPLES OF INFORMAL AUTHORITY IN ACTION

- *A hostile support group.* The office manager's clerical staff is slow to complete a report the office manager promised you today. The staff's reason for upsetting your arrangements with the office manager may go back to something you said or failed to say about the group. Even imagined slights can cause group hostility.

- *A hostile department.* The head of the sales department promises you two-week delivery to your potentially big new customer. Then the head of manufacturing, who strongly dislikes the sales manager, balks and says, "No way." Not only is the order now in jeopardy, but also the hope of future orders.

- *A hostile institution.* You agree to sell your business to a buyer who can put 50 percent down. You refer the buyer to your local banker to whom such a high equity loan has always been attractive. The buyer calls you back to say the deal is off because the bank turned down the loan. You call to ask what happened, and the banker says, "There was just something about that customer that bothered me."

- *A hostile associate.* The president of your company hires you with the promise to make you a department head in six months. During the first few months on your new job, you clash several times with an employee who has worked in the department for years and who turns out to be very important to the president. It seems the company's oldest, largest customer loves this person. The president explains that you'll have to wait two more years to be head of the department because right now your coworker would not stand for it.

GUIDELINES FOR FINDING THE INFORMAL DEAL MAKERS

1. *Never confine your important negotiations to just one person.* Whether you are negotiating for an important new order for your company or a promotion for yourself, always remember you are negotiating with many people.

   - The boss's assistant may require more attention than the boss.
   - The junior member of a purchasing team may become your hidden enemy if you overlook this person in your negotiations.
   - Tangent groups or people may be critical to your success, and you must seek them out to see exactly what or whom they influence. Such tangent groups can range from family members to public and customer groups. Outside departments can also be critical tangents. An advertising agency may sell a client's advertising and sales departments, but overlook important production people who could be key decision makers.

2. *Always focus on three levels in a negotiation:*

   - The people at your negotiating level.
   - The people below your negotiating level.
   - The people above your negotiating level.

   When you break the authority code, do not reveal that you know who calls the shots *informally* when you are in *formal* negotiations. Keep your formal contacts in the dark as you meanwhile use strategies that you know will have a positive influence on the tangent people in your negotiations. That way you cover all bases without causing your official contacts to lose face.

KEY TACTIC: If in Doubt, Get a Signature From Your
Negotiating Opponent

If the issue of who is calling the shots is cloudy, insist on a legal written agreement or memo of terms of agreement which includes this phrase under the signature line: "I certify that my signature is the sole approval required to make this agreement legally binding." In complaint negotiations and other important matters always seek your lawyer's advice as to how best to pin things down in writing.

UNDERSTANDING THE DIFFERENCE BETWEEN NEGOTIATION AND DISCUSSION

People may think they are negotiating when they are not. As these examples show, the consequences of such a misconception can be devastating.

MISTAKING DISCUSSION FOR NEGOTIATION: THREE EXAMPLES

- Thousands of people get trapped in a career rut by thinking that they are negotiating for their success when they are not. They fail to really negotiate with their superiors for the terms under which they might achieve success. Such people assume that promotion is a pure, logical, inevitable process. Bologna! Success does not happen until a person finds ways to negotiate with his or her superiors all of the time.

- NASA officials spent much of the night before the Challenger space shuttle disaster discussing safety aspects of the launch. Significantly, the decision to launch was made without a consensus. Some of the highest officials in NASA were not told of these unresolved positions.

  A key issue was the possible impact of below-freezing temperatures at the launch site on certain safety and performance devices. The parties to these critical discussions represented a variety of management levels at both NASA and certain manufacturers' locations. In fact, some top NASA people apparently had no knowledge of the discussion until after the accident.

  Two facts that emerged about how a life or death decision was made were these: There was no formal agenda for solving this type of difference of opinion about safety; There were no arrangements for resolving impasses, no established mediation routes of appeal, and no procedure for turning critical random discussions into formal negotiating procedures.

THE VALUE OF USING A FORMAL AGENDA IN NEGOTIATIONS

Discussions about a problem have nothing to do with resolving the problems through formal negotiation. An agenda helps air a variety of positions so that the parties can negotiate different viewpoints in an orderly fashion. Until this happens, nothing gets agreed. Discussion lacks the formality of signatures or a written agreement stating who agrees to what and by what authority.

Discussions pose the danger that people involved in the discussion may mistake it for part of an orderly negotiating procedure. A participant may think that a decision has been made, and that everyone is in agreement when this is not the case. Perhaps some of the people in NASA's prelaunch discussions assumed they were part of formal safety negotiations or that an agenda was in place somewhere to bring order to their differing opinions. Perhaps some NASA officials assumed there were high level, formal negotiations about the safety of the launch, when in fact the only discussions taking place were at random times and places without the highest level people.

RULES FOR DISTINGUISHING DISCUSSION FROM NEGOTIATION

Rule 1: Don't confuse decision making with agreement. Many decisions must be made all of the time without unanimous consent. Avoid the temptation of defending a poor decision with the excuse that everyone agreed to it, even if they did not.

Rule 2: Critical problems and the decisions related to them are best resolved by formal negotiation instead of random discussion. A measure of formality serves to clear the air.

Rule 3: Formal negotiations about how to solve a problem should include a structured agenda. All parties to the negotiation should have to go on record. A clear record of issues agreed upon and not agreed upon should be made and then signed by all parties. The parties should designate a procedure for mediating the remaining differences, and they should spell out the highest level of authority possible. If mediation does not produce a unanimous agreement, whoever makes the final decision must do so without claiming that all parties approved. The situation is similar to a judge deciding between parties after hearing all negotiating positions during a trial.

Rule 4: Just because a group of negotiators follows a certain practice, do not assume that the practice resulted from orderly negotiation. If your opponent in a current negotiation expects you to accept a prior practice, do not! Feel free to question who decided on the benefit of those practices and after how much formal negotiation. Often, you'll find little hard information about such things. So, before going forward in your negotiations, be prepared to renegotiate whenever you suspect that the origins of a negotiating practice is murky. We call this breaking the code about earlier habits and decisions which can affect current negotiations.

TECHNIQUES FOR WORKING OUT HONEST MISUNDERSTANDINGS

It is interesting to note that when two people fall in love for the first time and decide to marry or live together, they almost never complete a written agreement about who owns which assets in the event of a divorce or break up.

It is similarly interesting to note that when two people fall in love for the second time and marry or agree to live together, they almost always complete a written, witnessed, legal document to spell out who gets what and who does what for whom if things fall apart.

In both cases, the people are in love; they trust one another. But the second time around, many people add to their love and trust a mechanism for preventing misunderstanding. Experience has shown such people that agreements based on love and trust work better when procedures are established in advance to avoid honest misunderstandings. Likewise, experience has shown that any agreement on any subject works better for all parties if procedures supplement trust.

SEVEN EXAMPLES OF HOW PROCEDURES REDUCE MISUNDERSTANDINGS

- A patient trusts the family doctor but gets three outside opinions.
- An employee trusts the boss but still gets his or her signature on all important decisions.
- A newly hired person trusts the new company but insists on generous severance pay arrangements.
- A banker trusts a customer's balance sheet but arranges for a physical appraisal of assets listed by an independent auditor. The auditor physically locates and inspects all principal assets. At the same time, the bank's lawyers run searches to verify that these assets are free and clear, as understood.
- A buyer makes the seller put into writing everything that is being

sold or represented. Then the seller is asked to certify by signature the accuracy of the written statement. The signature is witnessed; and if the seller has a superior, the superior signs the statement and has it witnessed. Plus, the buyer's lawyer always checks the written agreement.

- A seller reverses the process just described, but includes special payment procedures and guarantees.

- Significant intracompany agreements of every kind—those between employees, departments—and varying points of responsibility should all be covered by jointly signed memos by the agreeing parties. These memos should specify what has been agreed and who has what responsibility. The original signed copies of such memos should be placed in a safe spot under the control of disinterested third parties.

In many antitrust cases, vice presidents have gone to jail because they were unable to locate files about price fixing that would have shown that their superiors were responsible. Of course, the superiors went free because their knowledge of what their vice presidents were accused of doing could not be proved.

GET IT ON RECORD!

When everyone is on record, you seldom hear the excuse that something is an honest misunderstanding. Could it be that many honest misunderstandings are really dishonest alibis? You can bet on it!

HOW TO SOFTEN UP YOUR OPPONENT BY PUTTING "CASH ON THE TABLE"

- When a young man asks his true love to marry him, he gives her an engagement ring. This is his way of putting "cash on the table" and, in a sense, finalizing the negotiations between himself and his intended.
- When you're dining out and tip the maître d' five dollars for a choice table, you are putting "cash on the table" to impress your dinner guests.
- You want your secretary to work extra hours this week, but you can't afford to pay her overtime. Instead, you place a single red rose on her desk before she comes in Monday morning. It's not cash, of course, but she appreciates your generous gesture—and puts in the extra time with a smile.

HOW TO GET RESULTS WITHOUT SPENDING A FORTUNE

The "cash on the table" principle may have nothing to do with cash at all. Instead, the "cash" you put down is a symbolic gesture of generosity designed to get your opponent to see things your way.

Provided that it's done in the right spirit, a small gesture of generosity may be more effective than a bagful of cash. It isn't the dollar value of your gesture that counts—it's the thoughtfulness behind it. In fact, the best time to put cash on the table may be when you're cash short.

Here are just a few of the ways smart business people have used generous gestures to bring employees and colleagues around to their way of thinking.

CASE 1: USING THE GENEROUS GESTURE AS A NEGOTIATION TOOL TO ATTRACT TOP TALENT

A department head had a very tight budget year in front of him, but he desperately wanted to hire a talented individual employed by a competitor. He met with the man several times. During their final session, he offered a salary which, he knew, was on the low side. But it was the best he had to offer.

As the candidate got up to leave, he said, "Let me think about it. I'll get back to you next week."

At that moment, the department head reached into his desk and took out a gift-wrapped book. "Give this to your wife," he smiled. "It's all about the bottle-collecting hobby she told me about when she had dinner with us last week."

His "cash on the table" gesture made a big impression. It said so much more than money ever could about the kind of man the department head was.

Yes, the man took the job!

CASE 2: IMPROVING PRODUCTIVITY WITHOUT OVERSPENDING

The head of a service organization needed to get more work out of his already well-paid staff. More money wouldn't motivate them to work more hours, and he couldn't afford to pay the extra money in any case.

The organization's offices were located in a city plagued by parking problems. All too often, staffers were forced to park blocks away or waste precious time looking for a parking space.

The head of the organization decided he could solve two problems with a single expenditure. He leased private parking spaces for his staff in the parking lot of a nearby building. Yes, the parking spaces cost money, but they were cheaper than across-the-board raises—and a whole lot more effective.

"That did it," the organization chief reported. "Just by renting those spaces, I got an average of one more hour's work per day from everyone. And they all thought I was a hero to boot."

Here's another example in a similar vein: A sales manager hit his staff with new and higher call quotas. To avoid disputes over the heavier work load, he also announced that from now on, the sales people could take home their company car on weekends. Yes, his gesture cost the company money, but it was insignificant compared to the sales increases generated from the higher quotas.

CASE 3: GETTING WHAT YOU WANT WITHOUT NEGOTIATING AT ALL

The buyer of a key assembly part was already paying the seller top dollar, and he had no more room to negotiate. Mr. Buyer, however, wanted Mr. Seller to provide more backup inventory at Mr. Seller's own plant. He knew, however, that to broach the subject would open up negotiations for a price increase he couldn't afford.

Mr. Buyer knew that Mr. Seller was an avid football fan, so he arranged to buy tickets to the Superbowl for a fraction of what the price increase for inventory would have cost him. By half time, Mr Seller was having the time of his life. Mr. Buyer picked that moment to ask, "By the way, Jim, could you see your way clear to keeping a few more of our items on your shelf?"

"Anytime," Mr. Seller boomed. "Just tell us what you want. It's the least we can do."

Mr. Seller placed more value on Mr. Buyer's generosity than he did on a price increase. And in the process, Mr. Buyer completely side-stepped a difficult—and costly—negotiation.

PUTTING CASH ON THE TABLE GIVES YOU A NEGOTIATING ADVANTAGE

By putting cash on the table—even if your offer has nothing to do with cash—you often gain a negotiating advantage that money could never buy. A thoughtful action tells your opponents what kind of person you are and makes them want to do business with you.

THE ADVANTAGES OF BEING A LITTLE MYSTERIOUS

- Remember the few boys and girls of your youth who were always slightly mysterious? You could never quite be sure how they might react, especially to things involving you.
- Remember how these rare, mysterious people kept you off balance?
- Remember the kids who came from families you knew nothing about, and the kids who went places and did things you never imagined?
- Remember the kids who owned things you never dreamed of owning and spoke words you'd never heard?
- Remember the kids who seemed to have it all: beauty, athletic ability, friends, and straight 'A's?

Even if just one of these memories seems familiar, perhaps you can understand how keeping a little mystery about you can work wonders in negotiations.

TYPICAL REACTIONS TO MYSTERY

Remembering how we felt about people who were mysterious to us when we were children illustrates how mystery about you can intimidate a negotiating opponent.

- If you have an outstanding record in one skill, many people will assume you are equally brilliant in all areas, provided that the one skill in which you excel is mysterious to others.

    Thus, many lawyers rise to the top in organizations where other people are not familiar with law. Coworkers attribute the lawyer with more general management skills than is actually the case.

- If you look and act successful, many people will not search further. They assume you have unique abilities which they may not even attribute to themselves.

- Your opponents may attribute strengths to you if you know and belong to worlds to which they aspire.

- If you take unexpected, mysterious action, your negotiating opponent may imagine strengths or feel fears about the reasons for your unexpected action. Thus, if you suddenly leave the room saying, "I'll have to make a phone call," your negotiating opponent will often read into your mysterious action either a hidden threat or a hidden strength.

- Take care not to seem like one of the boys, a groupie, or an organization stereotype. Many people will not know quite how to handle you. If by seeming different, you are able to get others to attribute more to you than they do to others, then you have a strong negotiating tool.

  For example, a foreman often stopped for a drink with his people after work. The foreman always seemed slightly different from his coworkers, as if separated by some invisible line. After one or two drinks, he always left. His staff, meanwhile, continued the outing for hours.

  Everyone liked the foreman, and he never pulled rank in any way on these social occasions. He just seemed separated by that invisible line. Whenever this foreman negotiated problems on work assignments with his people, he had an advantage. Not only did they think he was different but also they thought he was better because they credited him with strength that he didn't necessarily possess.

  In confidence, we spoke to the foreman about this situation. He admitted that he had his people fooled. "That's why I avoid playing softball with them," he grinned. "They expect that I'll be a star there, too, and I can't hit a barn door. But why disappoint them? Better to just avoid the game."

THREE IDEAS FOR CREATING A LITTLE MYSTERY ABOUT YOURSELF

Create mystery by being unpredictable: Vary your schedules, both business and social. Vary your work and physical habits before, during, and after an important negotiation. Also vary your moods.

Before negotiations, keep the people with whom you will be negotiating guessing about what you are doing and thinking. Thus, never look bothered, worried, tense, or anxious by the impending negotiation. Never let your opponents know who you are seeing, what you are discussing, or how you are spending your time and energies before negotiations. A car sales person would love to know what showrooms you already visited. A president would love to know what other companies you talked to about mergers before starting to negotiate with you.

During negotiations, use mysterious phone calls, interruptions which cause you to leave the meeting, and apparent strengths in areas you deliberately refuse to discuss: These tactics encourage your opponent to attribute more strength to you than you may have. Unexpected silence also can create tremendous mystery about you.

After negotiations, never let your opponent be sure of how you feel. Be polite, friendly, and rational, but not openly pleased or disappointed. This is especially true if you expect future negotiations with the same people.

Use status symbols to create mystery: Dress, speak, and act successful. You may have to adapt to meet the known criteria of your negotiating opponent. Thus, a stuffy, formal opponent may become curious about your strengths if you arrive at the meeting casually dressed, but with an exclusive club blazer which connotes status to your opponent.

The best status symbols for each negotiation vary. Do you need a big office for receiving a person you want to hire? A small office to suggest that money is tight during wage negotiations with outside union people and new hires?

The two best objectives in using status symbols to create mystery in your negotiations are:

1. Reinforcing the invisible strengths you guess your opponent already attributes to you, and

2. Causing surprise in matters upon which you may wish to cast doubts, such as your ability to pay, your respect for your opponent, your need for certain things from your opponent, or the kind of person you are. Use the surprise status symbols to keep your opponent questioning his or her prior guesses about you.

HOW NOT TO BECOME AN OPEN BOOK TO YOUR OPPONENTS

- If you have a unique skill or success record, don't tell everything about how you do it.

- If you have unique problems, whether they concern business, social matters, or family, don't go into detail and don't reveal your true frustrations.

- If you are impatient, anxious, fearful, or cocky, don't reveal these sentiments through body language, words, or deeds.

- Never reveal your best negotiating cards until last.

HOW TO USE THE "SUBJECT TO FINAL APPROVAL" TECHNIQUE

f the people with whom you are negotiating expect that your deal vill be subject to final approval from your superiors, you do not have negotiating tool. Such a situation lacks surprise, and your opponent loesn't wonder what's behind it. Surprise is the key to using the subject o final approval negotiating tactic. The purpose of this tactic is always o escalate your demands on your opponent.

Here are four examples of how negotiators surprise opponents vith demands for final approval:

- *A buyer does not seem concerned about a price that originally worried you.* You thought price was a problem and cut your bid as low as you could only to find you were wrong. Price was not a key in the buying decision. As an afterthought you say, "Of course, before we finalize this arrangement, you understand I have to gain approval for the sale."

  You know the buyers never understood such a requirement, but you say it anyway. Then you excuse yourself, supposedly to gain approval. You return with an escalated price. Had the buyer expected a final approval demand, he or she would have been forewarned and would have gotten cagey. Surprise gives you a chance to raise your price while the buyer is still in a sold frame of mind.

- *The seller is already counting the money, and you want to try to get more or pay less than what the seller wants.* The seller thinks the deal is firm, but you surprise him or her by saying, "I'll need to make a few inquiries to be sure I can get the money."

  When you return to escalate your demands, blame the new terms on the new party. "The bank insists that the car be rust proofed." Or, "The executive committee says you're hired, providing you give us a noncompetition agreement." Or, "The contract is approved, providing we get some additional service guarantees."

Once again, the need for approval must be a surprise. Other wise, your opponent will not reveal his or her position until yo reveal who is on the other side of the approval door. When thi happens, your opponent's guard goes up.

- *You want to break off crisis negotiations which are getting too steep f you.* Often, someone may be gaining on you in a crisis negotiatio situation. An employee may be solving a crisis for you, or a banke may be tiding you over on the understanding that the next move are up to you. When the crisis is past and you have nothin; more to give your employees or your banker, you say, "I'm workin on it, but I can't get the people upstairs to move."

In this way you have not really welched on your negotiate promises. Someone else is changing the deal, if only by stalling as in this example. Save this surprise until the last moment t get as much as you can when the crisis is upon you.

- *You need to stall to marshall your forces, but you are afraid a fin approval demand might lose the deal.* In these cases, you are no sure you can actually do or get what you agreed to do or ge Thus, you agree to pay more than you expected, and you nee time to try to raise the extra funds. Or, you may agree to promot someone, but your budget is still not clarified. Or, you agree t sell an item that you aren't sure you can produce on time.

In such instances, you buy time. However, a "subject t final approval" demand might upset the arrangement completely so you present it in modified form by saying, "There are som routine procedures which I have to complete; I'll get back t you as soon as possible."

Then, if all else fails, you can turn these routine procedure into the unavoidable snag. This allows you to blame someon else for your nonperformance. It is sort of after-the-fact fina approval that provides you with an excuse now. You did no wish to use the excuse earlier in case you could have put th deal together.

WHAT TO DO AS A NEGOTIATION APPROACHES THE CLOSING PHASE

Many buyers and sellers have second thoughts as an agreement gets close to being final. The ideal period between agreeing to a deal and closing it is zero time. But often, delays are caused by such things as title searches, contractual details, backup numbers, methods of funds transfers, routine sign offs, approval or release by third parties, and possibly presentations to directors, officers, or other people.

If you expect an opponent who has finally agreed to something to wrap up all of these details, you are at his or her mercy concerning time. The longer your opponents take to wrap up details, the greater the chance that they may change their minds about the deal. This means that you must always volunteer to take care of details. Do the boilerplate. Run those approvals through. Pull together the presentation, and fill in everyone else involved.

You will usually look like a nice guy for volunteering. But you are really being nice to yourself by speeding up the closing process and thus avoiding time for other people to have second thoughts.

SECTION 7

WHY THE RIGHT TIMING CAN HELP YOU SUCCEED

WHY THE RIGHT TIMING CAN HELP YOU SUCCEED

When you negotiate can be as important as with whom and for how much. In fact, paying attention to timing can increase your effectiveness before, during, and after negotiations.

Taking timing into account teaches you to be more responsive to specific circumstances. This section, for example, will help you answer these questions:

- Who should state demands first, you or your opponent?
- When are negotiations going too quickly?
- Why do sellers seem to be in such a hurry?
- When is the best time to begin negotiations?
- What can you do to vary the pace of negotiations?

WHY TO START TALKING AS SOON AS THE OTHER SIDE IS READY

People simply do not behave rationally all of the time. If you don't believe this, take a walk through your home and ask yourself, "Why did I buy that?" You'll be surprised how many items in your closets, garage, or basement simply do not make sense. But you bought them!

In much the same way, many negotiations will permit you to sell others on your demands because they are ready to buy your ideas for irrational reasons.

EXAMPLES OF GOOD DEALS THAT RESULTED FROM IRRATIONAL BEHAVIOR

- Within days of a hurricane, would-be buyers offer undervalue bids for beachfront houses. Many purchasers realize that the probability of a second hurricane in the same area is decades away. But the owners are frightened, and their emotions have not subsided long enough for them to realize this. So, the purchasers strike while the iron is hot.

- Many Florida homes are bought by people on their trips to the state. People buy when they are full of romance about the idea. Ask any top real estate negotiator. They all will tell you, "Sell them now, before they return home and the glow wears off."

- This entire area of seasonality reminds us that people often operate in herds. They are influenced to buy things irrationally in response to an emotional impulse related to the changing seasons.

  People should know that waiting until winter to buy a summer cottage might get them a lower price. Nevertheless, many buyers pay higher prices in the spring and summer. They could have rented a summer cottage this year while waiting for the soft winter market!

- People often sell good businesses at low prices because they are restless to do something else. Many sellers live to regret it. This same restlessness becomes apparent when people divorce, only to regret their action later.

• People may change jobs because they are curious about the road not taken. Later, they may find themselves longing for what they left.

WHY TIMING AND DISCRETION ARE ESSENTIAL AROUND EMOTIONAL OPPONENTS

The keys to irrational behavior involving negotiating decisions are time and discretion. Whenever you sense that a negotiation is possible and you suspect an irrational motive, don't give your opponents a chance to regain their sense. But, because you know they may eventually regret what they agree to do or buy, never tell anyone of your good deal. To do so will be to ask for trouble.

People may attempt to upset a deal which is sharply in your favor. Emotional opponents who are regaining control can live with an internal awareness that "they've been had." These same people may become tigers if they think that others are laughing at them, though.

Lesson: Strike when the iron is hot, then be quiet about your winnings from other people's irrational agreement.

HOW TO PICK THE BEST TIME AND PLACE FOR NEGOTIATIONS

Check for these danger signs:

- Your opponent suggests a time that puts unnecessary pressure on you. Reject the suggestion.
- Your opponent suddenly tries to change the time or place upon which you both agreed. If this causes additional pressure on you, reject the suggestion.
- Your opponent wants a negotiation location that is difficult for you to get to, too expensive, or which simply gives you bad vibes. Find alternate locations.
- Your opponent selects a negotiation site which is supposed to put you in awe of the opposition: impressive clubs, important lawyers' offices, the opponents' big bank or his home. Resist locations that might give your opponent a top-dog advantage.
- Your opponent tries to prolong negotiations to cause you fatigue. Do not permit this to happen; insist on a break or adjournment.

KEY TACTIC: A Strategy for Reversing Troublesome Situations

Selecting times and places that are ideal for you can reverse these red lights in your favor. Try this reverse tactic in each red-light situation. "How about my club?" "How about a place closer to my business?" "How about my office?" At the very least, arrange neutral times and places which do not give your opponent an advantage.

WHY IT PAYS TO PUT YOUR DEMANDS ON THE TABLE LAST

Perhaps the most widely discussed time to keep your mouth shut is during an IRS audit. "Never bring up anything else." "Only deal with the questions they raise." This kind of advice refers to negotiating situations in which the other side has made demands of you.

KNOW WHEN TO KEEP YOUR MOUTH SHUT

When all of the other side's cards are on the table, you may be surprised that issues you were sure they would demand were not mentioned. You win those points by simply keeping your mouth shut.

Another situation in the same vein involves a seller who tells you what you'll get for what price. Often, if you keep your mouth shut until all of the seller's cards are on the table, the seller will give you more than you ever expected. Of course, this same principle is true in other situations. Buyers may give you a higher price because you hold back on any price demands until you have smoked out the buyer's position. A valued employee may make demands of an employer which turn out to be modest compared to what the employer could have paid.

An employer may pay a new employee much more than would have been required because the employer failed to hear the other person's demands.

FIVE RULES FOR KNOWING WHEN TO TALK ABOUT YOUR DEMANDS AND NEEDS

Rule 1: Whenever someone demands that a problem be solved, let the other person define a solution first. It may be less serious than you anticipated.

Rule 2: Whenever a buyer finally offers a negotiated price, say nothing and wait as long as possible. Change the subject. Arrange to be called away from the meeting, or simply sit silently. Impatient buyers will often raise the price before you respond if you give them time for their anxiety to build.

Rule 3: Whenever a seller offers a price, use time to test the seller's anxieties. Often the seller will start to throw in extras if you find ways to delay your responses to the seller's overtures.

Rule 4: After smoking out your opponent's position as much as possible, lay your demands out in a sequence which begins with issues to which your opponent can most easily say "yes." No reason to get hung up early on the toughest demands in your bag. Remember that "yes" can become a habit for your opponent if he or she thinks the "yes" is not to a demand but to a mutually beneficial arrangement.

Then, after your opponent feels good about the mutually beneficial areas to which you both agree, produce your toughest final demands. Again, couch these demands in language such as, "This reflects reasonable self-interest for both of us."

Rule 5: Expect many negotiations to have a hidden agenda wherein your opponent consciously or unconsciously holds back his or her true objectives. Unless you keep your opponent doing most of the talking about his or her demands, you will never get through the formal agenda to this person's hidden agenda. This works the same way as most psychiatrists' methods. Keep listening until your opponent provides a clue about what the other person really needs or feels.

For example, a seller offers a low price, claiming it is "to get out of this particular inventory that doesn't fit my plans." You listen. You don't react to the price, but say, "Tell me about your new plans." As the seller talks, you listen. You find a clue. The seller's plans are seasonal, and thus the seller's real need is to get going now, before the season is over. The seller's offer to you is an emotional need to clear his or her mind as much as the need to get money out of the inventory that no longer will fit the seller's plans. Now you have discovered the seller's hidden agenda: to get on with his or her plans as quickly as possible.

With this new information, you might offer to take more of the already discounted inventory, but at a ridiculously low price. The price is low in monetary value, but not in terms of the value the seller attaches to getting going with something new.

WAYS TO CONTROL HOW LONG NEGOTIATIONS LAST: FIVE EXAMPLES

WHEN THE OTHER SIDE'S FRESH, BUT YOU'RE NOT

Your opponent is fresh, alert, sharp, and you feel tired, numb, or preoccupied. Your best tactic in this case is to always take a break or seek an adjournment. Give yourself enough time to recoup your strengths. Otherwise, your opponent may sense your weakness and want to keep you negotiating.

TROUBLE WITH A TEAMMATE

One of your team members isn't acting in his or her normal fashion. Maybe this person is fatigued, preoccupied, or hasn't done the required homework. Or maybe this person is incompetent. Whatever the cause, stop negotiations until you can get the person alone. Decide what is needed to restore or replace the weakened team member. Again, you may need a diplomatic false crisis to request a break. Just be sure to hide your real concerns from your opponent.

WHAT TO DO WHEN YOU EXPECT BIG CHANGES

You expect some outside change to affect your negotiations. The nature of the expected change will determine whether you should speed up or slow down your sessions. With our rapid communications, outside events can quickly influence our opponent's attitudes. A prospective home buyer may be convinced that interest rates are as low as they will go and wants to negotiate today. But your information suggests a further break in interest rates may be only weeks away. You speed things up to save your sale.

AN OPPONENT SENDS SIGNALS THAT YOU CAN'T READ

An unexpected change in your opponent's behavior bothers you; you can't explain it. Slow things down to give yourself more opportunity to understand what's behind your opponent's change in behavior or attitude. Is it a test? Is your opponent facing a new problem?

TIPS FOR PICKING UP THE PACE WITHOUT BEING OBVIOUS

You are concerned about something and hope your opponent doesn't realize it. You speed things up, but in a way that is not obvious to your opponent. Do not appear to be pressing. For example, one negotiator deliberately takes off his jacket and says, "Might as well be comfortable. This will probably take us a long time." He does this when he is in the greatest hurry. Then, as he moves things along rapidly, his opponents tend to overlook the pace. After all, he looks so relaxed.

WHEN TO SLOW DOWN NEGOTIATIONS

Many people pride themselves on being speedy decision makers. They see a problem or an opportunity and quickly decide how to solve the problem or seize an opportunity. They move fast and often boast that they "do things quickly without wasting a lot of time."

On the other hand, many of these speedy decision makers make lousy decisions. Poor decisions usually result from not allowing enough time in which to consider possible consequences and alternate decisions.

We all make decisions and, unfortunately when we do, most of us limit ourselves to examining two or three possible consequences. We take Step 1, in which we ask ourselves, "What will happen if I decide in this way?" Then, we usually take Step 2, which is to ask, "And if that happens, what will be the consequence?" Far fewer people take Step 3, which is to ask, "What happens if the results anticipated in Step 2 becomes a reality?"

This process gets too complicated for many people when they realize the time and effort involved in evaluating each alternative before they decide what to do. Many people also are unable to imagine very many possible decisions. Such individuals may ask themselves questions as in Steps 1, 2, and 3, but they examine only a few alternatives. The worst decision makers conceive of only one or two possibilities and examine these choices on one or two consequence levels.

HOW TO MAKE BETTER DECISIONS

People have produced all sorts of courses, books, and cassettes to teach better decision making. Most of these products are worthwhile, if only as reminders of how random the decision-making process can be if we fail to bring order to it.

But short of taking a cram course, the best way to improve our decision making is to provide more time to contemplate our decisions before we make them final. Thus, you may be less creative than someone else in coming up with possible decisions, but if you have more time you will come up with more possible decisions. Normally, you may examine each of your possible decisions in only one or two steps, but with more time, you may find Step 3 worthwhile. And, why not carry the process on to Steps 4 and 5?

No matter what your present level as a decision maker, you can move yourself to a higher level by simply giving yourself more time.

---

*KEY TACTIC: Wait for Your Opponents to Help You
Unknowingly*

A good reason for taking time on important negotiation decisions is that your stalling by silence or an interruption gives you and your opponent time to think. Your opponent throws a new idea on the table. Often, this may be a possibility that you have not considered.

TWO PROFITABLE WAYS TO USE BREAKS IN NEGOTIATIONS

Calling for help: Negotiations can be about quite different subjects, and this affects your effectiveness. You may be an ace negotiator on manufacturing issues but know too little about finance to successfully negotiate in that area.

Too many people think of themselves as good negotiators without realizing that most of their negotiations have been in one or two fields. They assume that they are good negotiators in any subject area. This is obviously not true.

When you are having trouble coming up with several decision possibilities or thinking through several consequence steps for each possible decision, the reason may be inexperience rather than an inability to negotiate. You can compensate for inexperience with outside help. So, take your time and call for help when necessary.

Taking your time: Many people negotiating in areas in which they lack experience fail to take time to seek outside help. They wing it. This is fine if you always know where you're going while your opposition is slightly fuzzy. The trick is never to have the situation reversed on you. Always take the time required to be very clear on everything.

A CHECKLIST FOR UNDERSTANDING THE NEED TO SLOW
DOWN

1. Slowing down negotiations is quite different than hurrying to wrap up the details about what has been agreed. Once agreement

is made, it often may be in your best interest to speed up the closing details.

2. Slowing down negotiations refers exclusively to what your final decision will be on any item on the negotiating agenda. You need time to examine many possible decisions.

3. Even when you feel no need to slow down, it pays to do so on the chance that your opponent will volunteer a new possible decision. Always test your opponent with slowdown tactics. These can range from silence to adjournment.

4. In areas of negotiation which are new to you, slow down enough to get experts by your side. This does not make you appear to be a poor negotiator. Rather, it proves that you are sharp.

5. Accelerate negotiations whenever you find an opponent who is willing to wing it in areas where he or she is obviously weak, but where you are strong.

REASONS TO KEEP A BUYER SHORT ON TIME

A seller usually has had plenty of time before a negotiation to think about what to sell. Often, the only questions to be resolved in the seller's mind are, "How much?" and "How will I get my money."

WHY BUYERS ARE DIFFERENT FROM SELLERS

A buyer, on the other hand, usually has only vague notions about what may be on the market. Thus, the buyer wants a car, computer, or house, but knows little about the alternatives available. This means that when you have a buyer who says yes, you had best stop talking and wrap the shoes, as the saying goes. If you don't stop talking, you may confuse the buyer by inadvertently suggesting something he or she didn't know about. The buyer may use the delay to discover other alternatives. The buyer may get cold feet for numerous reasons—anything from having a head cold to concern about balancing the checkbook.

SIX IDEAS TO SPEED UP A BUYER'S CLOSE

Depending on what has been sold, one or more of these ideas may help you:

- Offer to do as many of the time-consuming details as possible yourself. These may relate to legal, accounting, banking, inspection, or approvals.

- Insist on a substantial down payment now to hold the deal. The longer the closing interval, the higher the down payment. If there are steps to be taken related to closing details, try to get more money down at each step.

- Use legal paperwork to protect your sale. Do not rely on a handshake or promise beyond the shortest reasonable time, the time it takes to draw up an agreement.

- In your original negotiations with a potential buyer, do not permit many, if any, contingencies to become part of your deal. If you permit too many contingencies for too long, you have not made a deal, only a conversation.

- Arrange for delivery as soon as possible, whether it be manufacturing parts, consumer products, real estate, or service. Depending on what the buyer bought from you, you may have to extend normal credit terms, including delayed payment. However, if you speed delivery, you speed up the point at which the payment clock starts ticking. You also reduce the chances for a stop order or a cancellation.

  Always have a legal paper to be signed by the buyer at two points in time: when the order is placed and upon delivery. Depending on what you're selling, your lawyer can help you decide how to make the paperwork look routine and painless and yet be solid as a rock from a legal perspective.

- Consider someone who is hiring you as a buyer. The same principles apply. Do not let things drag after your final agreement. Do try to get some things in writing as soon as is diplomatically possible. Written terms may cover severance arrangements, compensation, bonus, or commission.

Particularly with fees or commission arrangements, insist on a written legal document before you provide any service for the buyer. Until you do this, don't even hint at the names and places you plan to sell. Otherwise, you may find yourself "odd man out."

WHY TIME IS OF THE ESSENCE TO SELLERS

This section deals with people who have decided to sell. When you proposition someone who has not even considered selling, the person may not be in a hurry. However, expect this to change when the person decides to sell.

NINE REASONS SELLERS BECOME IMPATIENT

It always pays to pause long enough to look for clues as to why a seller seems in a hurry. Consider these possibilities.

- You may be offering too much.
- The seller may know something that you don't know.
- The seller may have a special use for the money now.
- The seller may doubt your ability to close the deal and want to test you quickly.
- The seller may want out at once because of a physical or psychological problem.
- The seller's boss may be imposing a quota based on sales during a certain time period.
- The seller may need a personal confidence builder during a dry selling period.
- The seller may have just lost an important sale.
- The seller may simply be an impatient person who hates to wait for anything.

Consider the negotiating advantage you can enjoy if you spot one or more of these motivations in your opponent.

WHAT YOU CAN LEARN FROM A SELLER'S IMPATIENCE

- You may be on to a bad buy if you suspect that the seller is impatient because you are offering too much or that the seller knows something that you don't.

- You may be on to a good deal if you suspect that the seller needs money, wants out badly, or just lost a prior sale.

    Kinds of seller impatience which are not going to help you much are those resulting from the seller's testing of your ability to pay; a seller's normal sales quota; the seller's need for a confidence builder; or simply the seller's impatient personality. But if the seller has a special sales quota *problem* or *bonus* opportunity— you may be in luck.

KEY TACTIC: Try the Triangle Approach

This is a perfect place to use the triangle approach to your negotiations. Find someone who also knows the seller. Talk to this person about the seller. Use the above listed reasons for impatience as a checklist in your discussion. Use two or more triangles if possible. This allows you to check the validity of the information you are receiving from each third party.

HOW TO USE TIME TO TEST YOUR OPPONENT'S PATIENCE

WHAT AN ANXIOUS OPPONENT IS TELLING YOU

Your opponent seems anxious about your negotiations. Perhaps this person is anxious to sell, to buy, or to get things settled. This can be normal anxiety, or it may be related to some reason that your opponent has concealed from you. For example,

- A money shortage.
- A personality problem with you.
- Personal problems.
- Someone who is watching his or her negotiation with you.
- Psychological problems.

Such influences on your negotiating opponent tend to become apparent if you slow down negotiations. Consider what might happen when you do this.

- Time may test your opponent's patience to the point where he or she reveals something new, often without realizing that you have a new card to play.
- Time gives you a chance to dig a little deeper for information about your opponent. You may find clues about the anxiety. Call people who know your opponent. Have informal chats with your opponent's staff. Ask what your opponent's competitors know.

WHAT TO DO WHEN AN OPPONENT HAS ALL THE TIME IN THE WORLD

Your opponent seems in no hurry to complete negotiations, and you can't understand why. Arrange a false crisis in your negotiating position. Say something like, "I've got to leave the country as soon as possible. Maybe we should postpone this until I get back." By doing this, you test your opponent to see if his or her relaxed approach has been a deliberate test for you or a put-on to wear you down. If it has been one of these two situations, you'll be surprised how fast your opponent wants to move now.

If your opponent grants the long delay, you have not lost anything and you saved a lot of time by knowing that your opponent is not ready to negotiate. He or she has only been pretending, for whatever reason.

WHAT A PROPERLY TIMED CASUAL AFTERTHOUGHT CAN DO FOR YOU

- A manager reaches to answer the telephone and says to the people in the office, "Think about what I've been asking you. Think about it."

  The manager emphasizes the last three words, then picks up the telephone. Thus, the people listening have no way to respond at that moment. Like it or not, they will think about it as long as the manager stays on the phone.

- As a customer leaves the small retail store, the owner calls out, "Wait a minute, let me open that door for you."

  While graciously holding the door, the owner waits for the customer to say "thank you," and then the owner loudly whispers, "That's a stunning outfit you're wearing today." The owner pays his compliments in circumstances which will not embarrass the customer. The kind words all appear to be an afterthought to opening the door. But this clever retailer does the same thing to many customers every day. No one would dream that this is the case, because it appears so impromptu. As a result, more and more customers happen to think of additional items to buy in the store.

- A small-company president needs a rest, and other employees know this. On the other hand, this is a very busy time for the company, and the president feels guilty about leaving for "even for an hour." So, the staff urges, "Go. Take a whole week off. We insist."

  Everyone knows what a heavy workload they will be assuming to cover for the president, but they insist that he go nevertheless.

  As he leaves, he calls his staff into his office and explains how much their sacrifice means to him. The staff members beam as they follow him to the elevator. As the elevator doors are closing, the departing president beams back and waves an airline ticket. "Oh, I meant to tell you," he says, "they could only get me tickets back on the twenty-eighth." The doors close as he speaks the words. The staff gasps. That's almost three weeks away, but what can anyone do? The boss has gone.

These examples show the critical use of timing in planning a casual afterthought. While they appeared to be nonchalant, they are not. They are carefully contrived to get agreement that might otherwise not be forthcoming.

Properly planned and timed casual afterthoughts gain agreement because—

1. Your use of surprise leaves no alternative for others.

2. You arrange to make circumstance appear to have caused the situation, not your planning.

3. No one would ever believe you are such a conniver. No one!

SECTION 8

PROVEN TECHNIQUES FOR AVOIDING MISCOMMUNICATION AND ILL WILL

SECTION 8

PROVEN TECHNIQUES FOR AVOIDING MISCOMMUNICATION AND ILL WILL

Good golfers develop rhythm and swing. Tennis players concentrate on rhythm and stroke. Likewise, good negotiators must cultivate rhythm and procedures. As with a golf swing or tennis stroke, negotiating procedures must become automatic if you are to develop a winning game.

Athletes often use memory tricks to make their responses automatic, instinctive. In the same way, you can develop winning procedures and make them second nature. This section utilizes a memory tool for doing just that.

A handy memory tool: View your negotiating opponent's suggestions, actions, and agreements as either *red lights*, which cause your adrenaline to flow, or *green lights*, which mean that the negotiating course is momentarily free of hazards.

A word of caution: Many sharp negotiators deliberately provide us with a string of green lights in early discussions. They do this to make us fall "asleep at the wheel," so to speak. Then, as we doze, perhaps we won't notice the red lights they are running past us. In negotiations, as in driving, you may occasionally get by running a red light, but if it becomes a habit, you are sure to suffer!

TIPS FOR REDUCING YOUR OPPONENT'S EVASIVENESS

Red light: Your opponents skip the next item for discussion despite your agreement to include it on the agenda. For example, in a negotiation for a new job, you might hear, "About severance pay, we can get to that some other time."

Do not let this happen. If you and your opponents have agreed to an agenda, cover all topics in logical sequence.

Red light: Your opponent suddenly needs to interrupt negotiations. "Sorry, something has come up which requires my attention. Excuse me for leaving," he may say, offering a typical excuse.

Never be gracious. Always show surprise, smile, and say, "If we can't continue this now, we'll have to adjust to my schedule next time. Give me a call, and I'll let you know. I can't agree to anything now." This re-establishes your control and ensures that opponents who test your patience with interruptions will not take you for granted.

Red light: Your opponent refuses to answer a question directly. This refusal can take a number of forms: pretending not to have heard, being conveniently distracted, changing the subject, or outright deadpan.

Respond with patience and apparent good humor as you say with a smile, "Let me again ask." Opponents will often watch you to find some form of intimidation that works on you. If you appear to be intimidated when an opponent ignores your questions, the opponent will lose respect for you and will pour on the evasiveness with more intimidation.

HOW TO KEEP MISUNDERSTANDINGS IN CHECK

Watch out when your opponent—

- is hurrying.
- seems preoccupied.
- uses obtuse language or technical jargon.
- uses someone else, such as a spokesperson, lawyer, accountant, banker, or consultant.
- has a sudden mood change.
- tries to add new issues to an established agenda.
- becomes absentminded, presenting illogical arguments and rambling from topic to topic.

All of these situations are red lights. Your appropriate response is to feign humility as you say, "Bear with me. I have to write things down to be sure I have them straight. Now let's see what we've agreed so far."

Slowly, deliberately appear to be thinking aloud as you review the items you want to clarify. Write notes to yourself as you speak. Use this same technique when someone informally arranges to meet with you about a negotiation. Use the notes to establish a final agenda, which becomes your record of what is to be negotiated.

A CHECKLIST FOR DISCOVERING PROBLEMS BEFORE NEGOTIATIONS BEGIN

Red light: You suspect that someone else may be behind your negotiating opponent, some greater authority who might second-guess your deal or insist on approving it. You must check out this suspicion before you begin negotiations. Try to flush out the facts and get them on record. Who sees what? Who contributes what to the negotiation? Who approves the negotiated agreements?

Red light: The security of your negotiations must be upheld. You want to guard against leaks to competitors, other people in your company, and others in your community. Before talks begin, arrange specific rules and procedures to protect security. If you don't do this before beginning negotiations, your opponent may deliberately arrange leaks to pressure you.

Red light: You suspect that your opponent's motive in your proposed negotiations is not the reason he or she has given. The motive may be—

- A delaying tactic.
- A political tactic to please someone else.
- An excuse to damage you by distracting you from something else.
- An excuse for you to damage yourself by prodding you to lose your cool.
- A strategy to serve another goal, such as creating an impasse that would justify other extreme action.

If you discover a potentially damaging situation before negotiations start, refuse to negotiate until the dangers to you or the benefits to your opponent have been eliminated.

WHY IT PAYS TO COMMUNICATE ADULT-TO-ADULT WITH YOUR OPPONENT

Negotiation involves communication, and communication during negotiation should always be adult-to-adult. Many negotiations break down because one person is acting like a child while the other is acting like a parent.

HOW PARENT-CHILD ROLE PLAYING STIFLES NEGOTIATION

- The union's negotiation leader wags a finger across the table like a parent and says to the company negotiator, "You should be ashamed of yourself. You should know better!"

    The company negotiator jumps up, storms out of the room, and shouts, "I'm sick and tired of your lecturing me," just as a child might behave.

- An assistant is overwhelmed by her workload and wants her boss to get more help. She angrily bursts into her superior's office with tears streaming down her face. "You promised me you'd get someone to help me, and you forgot all about it. You can find yourself someone else. I'm through." As she speaks, she involuntarily stamps her foot, exactly as she did in childhood with her father.

    "Don't you ever pull this kind of behavior on me, or I'll see to it that you never work for this company again," says her boss, sounding like a parent threatening the child in a woodshed.

    The assistant rushes out to clear her desk, saying "I quit!"

In both examples, everyone lost. In the first example, a long and costly strike ensued and hurt all parties. In the second example, the boss lost the most productive assistant in the department, and she never found a comparable position in a new firm. Why? Because the parties in both instances played the parent-child game.

FIVE RULES TO ELIMINATE PARENT-CHILD AND CHILD-CHILD COMMUNICATION FROM NEGOTIATIONS

Rule 1: Don't let your hostile emotions show. When you feel you are about to explode, smile and be quiet. Remind yourself to remain adult about the situation.

Rule 2: If your opponent starts to play the game as a parent or child, stay cool. Take time to get yourself under control. During this time, keep a smile on your face, and then use humor about yourself and the situation.

For example, you might smile as you say, "Hey, for a minute there I thought I was watching a play about a couple of kids fighting or a parent lecturing a kid. We're both old enough to know better and smart enough to know we've got to approach this thing like adults." Continue to smile and show compassion in your tone and facial expression. Never be hostile.

Rule 3: Remember, if someone acts like a parent or a child, the action may be a deliberate attempt to rattle you. Don't get shaken. Don't respond as a child or even a parent, ever!

Rule 4: Watch how you say things. Avoid lecturing your opponent. This may trigger your opponent to act like a child.

Rule 5: When your efforts or your opponent's efforts to regain composure fail, arrange time for cooling off. Simply suggest, "Let's take a break." At other times, arrange to be interrupted by some outside event. "Excuse me while I take a phone call." Or, look at your watch and say, "Wow, I didn't realize what time it is. I really have to duck out because. . . ."

When you duck out, it can be for a few minutes, a few hours, or days. But do this in a way that seems unrelated to the problem in your negotiating environment, the problem of someone losing adult behavior and logic. It cannot be stated too strongly: a smile, not a smirk, is your best tactic for restoring adult behavior. Sometimes a smile is the only response necessary until things cool down.

Always avoid escalating emotions during negotiations. Nothing escalates emotion faster than when one or both of the parties abandon their adult roles and behave like a parent or a child. When this happens, negotiation gives way to recrimination. Progress slows and reaches an impasse or stagnation.

WHY IT PAYS TO STAY WITH YOUR SET AGENDA

Red light: Your opponent changes the focus of discussion, then replaces your agenda with one you never approved. Suppose, for example, that you agree to negotiate a price on apples, but your opponent shows up to talk about bananas. "Hey," you must respond, "I never agreed to talk about bananas, and I certainly won't now until we complete our apple negotiation."

This is the way negotiations get sidetracked. Agree to an agenda with your opponent before negotiations begin, and then stick to it.

Often, your opponent flashes this red light at you to see if you—

• notice.

• care.

• can be confused.

• can be delayed.

• are willing to talk without preparation.

• can be thrown off balance emotionally by the new issue.

Red light: If your opponent sticks to the agenda but tries to horse-trade by saying, "What if I give you point #1? Will you give me point #6?" Your opponent hopes you will not notice that #6 is much more valuable than #1. Your response must always be, "Let's cover each point on its own merits. No deal!"

Red light: If your opponent says, "What if I leave and refuse to talk further?" Smile and say, "Hey, two can play at that game. So, what's your pleasure? Do you want to continue to talk?"

Never beg your opponent to stay and keep negotiating. When you do this, you might as well be living under a dictatorship. To stay would not be negotiation. You would be listening to "the way it's going to be."

TIPS FOR PERSUADING AN OPPONENT TO SEE THINGS YOUR WAY

Red light: Your biggest customer suggests that you review your recent price schedules because your competitor has a ten percent price advantage on comparable products.

You must seek ways to show the customer how your company provides an overall value that your competitor lacks. Your customer is talking about a ten percent price advantage in your competitor's offering. You direct attention away from price and toward other areas where you know your company is superior. Mention your company's stability, and thus raise doubts about the competitor's stability. Mention your company's service. This casts doubt on their service.

The slant you present as a persuasive argument can be as simple as, "Would you really feel comfortable with them. They're certainly not your kind of people." The purpose of the slant is to cause your customer diplomatically to see the competition from a different perspective. Never slander your competition. Rather, suggest indirect, indefinite problems that your customer might encounter with the competition.

Red light: Your boss has been informally negotiating with you and two of your coworkers about the one available promotion. You sense that one of these people is the odds-on favorite to get the job. "The boss sees himself in that guy," you say to your wife.

"You've got to be kidding," she says, "I can't imagine how you could say that. Look at their wives. They couldn't be more different. Your boss's wife can't stand his wife."

Now you have a possible slant to help you. Subtly suggest to your boss that the person promoted will have to spend more time at conventions and business trips with him and his wife. Maybe the boss will perceive a problem that he has not considered.

Do not commit character assassination, but indirectly slant the discussion toward your point of view. You might say, "Whichever of us gets this promotion is going to be doubly lucky. Not only will he have a better job, but he and his wife will have the chance to become close friends with you and your wife. All of those trips together will be a bonus because your wife is such an outstanding person."

REASONS TO RESIST "EVEN-STEVEN" TACTICS

Red light: Your opponent gets very angry in response to anger you have shown. It is your fault when this happens. You started it; now you must reverse your approach by removing your signs of anger. This will help your opponent cool down.

Red light: Your opponent starts to name-drop nervously. This is really a compliment. Your opponent is showing a need to even some advantage he or she sees in you. Usually, though, having your opponent feel intimidated is not a good basis for negotiation. You must find ways not to look so strong to your opponent, or not to look so stuffy or remote. Once you hide your advantage, your opponent's Even-Steven tactics will cease. So, too, will your opponent's feelings of intimidation. Never let name-dropping accelerate into a "let me see you top this one" situation.

It is perfectly okay to arrange to come up even with an opponent whose strategy is to intimidate you. But this is quite different from discovering that you inadvertently intimidated your opponent, thus causing him or her to try the Even-Steven name-dropping.

Red light: Your opponent displays a childlike approach to negotiations. Your opponent, in effect, is pouting and saying, "You won that last point. Now it's my turn!"

This Even-Steven approach is based not on logic but on childlike emotions. Never yield to your opponent's emotional deterioration. The moment you do, you're playing the same childlike game. Instead, go back over your last point of agreement. Your opponent clearly perceives this as your victory. Reset the mood of the agreement on the victorious point so your opponent now sees it as less of a clear-cut victory for you, but a compromise. Thus, you might say, "I've been thinking about that last point we agreed upon. I'll let it stand, but I'm not so sure I'm really pleased with it the more I think about it. But what the heck?"

This gives your opponent a reason to feel better because you may not have won. Now it is more fun for your opponent to continue the game in an adult frame of mind.

THE VALUE OF LETTING YOUR OPPONENTS THINK THEY ARE MAKING YOU SWEAT

Red light: Your opponent is obviously getting careless and yielding more than you ever hoped. Especially now, look very serious, concerned, and unsure. This will signal that you are sweating, and it will reinforce your opponent's carelessness.

Red light: Your opponent expresses anxiety about what other people, including those in authority, will think of your agreement. Find ways to let your opponent understand that everyone will know that he or she made you sweat.

You might say, "Wait until I tell your boss how hard you've been with me on this. When word gets out, they'll think I've gone soft." Or, "People who know about such things will understand how much I've compromised to make this work."

Red light: Your opponent has been so generous to you that you hope you will have future opportunities to negotiate with this person. After a negotiation, many opponents will carefully try to read you as you leave. This is a way of measuring themselves. If you are too jaunty, relaxed, or friendly, they will get worried and begin to second-guess themselves. Even if their second-guessing does not upset your agreement, it may put your opponent on guard the next time you negotiate together. To avoid this possibility, always use body language and words which suggest that—

1. You are pleased the negotiations are over, "because this always takes a lot out of me."

2. You are worried about what others will think. "I hope my boss doesn't chew me out for this."

3. You are second-guessing yourself. "I don't ever want to think about this entire thing anymore. What's done is done."

Carefully contrived protests will make your opponent want to negotiate with you again, which is exactly what you want.

PRACTICE DRILLS TO HELP YOU PREPARE FOR A NEGOTIATION

A CHECKLIST OF RED-LIGHT SIGNALS

- You're not sure who your opponent really is. A jerk? A sweetheart? A numbers person? A big picture person?
- You're not sure of your opponent's tactics. Pressure? Intimidation? Good cop/bad cop?
- You're not sure of your ability to communicate certain complicated issues. How can you make them clear to anyone?
- You're not sure how much time will be available for negotiations such as a key sales call.
- You're not sure of your ability to stay cool if certain topics are mentioned.
- You're not sure of your ability to handle surprise questions or issues.
- You're not sure of your ability to go in strong when you're nervous about your problem.

THE ADVANTAGES OF PRENEGOTIATION DRILLS

If you see any possible red lights in one or more of the situations on the checklist, drill yourself before negotiations begin.

Even top lawyers assemble panels of people who match the profiles of their real juries as a means of testing different arguments. The panels tell the attorneys what will and will not work.

Our nation's presidents stage mock press conferences with their staffs before confronting the real media. In sports, top teams use their opponent's plays to practice for a big game.

Ask people to role-play a negotiation with you. Try to imagine the worst that might happen and role-play these difficult situations. Ask others in your group to watch the role-playing exercises and critique your performance. Talk each performance over with your critics. Keep working until everyone thinks you are ready.

One sales manager drilled a top sales person using a stopwatch. The manager taught the sales agent to think clearly under time pressures despite a customer's nasty behavior.

HOW NICENESS WORKS TO A NEGOTIATOR'S ADVANTAGE

A CHECKLIST OF RED-LIGHT SIGNALS

- Your opponent thinks of you as tough.
- Your opponent thinks of you as unreasonable.
- Your opponent thinks of you as foreign to him or her.
- Your opponent fears you.
- Your opponent distrusts you.
- Your opponent fears your power.
- Your opponent dislikes you.
- Your opponent dislikes your associates.
- Your opponent knows nothing about you.

All of these signals suggest that you might be heading for a more difficult negotiation than is necessary. Still, there are techniques for overcoming this difficulty.

WHY PEOPLE WHO KNOW YOU BEST MAKE TRICKY OPPONENTS

Ask people, "Who would you rather negotiate with, a jerk or a nice guy?" Most people answer, "The nice guy, of course." Yet the hardest people to win negotiations with are—

- Friends you respect.
- People who have done you favors.
- Family or people you love.
- Role models who represent your beliefs and values.
- People you see as nice guys.

By knowing this, you can understand how you would profit by the same principle. You can make winning more difficult for your opponent by appearing less difficult yourself.

If your opponents think of you as a difficult negotiator, they will prepare for the worst. Your opponents will train by sharpening their arguments, tactics, and support positions. If your opponents think they can identify with you, if they think of you as someone nice, you have a real negotiating edge. Your opponents will drop their guards.

HOW TO FIND COMMON GROUND WITH OPPONENTS BEFORE NEGOTIATIONS

Writing letters: Some sharp people precede negotiations with letters enumerating everything they have in common with their opponent, or at least what they want their opponents to feel they have in common. An excuse for writing such a letter could be to confirm who will be at the meeting, the time and place of the meeting, or meeting details such as room number or lunch arrangements.

Having stated your excuse for writing, say something like, "This reminds me to mention that I really look forward to our work sessions together. It is seldom nowadays that you can be sure whom you are doing business with. We have so much in common that the meetings will be more like social get-togethers than hard-nosed bargaining. I do enjoy meeting with people I like."

Telephone calls: Some people call opponents before negotiations. For example, "I just wanted to confirm the time for our meeting and to ask you if you would be my guest for lunch. I told my banker about our meeting. My banker says you are one of the best executives in your industry. Of course, I know this, but I thought you'd like to hear it."

Messages through third parties: Have someone you and your opponent both know contact your opponent. Select someone who is closer to you than to your opponent. Ask your contact to call or write your opponent "to emphasize all of the things the two of us have in common." Sometimes your contact will permit you to dictate a draft of your message. Offer to do so to save your contact's time.

An opening speech: The trick in delivering an opening speech is not to let it look rehearsed. For example, "As I arrived here today, I realized how pleased I was to be coming. And, for reasons having absolutely nothing to do with the purpose of our meeting. I was pleased to be seeing someone whom I respect for so many reasons and about whom I continue to hear so many good comments from all quarters. Actually,

I feel more like a guest than anything else. I'm just glad to have an excuse to be here."

In any opening speech, find ways to list as many common denominators between your opponent and yourself as possible. This has nothing to do with reasons for negotiating; that comes later when negotiations commence.

FINDING THE RIGHT TIME TO STATE THE ISSUES

Look for these red light signals:

- Your opponents seems to be getting emotionally sidetracked.
- Your opponents seem to be getting intellectually sidetracked.
- Your opponents are frequently interrupted.
- Your opponents act pressed for time.
- Your opponents are taking an unexpected break in your meeting.

Any of these signals remind us of how useful having a short, pithy speech on reserve can be when we want to summarize issues. Your speech can even be a written summary that you carefully keep out of sight until needed.

If the situation heats up emotionally, arrange a break and then use your speech before resuming discussion of the issues. You could use the speech after a normal break if you think it is warranted. Another option is to use it during the meeting whenever the conversation rambles on or gets interrupted.

Your opponents may say, "Oh, here you go again." This is exactly what your speech is for—to have them notice that you want to stick to the issues. Simply put, your speech is a restatement of the meeting agenda which your opponent and you set together. Your speech, though, is less formal than the agenda. Often, a detailed, three-page agenda can be boiled down to a few sentences that categorize the issues. You may not have to use your "stating the issues" speech, but this does not mean you should not have one ready just in case.

WHY GOOD NEGOTIATORS LEAVE THE WORD "ENEMY" OUT OF THEIR VOCABULARY

Look for these red light signals:

- You feel tight going into a negotiation.
- You are fearful going into a negotiation.
- You are vengeful going into a negotiation.
- You are powerful going into a negotiation.
- You feel furious going into a negotiation.
- You feel coldly destructive going into a negotiation.

If you feel any of these things going in, you are not ready to negotiate. You may be prepared to dictate, punish, humiliate, or defend against the other side, which you perceive as the enemy. One thing you are not, however, is ready to negotiate!

You may have ample reason to harbor negative feelings about an opponent, and you may really want to dictate, punish, or in some way trouble your opponent. But even when these feelings precede a bargaining session, you must be detached emotionally when negotiations begin. When you sit down at the table, you should have no emotional drives except being up, being sharp. Replace negative emotions with goals and objectives. You become an actor in a play. You become only that which you want your opponent to see, a logical, pleasant negotiator who is in control.

Far too many people think they can win negotiations through intimidation. This is never the case. When direct intimidation is your tool, negotiation is not your objective.

Intimidation is like using a sledgehammer to beat your *enemy* into submission. When this happens, your agreement with this opponent may be temporary or laced with the other person's schemes to get even.

On some points in some negotiations, however, you plan and use theatrics. You appear to get angry, to wield power, or to show fear. These are tactics which you use carefully and sparingly for effect. You are not feeling the role you are playing.

After negotiations, you can allow yourself to experience your feelings. You can indulge yourself in the satisfactions related to your original feelings about your opponent. But during negotiations, your mind, not your emotions, is your tool. You have no enemy during negotiations. You have only an opponent with whom you plan to reach an agreement. If you outmaneuver your opponent, it will be with logical, not emotional, strategies—top negotiators know to check their guns at the door.

SECTION 9

THE HUMAN FACTORS IN NEGOTIATIONS: WHAT THEY ARE AND WHY THEY MATTER

SECTION 9

THE HUMAN FACTORS IN NEGOTIATIONS: WHAT THEY ARE AND WHY THEY MATTER

We negotiate with one another in matters large and small in response to underlying human needs. Too often, though, our negotiations break down because we fail to understand other negotiators' changing needs. In this section, we will consider the human aspects of 18 key negotiating situations. Insight gained in such cases can dramatically improve our negotiating results. Two important hazards we'll consider are—

- Confusion about negotiating mechanics.
- Misunderstanding an opponent's feelings.

Too often, we get bogged down in the mechanics of negotiations and confuse the human needs that were the catalyst for the negotiation. A divorce, for example, illustrates five problems with confusion.

The third-party spokesperson problem: Both husband and wife retain a lawyer. From this point on, the lawyers do the talking for the couple. How can attorneys understand both parties' needs and feelings? Will they oversimplify the situation and stereotype the divorcing partners? What's to stop the attorneys from saying, "I handled a case just like this last week."

The expert problem: If the divorcing couple has children, lawyers will usually send them to a psychologist or psychiatrist. The purpose of this visit is to get a professional's findings, that is, a report which can guide the judge as to what is in the children's best interest. How, though, in one or two meetings, can the expert really determine the children's human needs? Nonetheless, an expert now becomes a central player in what was a family negotiation. Lawyers, judge, and experts may negotiate about the family's future based on their feelings, not those of Mom and Dad.

Loss of human spontaneity: Since the husband and wife are talking mostly through their lawyers, the divorce process leaves little room for

248

human spontaneity. If one of the parties wakes up one morning with an unexpected need to talk to the other person, the process usually rules this out. "Calm down," the lawyer may say, "You're letting your heart rule your head." All the while, the best negotiating tactic may really be to respond to the need to reach out to the other person, but the mechanics of the situation discourage this reaction.

A hostile environment: Good negotiations often result when both people select the time and place where they will talk. In a divorce, however, meeting arrangements usually revolve around the judge's calendar. The result can be an unseemly hostile place in which to conduct negotiations.

Unsolicited outside advice: Because divorce is so entangled with legal proceedings, it usually brings forth unsolicited advice from well-meaning third parties. Likely candidates are friends, acquaintances, business associates, and distant relatives. Typically, third-party advice is of a procedural nature, not advice about coping with human feelings. Listen for—

- "Let me tell you about this lawyer I've heard of. She's supposed to be a whiz in child-custody matters."

- "What you need is a lawyer who will protect you from your husband's tricks."

- "I have an accountant who knows how to dig up all of the hidden resources; he'll spare no mercy."

Such advice can misdirect negotiations. For example, the whiz child-custody attorney may win her day in court, but will she consider the needs and wants of the children? A wife wanting to avoid trickery will enter a negotiation in a defensive position, which may not be in her best interest. In the last instance, the spouse may really have no hidden resources. The digging itself may cause embarrassment.

WHY PEOPLE'S NEEDS ARE MISUNDERSTOOD

Everywhere we look, old values are being eroded by new realities.

- Not long ago, gambling carried a negative value. Today many states have institutionalized the practice.

- Sports and religion were not always commercialized activities, but today they are big business on television.

- Not too long ago, the nation's youth looked to family, school, and community as models for their values. Today, we have television to contend with.

What this rapid change in values means is that in negotiations you must not assume that the values you hold are always at work in the other person. People are different. Today's top negotiators must be flexible in their approach to human needs. Today's negotiators must develop an ability to sense differences in their opponent's values and their own.

TWO KEY NEEDS THAT ARE BECOMING MORE IMPORTANT

First, we feel a growing need for security in a world which projects greater and greater feelings of insecurity and loneliness. Second, our need for ego gratification is growing. Television ads tell us, "Yes, you can be all you want to be!"

In all of our negotiations, we must at least consider how these two attitudes can be used to gain our negotiating goals. In employee negotiations, for example, no longer can we expect a positive response to statements like, "Competition is the way you get ahead around here." Remember, people tend to be getting progressively more insecure and lonely.

No longer can we assume that employees' loyalty to the company and dedication to the job are the strong values they once were. Today, many people's deepest loyalty and dedication are to themselves. If we are to negotiate mutually agreeable settlements of people problems, we had best consider gut feelings such as these when we set our agenda.

HOW NEW VALUES AFFECT OUR NEGOTIATING VOCABULARY

- Not long ago, when an unmarried man and woman were sleeping together on a regular basis, they were having an affair; now, many people think of this arrangement as a relationship.
- Not long ago, you might have said that a job "pays well." Now, it "provides fulfillment."
- Once we might have told disputing employees, "Control your tempers." Now a manager might ask, "What's the source of this confrontation?"

The gist of how our changing values affects negotiation lies in how we relate to different people in different negotiations. For some negotiations, pop vocabularies might be great; in other situations, the language of old values still works. The key is to avoid getting mixed up about who expects to hear us express which type of values. Choose the wrong vocabulary for a given negotiation and your opponent may think you have the wrong values. Choose the right vocabulary, and you build a bridge of common values with your opponent.

WHAT YOU WANT YOUR OPPONENT TO FEEL WHEN THE DEAL'S BEEN MADE

You want your opponent to feel three things after completing an agreement with you:

- That the mechanics of the negotiation haven't stifled your opponent's ability to communicate his or her needs and feelings.
- That the values expressed in the negotiation haven't portrayed you as a sharply different human being than your opponent.
- That both your opponent and you have won something. This means that you find ways to identify with your opponent's human needs. You might relate to your opponent's ability or status or your opponent's need to feel some sort of gain, whether it is money, survival, or future possibilities.

Here is a tough example. If you persuaded several employees to accept a cut in salary, show how it hurts you as much as it hurts them. Emphasize your humanity, your compassion. Explain how the salary cut will prove to be an immediate survival tool; no one is being fired. Explain that no one will lose status or appreciation of his or her real abilities. The salary cut was required by outside reasons having nothing to do with real worth.

Show how the future may be brighter because of today's cuts. Don't say how this will come about. Let them read into the future promise what they wish. Never treat the salary cut as an automatic or mechanical act. Do not let your people assume that their needs have been lost or ignored in a bureaucratic maze.

Carefully choose the time, place, and whether other people should be present for these tough situations. You risk losing your opponent's confidence in you if you select a sterile location or inopportune time for your negotiation. A private lunch or dinner, perhaps at a location pleasing to the other person, could be a nice place for such a meeting.

HOW TO COUNTER ATTEMPTS TO INTIMIDATE YOU

Earlier in this book we discussed how confusion can result when negotiating procedures have a negative impact on the negotiating parties' human needs. Often, your opponents can turn such mechanical considerations on you as a form of intimidation. Consider these examples.

FIVE COMMON INTIMIDATION PLOYS AND WHAT TO DO ABOUT THEM

- You are forced to deal with a designated third-party spokesperson for your opponent. The third party could be a lawyer, accountant, or consultant. In any case, the situation can be very intimidating. If you feel intimidated, find yourself a spokesperson to deal with the other side's spokesperson.

- You are subjected to the opinions of the other side's expert about your negotiations. This information may come from professionals, consultants, reports, or other sources. Use these tactics if you feel intimidated. Do not comment on the expert opinion when it is presented. Instead say, "I'll give this to my people to study." Then, find your own expert to comment on their opinion.

- Your opponent rigidly tries to control negotiating procedures, including how much time is devoted to discussion on various points. Your opponent also tries to limit questions related to agenda items earlier agreed upon. Thus, your opponent tacitly says a third-party approval is required. Your opponent also tries to limit the people or support materials you introduce into your negotiation.

    Counter any procedural controls your opponent may try to use to intimidate you with a smile and the words, "You have to be kidding." When you smile and say this, your opponent knows the attempt to intimidate you failed.

If your opponent persists in having his or her way about procedures, look for trade-offs. Thus, if you hear, "We have no more time to spend on this item," you say, "Then let's table it until we have more time."

If you hear, "We don't want your lawyer present," say, "Then we'll have to make any decisions on this subject to my lawyer's review later."

- Your opponent tries to set you up with meeting arrangements that are physically difficult for you. The difficulty may stem from the time or place of the meetings. Your opponent may try to place you in a hostile environment or surround you with hostile people. The other side may select surroundings to impress you with a show of power.

  Try first to establish a neutral basis. This usually will be possible if you use diplomacy to explain why the earlier suggested meeting arrangements will not work. If this fails and the meeting arrangements go forward as your opponent suggested, add people or circumstances to match your opponent's intimidation attempts.

- Your opponents encourage outsiders to pressure you to cooperate with them. For example, your opponent arranges to have your banker, friend, or family member offer unsolicited advice to influence you.

  This cannot be allowed to go unnoticed. Immediately upon learning of such efforts, call a special meeting to discuss the breach of security. Explain that negotiations cannot go forward until your opponent assures you of 100 percent security. Be diplomatic, but be firm. If a face-to-face meeting is out of the question, use the phone.

  At the very least, your opponent will now know you have seen through this form of intimidation and that it is no longer effective.

WHY OPPONENTS TEST YOUR VALUES

In addition to attempts to intimidate you by dominating procedural aspects of negotiation, some opponents try to intimidate by confusing your values. An opponent who knows you are sympathetic to unions may deliberately test you by saying something like, "These striking workers have to be kept in their place."

Your opponent is trying to get you to show uncertainty or to lose your cool. In either case, you would be setting yourself up for more intimidation. Your response should always be firm, but nonconfrontational. Smile and say, "Of course, you know I don't agree with you on that."

The point is to keep clearing the air each time your opponent hits you with a statement which does not fit your values. If you go along with an opponent's intimidation attempt that is based on your values, you allow your opponent to dictate rather than negotiate. This is only your recourse when an opponent is trying intimidation. Be careful, though. Often an opponent may simply be showing his or her limitations by such remarks. If so, ignore the comments and stay with your basic negotiating objectives. After all, a seller's values may not be your cup of tea, but this does not have to deter you from your objective to make a deal.

WHEN TO USE INDIRECT INTIMIDATION

Expect opponents to attempt intimidation related to your values and negotiating procedures, but avoid using such direct attempts to intimidate your opponent. This is not to say that you should abandon any intimidating tactic. Indirect intimidation may be appropriate on occasion.

You may find subtle indirect ways to have your opponent experience fear of resisting you or fear of missing a future opportunity. The key, however, is that such fear must originate in your opponent's own mind through his or her own ideas. This is quite different from making overt threats. Never do that!

HOW TO CONTROL NEGOTIATOR'S ADRENALINE HIGH

Some opponents charge into a negotiation with great excitement. Others blast in with anger. Still others wear a cool facade that masks a tiger quietly stalking its prey.

In any of these situations, your opponent's adrenaline high may be something you need to control. To do this, you have two areas, mechanics and values, with which to work.

HOW TO COPE WITH AN EXCITED OPPONENT

An excited opponent may become careless. If you suspect this is the case, try to build your opponent's excitement. Try doing this through these tactics which are related to negotiating mechanics. Select an exciting place for your meetings. Invite exciting experts to help build your case. Deliberately speed up the tempo of the negotiations. Encourage your opponent's spouse, associates, and friends to tell your opponent how enthusiastic they are. For example, say, "What a great deal if things work out!"

To work with your opponent's values, speak in his or her value vocabulary. (See Section 5–3 of this book.) Find ways to use your opponent's values to feed his or her excitement by saying such things as, "Wait until your boss hears about this. You'll probably get promoted!" Instead of saying "boss," fill in the blank with the name of the person or group which means the most to your opponent.

TACTICS FOR DEALING WITH ANGRY NEGOTIATORS

You must lower an angry opponent's adrenaline level. You could change negotiating mechanics by walking away—not out—and turning your face away, as in deep thought. You could arrange a meeting break to cool things down. Or, you might ask an expert of your choice to talk to your opponent on your behalf. Another alternative is to ask an appropriate outsider to help calm your opponent down. This person might be a spouse, friend, professional contact, or intimate associate.

Unless you are absolutely certain of some of your opponent's value needs, you had best not use a tactic related to values. Depending on how well you know your opponent, you might say, "Can you imagine if your boss could see you now?" In this case, you know your opponent respects his boss, that he fears the boss's rebukes, and that he knows the boss would not approve of this angry behavior.

To another angry opponent, you might say, "If your old coach could see you now." In this case you know your opponent's esteem for the coach. You know that the coach always preached self-control. You know that your opponent will try to regain control, not for you, but for the coach.

WHAT TO DO ABOUT A COOL, CALM OPPONENT WHO IS READY TO STRIKE

You sense that your outwardly cool opponent may be a stalking tiger. This person's adrenaline level seems to be producing high alertness. Your tactic should be to get your opponent more relaxed by lowering his or her emotional intensity and intellectual sharpness. Again, you can work with issues about both mechanics and values.

Try to arrange the most relaxed times and places for your negotiating sessions. Use your opponent's value vocabulary to put him or her at ease about the kind of person you are.

You may wish to introduce an outside party with a sense of humor. The outsider's purpose is to further relax the negotiating environment.

Another mechanical device is to include deliberate and fun distractions such as a tennis break, a drink, or a sporting event you watch with your opponent. Such activities lower your opponent's level of intensity.

When facing an outwardly cool, inwardly churning opponent, beware of thinking that you understand this person's inner needs. Better to use values in a different way. Instead of trying to match values, use values as questions to get your cool opponent talking. Pick an outside event, news development, anything. Ask your opponent's opinion without showing any opinion yourself at first. As your opponent talks, nod your head, smile, and listen intently. Few people can resist hearing themselves talk if conditions are right. Getting the stalking tiger-type to talk will relax your opponent and give you useful information.

THE BEST WAY TO CORRECT A MISTAKE YOU MAKE DURING NEGOTIATIONS

The mistakes negotiators are prone to make fall into three categories: mechanics, value, and logic. Mistakes related to the mechanics of negotiations can involve the wrong time, the wrong place, ill-chosen experts, and outside advice which applies the wrong type of pressure to your opponent. Change negotiating mechanics that don't fit!

A mistake related to your assessment of your opponent's values would be speaking the wrong value vocabulary. This would cause your opponent to back off from you emotionally. Perhaps your behavior made your opponent question your values. You may have flirted with a waiter or waitress during lunch thinking that your opponent would find it amusing. Instead, you realized that your action was an affront to your opponent's values.

Another mistake would be dropping names of people you thought your opponent held in high esteem, only to hear your opponent say, "I can't stand those people!" Back off from your value assessment and look for better information.

Mistakes in logic stem from strategic exchanges of logic between your opponent and you. Here is a simple example of a logic mistake. You are negotiating to buy a car. Logic tells you the car cost the dealer about $5,000. This estimate becomes the basis of your strategies. When negotiations are stymied, you discover that the car costs the dealer $7,000. No wonder you were getting nowhere.

When you make a logic mistake, start over. Most people will forgive logic mistakes if you look them in the eye and tell the truth. You have nothing to lose by admitting a logic mistake and a great deal to gain. Your opponent will understand that you really are logical, whereas up to this point your mistake was creating doubt in his or her mind.

HOW TO ASSURE OPPONENTS THAT THEY GOT A BARGAIN

This situation is not quite the same as the one described in Section 9–1, "What You Want Your Opponent to Feel When the Deal's Been Made." In that section, we emphasized—

- Your opponent's need to know that he or she has communicated his or her feelings to you.
- Your opponent's need to see you as a human being.
- Your opponent's need to feel as if he or she has won something.

The need for a bargain is a summary rationalization need that relates to these three cited factors. It is also a feeling that he or she can live with your agreement. It is not enough for your opponent to feel good about a concluded negotiation. Your opponent must have at least one reason to give a positive answer to the question, "Could I have done better?" To feel good about a concluded negotiation, negotiators can't help but ask themselves this question. To leave the negotiation feeling good and to continue to have good feelings about the agreement, an opponent must have some reason to believe that he or she got a bargain.

EXAMPLES OF BARGAIN RATIONALES

- "That could have been the last buyer to come along. I was lucky to have this chance."
- "These people would never again have been in that kind of selling mood. I caught them at the right time."
- "I'm glad they hired me on these terms and before they learned about someone else who might be available."
- "Thank goodness, it's over. I wouldn't ever have the strength to go through that again!

- "Conditions might change and make this kind of agreement impossible in the future."
- "No one else could understand what I understand, so I alone know what a good deal I made."
- "You can be too greedy in life. It's not the way to live."
- "If I hadn't done business with them, who knows how much tougher the next group would have been?"
- "There's a time when you just know what you did was right."
- "There, but for the grace of God, go I, if I hadn't made this agreement.

Bargain rationales are never completely logical or based on reality. Their purpose is to put logic and reality to bed, once and for all, after an agreement is reached. Bargain rationales can be skewed to replace the question, "Could I have done better?" with "Think how much worse it could have been." A smart negotiator knows that the bargain rationale has to be the opponent's idea. Smart negotiators will never overtly state a bargain rationale for an opponent, but they are not above planting seeds.

HOW TO PLANT THE SEEDS OF A BARGAIN RATIONALE

- After a labor negotiation and when people are getting ready to leave, hold up today's newspaper, point to an article about a Third-World country where people are starving, and say, "We've still got a lot to be thankful for in this country. Look at those poor kids."
- After a negotiation that was exhausting for everyone, mention the television soap opera your opponents watched last night and say, "How about that heart attack on last night's show? It should remind us all not to ask too much of our energies."
- After a tough price negotiation, say, "My father grew up in the Depression. If he could see the price of things today, he'd never believe this money I'm paying. But then again, maybe I can't believe we could ever have another depression."

These examples do not fit logically into the concluded negotiation; they are seemingly random remarks. Yet they may be the right seed from which your opponent conjures up a handy bargain rationale.

UNDERSTANDING WHAT OPPONENTS NEED APART FROM NEGOTIATIONS

The signs of human need and how it relates to buying and selling are all about us.

- People enter a retail outlet to buy something just for an excuse to talk to sales people. Such is the power of loneliness.

- Employees leave successful jobs to have a new experience. Such is the power of curiosity.

- Consider those people who sell a comfortable, attractive home of long standing to buy a smaller, less comfortable, more expensive condominium with highly sophisticated security arrangements. Such is the power of fear.

- People sell profitable small or medium-sized businesses to which they have often devoted much of their lives because they feel a need for a change. Such is the power of restlessness.

- Employers hire people at high salaries to associate the new person's reputation to their organization. Such is the power of status.

- Consumers continue to buy products long proved inferior to new developments. Such is the power of habit and loyalty.

- Television commercials for products ranging from beer to cars to foods sell romantic images scarcely related to any real value or function. Such is the power of sex.

- Thousands of highly successful sales people offer real estate, insurance, securities, cosmetics, computers, and much more solely on their charm and personality. Such is the power of friendship.

- Heavyweight professionals in banking, finance, law, and accounting have long waiting lists of monied clients who could care less about more wealth, but who want to be near prestigious associates. Such is the allure of power.

These examples remind us to broaden our negotiating strategies to include human appeals which go far beyond the issues we are negotiating. If you can offer a promise beyond the realities of what you are buying or selling, you can often win for highly illogical reasons.

IDEAS FOR APPEALING TO OPPONENTS' ILLOGICAL NEGOTIATING MOTIVES

- *The promise of friendship.* Negotiations should never be truly routine, at arms length, or formal. Always seek to offer friendship beyond the completion of the negotiation.
- *The promise of adventure and excitement.* Even a machine or a financial investment can seem exciting. The promise of the new experience can be more enticing than financial rewards. Many computer sales people will testify to how excitement about the new world of computers sells normally hard-fisted customers.
- *The promise of status.* The desire for status explains why certain neighborhoods, towns, and cities enjoy residential and commercial real estate values beyond logic. Find a way to offer your product or service as a status symbol, and you can often name your price.
- *The promise of romance.* This factor often has nothing to do with reality. Associates who labor long hours for bosses who underpay them often have a hidden romantic dream which they may not even admit to themselves. A car, house, or vacation may be sold because of a clever sales person's romantic myth.
- *The promise of power.* People often buy and sell to get closer to power. They may buy a vacation home they really don't care much about because their new neighbors are leaders in worlds to which they aspire. People arrange mergers with people whose power they want to share. People may sell to other people at bargain prices to gain future access to the buyers.

The illusion of power becomes a reality to many people who encounter a clever negotiator. Such people don't care about what is actually promised, but rather what the negotiator leads them to assume will be future power benefits. For example, a real estate person name-drops about the neighbors who symbolize leadership and power, but doesn't introduce the would-be buyers to the neighbors. This desire becomes the buyer's illusion.

HOW NEGOTIATORS USE ILLUSION

Sharp negotiators not only permit their opponents to hold false illusions but they also find ways to encourage such illusions.

- The car may not run too well, "but you look so dashing behind the wheel."

- The basement may be full of water, "but the drama of the living room will sweep your friends off their feet."

- The price may not be quite what was expected, "but the buyers are such nice people."

- The merger may not really be a logical fit, "but these are the kinds of powerful people we always wanted for partners."

- The computer may not really be needed, "but it's nice to show everyone that we're up-to-date, too!"

- The business shouldn't really be sold; it's too profitable. "But we're sick and tired of doing the same old thing. We're restless; we need a change."

The adage "Never sell the steak, sell the sizzle" tells us everything. All we have to do is find ways to bring a sizzle into any negotiation. To find the right sizzle for a specific negotiation, look for your opponent's human needs. Try to uncover your opponent's dreams, frustrations, and self-image. Plant seeds based upon these human needs, and find ways to encourage your opponent to create illusions which lead him or her toward your goals. After all, you aren't promising these tangent benefits to your opponents; they are promising them to themselves.

HOW SPECTATORS MAY TIP THE OTHER SIDE'S HAND

- Your opponent seems quite affable in person, but you noticed that this person's secretary treated you with a degree of hostility. Does your opponent feel that way beneath the smile?

- You meet a junior member of your opponent's negotiating team in the washroom during a break. You smile and say, "Well, these things always take time, but we seem to be making progress." The other person responds, "We have to be in L.A. tomorrow. We never expected this to take so long."

   You may be able to use your opponent's L.A. appointment to your advantage. Your opponent may become impatient or careless because of the appointment. For openers, you stretch the meeting break. When you return, slow things down to see what opportunities your opponent's time bind may provide.

- You notice that all of your opponent's people seem to be getting tired, except their leader. The leader is still outwardly fresh, but since the team seems tired, maybe their top negotiator feels the same way. You can use this information to play your hand.

- Your opponent brings in an expert who is obviously trying to please you. This suggests that the expert is acting either as instructed by your opponent or in a manner that your opponent never intended.

   The second situation offers the most promise. Perhaps this expert has inadvertently tipped your opponent's desire to please you. If so, you're on to something! This becomes a strength that you didn't know you had.

- One sharp negotiator creates mechanical problems during a negotiation. These problems are designed to test the mood of people around your negotiation. Thus, a cup of coffee, which an opponent's staff member is serving, is deliberately spilled. If the staff member is less than pleasant about the accident, this clever negotiator gets a signal.

A series of phone calls cause deliberate interruptions. At each interruption, this negotiator reads the body language of everyone present for such things as patience, impatience, hostility, and frustration.

"I can tell from these reactions exactly what the real mood of the negotiation is at a given time," the negotiator has said. "These signals tell me when to pull back or press harder."

- Another successful negotiator has become an expert in peripheral vision. "I look away and give opponents plenty of time to send signals to one another. Sometimes they act as if I've left the room even though I may have just gone over to straighten a picture on the wall."

Sharp negotiating opponents will usually take great care not to send you any "free" signals. But, the people around your primary opponent are usually much less aware than their leader. It pays to look for clues from these people.

HOW WEARING DOWN THE OTHER SIDE CAN BACKFIRE

It can be amusing to watch how the mechanics of a negotiation backfire. For example, one negotiator deliberately arranges a lot of late evening social activity for opponents. This is a tactic to tire opponents and to make them careless the next day.

In one instance, an opponent arrived the next morning alert and ready for vigorous discussion, while the negotiator was but a shadow of himself. He took the medicine intended for his opponent. This backfiring occurred in the mechanical aspects of the negotiation. The same problem can show up in values and human needs areas when one opponent tries to wear down the other. Thus, the person who starts to act mean may wilt when the opponent gets really tough.

People who try to corrupt their opponents' values or needs may find that the corruption is weakening their position. Such was the case when a negotiator decided to wear down an opponent by deliberately attacking those human values most important to the other person.

"He expects this to be an orderly negotiation," the first negotiator reasoned. "So, I'm going to shake things up from the start. I'll be rude, crude, and everything that he dislikes. By doing this, I'll put him in such a state of shock that he'll agree just to get the matter over with."

As it turned out, the man who was the brunt of these attacks on his values of civility launched three separate lawsuits against his opponent that were based on charges of libel, damage to reputation, and coercion.

The suits had little intrinsic merit, but they kept the maverick negotiator tied up in legal red tape for three years. The person who began as the aggressor experienced a fit of depression and was worn down. His own need for action was stifled under the weight of legal problems.

Lesson: Before you decide to wear down an opponent, consider how much pressure you can take if your tactic backfires.

HOW TO BAIT THE HOOK WITH FLOWERS FROM ANOTHER SUITOR

Negotiators always think what-if about certain negotiating demands.

The job seeker thinks, "What if they have a better applicant?"

The seller thinks, "What if they know about a better competitive opportunity?"

The buyer thinks, "What if they get a better offer?"

The boss thinks, "What if they find a better job?"

The banker thinks, "What if they move their account out of our bank?"

The lawyer thinks, "What if they decide it's better to file a counter-suit?"

THE KEY TO UNDERSTANDING NEGOTIATORS' AMBIVALENCE

All negotiators are ambivalent about their opponents' alternatives. On the one hand, people train themselves not to be threatened by their opponents' competitive tactics. When a buyer says, "I have another alternative," a good negotiator will smile and think, "Here it comes again, the old competitive tactic."

On the other hand, this ruse may be true this time, and every negotiator feels some degree of uncertainty about an opponent's possible alternatives.

HOW YOUR OPPONENT'S AMBIVALENCE CAN INCREASE YOUR OPTIONS

"Will you?" "Won't you?"

"Is it a bluff?" "Is it for real?"

What can these conflicting feelings in your opponent do for you? The answer lies in certain tricks related to human needs.

Step 1: Combine a smile with the truth about your options. People need to think the best things about themselves. If you don't believe it, try this on your friends. Explain to a friend that you are now going to tell the truth about how you really feel about this person. Then smile as you say, "I think you are detestable." Watch your friend's reaction. Because you smiled and because we don't think of ourselves as detestable, your friend will laugh and be flattered because you are playing a joke. You are noticing the other person. Your logical explanation about the truth is ignored, as are your words.

So, too, will negotiating opponents have trouble believing that you have an option better than theirs. When you smile and say, "I have a better alternative," they will simply not believe you are telling the truth.

The purpose of Step 1, the smile plus the truth, is to plant a subconscious seed of doubt that persists, although opponents ignored the truth in their conscious minds. Your opponents feel flattered because you smiled and joked with them. Of course, you really were not joking.

Had you said the same thing without smiling, your opponent's reaction would have been much different. Your opponent would resent the truth and probably assume that you were bluffing. By smiling instead, your true options were heard on a subconscious level, and they were not resented because your opponent sees this game as flattering.

Step 2: You have put your option on the table with no resentment; the seed of doubt is working within your opponent's subconscious. Now, arrange to receive "flowers from another suitor." The key is not to verbally restate the truth about your option. Instead of words, use a symbol. Depending on the negotiating circumstances, these symbols might be used:

- You happen to make a competitor's letterhead visible.

- You receive a call from another company where you have another job interview scheduled. Of course, your opponent in your present job negotiation interview hears your conversation.

- In jointly arranging the time of your next negotiating session, you call in your assistant who happens to say, "Remember that on Thursday you're meeting with the Rogers Company." Of course, your opponent hears this and knows that Rogers is a potential competitor.

- One of your negotiating team members seems to slip as he or she says, "Remember, we still have to get back to them."

WHEN TO USE HUMOR TO RELAX YOUR OPPONENT

- Use humor if the mechanics of your negotiations are causing your opponent any anxiety. Use humor to reassert your humanity and to soothe your opponent's feelings. Thus, you might say of the lawyer's presence at a negotiation, "They are getting rich on us."

- Use humor if the mechanics of your negotiations are boring your opponent. You might say, "We live in a world of technical expertise and bureaucratic procedures. It's tough to just talk to one another."

- Use humor if your opponent has been unwittingly embarrassed, insulted, or confused by a value statement made by you or one of your associates. For example, "Accountants are overpaid."

  Immediately, if you sense that you have violated your opponent's human needs or values, make light of the situation by saying, "That was meant to be a joke, but I never was much of a comedian. Even in school, they gave me the hook at our local amateur contest."

WHY HUMOR DOESN'T HAVE TO INVOLVE LAUGHTER

Humor doesn't always have to evoke a laugh. Humor can simply be a sentence which shows how silly you both know something to be. When you say of the lawyers' presences at a negotiation, "They're getting rich on us," you don't expect a laugh. Instead, you're sending your opponent a signal that says you too feel much of the legal paperwork is silly, albeit necessary.

A sense of humor is really an awareness of the contradictions in life. When you share with your opponent a common knowledge of these contradictions during a negotiation, you show that you are human and that you know that your opponent is human, too. This helps!

THE HIGH COST OF A STUFFY NEGOTIATION

The tactic opposite of using humor during negotiations is to be stuffy. The stuffy approach ignores your opponent's need to be liked and understood. This approach fails to relax your opponent. It discourages opponents from opening up to give you more information. Thus, you have less fuel for the negotiating fire.

Often, a stuffy negotiation leads your opponent to say of you, "Never again." Too bad, because the best negotiating results often come the second time around.

REASONS TO LOSE A FEW ROUNDS BEFORE WINNING THE BIG ONE

Sometimes your negotiating opponent wants to meet your demands that stem from human needs, but outside circumstances make this impossible for the time being. For example,

- There simply may not be any money in the budget to give you a higher salary.
- There may not be a way to remove someone currently in charge to give you more authority.
- The time and place you want to negotiate may be your opponent's worst time.
- Your opponent may want a fair method of payment as much as you, but this person may also be temporarily strapped.
- You may be unable to win a service negotiation at the moment because your opponent's service people are ill or are on vacation.

It is foolish to blow up negotiations about an issue when outside circumstances truly make it impossible for your opponent to meet your demands. Why start a lawsuit about service if your opponent may be able to meet your demands in a few weeks?

Why quit your job in an emotional fit if your salary negotiation goes against you now? After all, your boss has said, "Next year's budget may present a better chance." Why not wait a little longer?

A word of caution: Sometimes an opponent is childlike. If so, don't risk a childish outburst early in negotiations. Instead, get your emotions under control and let the early part of the game be fun for your opponent. Give a little, at first. Then, when the fun is too great for your opponent to give up, change the rules of the game and win most of the marbles.

KEY TACTIC: Ask Yourself Why You Lost

Sometimes you lose a few because your original strategies and assumptions were wrong. You didn't mean to lose in these early rounds, but you did.

The trick then is to analyze why you lost and correct the problem. You'll stand an excellent chance next time. It is far better to grow from a failed negotiation on something minor than to fail later on something really important. This is another reason to save your important negotiating demands until last, if possible. Construct a negotiation agenda that will let you test and meet your opponent on small points early on, before the big game begins. If you lose some of the little issues early, you may gain insights for a big win later.

WHAT FUND RAISING TELLS US ABOUT NEGOTIATING TECHNIQUES

We were recently talking to a man who headed a fund-raising drive for his university. The drive raised almost $50 million in less than three years. Here are highlights of the conversation.

- "We never knew what we could really get from someone before we tried. Time and time again, we miscalculated, sometimes by millions of dollars."

- "Different people gave for completely different reasons. We originally thought we knew why most people would give, but we were dead wrong. You simply can't put a formula on it."

- "In my biggest gift experiences, I never put a top figure on a gift. If a person said, 'How much should I give?', I would always say, 'At least so much.' In other words, I made what was really my top figure sound like their bottom figure. This way, I usually got much more than I ever dreamed."

- "Little things were important. Sometimes a big gift would depend on a very small detail, such as which bank would receive the funds for the university. People are funny. Sometimes, someone's ancient animosity about a little thing threatened a large donation."

- "Another key factor was who asked for the money. A rich person expects to be asked by another rich person. It's not the old story of peer pressure; it's something else—the need for respect. One millionaire visiting another millionaire indicates respect. The person who gives doesn't do it to look good to a peer, but for other reasons. Rich people feel more comfortable telling other rich people what these reasons are."

KEY TACTIC: Ideas for Adapting Fund-Raising Lessons to Negotiations

- Never be sure that you know what your opponent may be able to give.

- Never be sure that you know why your opponent will meet your demands.

- Never limit negotiations by putting a top on your demands. Always say, "at least," instead of limiting your demands by too tight a definition.

- Never let details upset an otherwise successful negotiation. If your opponent is hung up on some outside detail involving a person, institution, or function, change the situation to save the big deal.

- In top-money negotiations, try to have a rich person sit down with another rich person. It may be taken as an insult if less affluent negotiators show up, capable though they may be.

- In negotiations involving specific skills, match skill people to avoid insulting someone by introducing people of lesser ability. Thus, a rich company owner may be ideal for negotiating a large bank line of credit, but completely wrong for negotiating how patent-right earnings are to be split with company scientists.

HOW FADS CAN REINFORCE YOUR BARGAINING POSITIONS

But for a fad, the purchase price of Manhattan Island might have been quite different. Trinkets and hats had little intrinsic value in European societies, but they created a new fad among the Indians. After all, the Indians already had plenty of land, clothing, weapons, food, and leisure activities.

UNDERSTANDING THE OPPONENT WHO HAS EVERYTHING

Many opponents may seem to have everything. A tactic appropriate in such a case is to use the appeal of fads, as in these examples:

- The owners of a large, prosperous company couldn't care less about computers. After all, they grew rich without them. But once computers became a fad, once all the other CEOs got one and boasted about them at the golf club, a memo went out from the head office which said, "Get one!"

- Business leaders will often do a lot to be in the company of important sports celebrities of the moment.

UNDERSTANDING HOW FADS INFLUENCE ALL SORTS OF NEGOTIATIONS

When the number of business mergers explodes, the underlying reason may be that the urge to merge has become the hottest new fad. When the investing public starts gobbling up new financial instruments, such as zero coupon bonds, a new fad is behind it all.

The take-off of a brand new type of product is another signal of a fad in the making. From hula-hoops to compact disc players, the momentum of a fad makes the product much more appealing to many people.

In today's television saturated world, faddish social attitudes and behavior influence our work-related negotiations. For example, young people negotiating with older authority figures are often preconditioned by faddish television portrayals of people in authority. Preconditioning can be helpful or harmful to real-life negotiations, depending on current fads. Are most cops characterized as dumb or heroic? Are business people dynamic empire builders or dull conformists?

Like it or not, fads do impose the influence of show business on negotiations. For this reason, good negotiators must be part sociologists. They must know what people feel deep down inside, and they must be up-to-date on their fads. Yesterday's trends don't work. To understand why some negotiating techniques have lost their efficiency, look at today's fads. Now the Indians selling Manhattan might opt for Keogh plans instead of trinkets.

HOW TO FIT INVISIBLE PROMISES INTO YOUR STRATEGY

One of the best company labor negotiators we know has a favorite phrase. His twinkling eyes and benevolent face seem made to order for the words he so frequently repeats, "Who knows?" Most of his opponents are never quite sure what he means when he says this. The words seem to promise so many possibilities at some future time and in some future ways.

HOW INVISIBLE PROMISES WORK

- "Can we have a pension review now?", an opponent asks.
  "No," he smiles, "but later on, who knows?"
- "Can we expect that all new plants will come under our jurisdiction in the future?", the union leader asks.
  "It's not on this year's agenda, but who knows?"

Invisible promises are in the mind of the negotiator from whom they seem to flow. This is so because a needy person will always grasp at straws, even imaginary ones, for encouragement.

SEVEN HELPFUL HINTS FOR USING INVISIBLE PROMISES

Rule 1: Never reject the other side's demand permanently. Instead, reject if for this year or for the time being. Let your opponents read what they will into future chances for the demand.

Rule 2: In sales, never assume that you know what others see in what's being sold. Always say something like—

- "This could present unlimited possibilities to you."
- "Tomorrow, this may not be available. Who knows?"
- "Only you could really appreciate the appropriateness of your purchase."

You're not making any promises about anything here. But you are suggesting hidden promises. You leave it up to the buyer to write his or her own scenario.

Rule 3: If you have made a failed demand, never go away meekly. Instead, say, "Next time it will be very profitable to look at this subject again. Circumstances are changing which may make it worth your while."

Your opponents don't know what to make of this. At the very least, they will accept the possibility of a future review because they—

- Either start to imagine how future events might prove you right, or
- Think you know something that they don't know.

So, why slam the door on future negotiations?

Rule 4: Always hold out the invisible promise of friendship. Leave any negotiation session with your opponents sure that you want to be friends, sure that you respect them, sure that you understand them. People believe in friendship. "Good things can happen among friends," they reason, "so, who knows what this friendship can mean in my future."

Usually, people to whom you seem to promise long-term friendship will race along in their thinking to see how they can benefit from the friendship. They will often make themselves a number of invisible promises based on your friendship. Also, because most people find it harder to negotiate with friends, your invisible friendship promise works for you from its inception.

Rule 5: After reaching an agreement that is satisfying to you, stop talking. Maybe your opponent agreed because of an invisible promise. If you keep talking, you may unwittingly refute the promise.

Rule 6: Beyond what is needed to protect you, put as little as possible in writing. This allows your opponents more opportunity to create invisible promises for themselves. This is not to recommend making a promise in bad faith. You do not make an invisible promise. Your opponent creates it from the vacuum of unlimited opportunity you present by not putting everything in writing.

Rule 7: Find models to whom you compare your opponent. For example,

- "You seem to have the Midas touch."
- "You never seem to miss what other people always miss."
- "You obviously know exactly what you're doing."

Such statements lead your opponent to visualize hidden promises in your agreement.

REASONS TO BEWARE OF HASTY NEGOTIATIONS AGAINST SOMETHING

Negotiations against something are potentially difficult in two areas:

1. One side may lose control of the mechanics of negotiation.
2. One side may be able to dramatize the human need aspects of negotiations in ways that create public sympathy and which add new dimensions to the original negotiations.

A CASE OF SURPRISE CONFRONTATION

A recent strike by TWA airline attendants produced an interesting example of how one side can use negotiation mechanics in a way that the other side may not anticipate.

In full color and in intimate detail, national television news showed TWA's top executive outside the magnificent iron gates of his handsome estate. The lush estate grounds and mansion provided dramatic contrast to close-ups of striking TWA employees who had marched to the estate. The symbolism was gripping. The nation's television viewers watched the drama unfold as a TWA employee spokeswoman recited the striking attendants' grievances.

WHY NEGOTIATIONS AGAINST SOMETHING ARE BECOMING MORE COMMON

- Millions of people watch highly publicized labor protests, and many viewers remember these methods in their own negotiations. Such confrontational tactics can become models for anyone entering negotiations.
- The fact that tactics are seen on television lends them respectability. Thus, reservations against such tactics may be lowered or eliminated in viewers' minds.
- More and more local television news shows are providing editorial

opportunities to air the views of both sides of a highly disputed negotiation. This factor can heighten negotiation confrontations.

• More and more legal matters are being restated on the courthouse steps. Opposing lawyers often seize on the power of television to state their side of a case.

• Congress expanded television coverage of legislative sessions, and it is reasonable to think that this will increase confrontational rhetoric that will be designed "to play well in Peoria." Again, have we created a new model of behavior for millions to see and copy?

PUBLIC PRESSURE AS A NEGOTIATING TACTIC

You must be aware of the increasing use of public pressure as a negotiating tactic for human need negotiations against something, against someone, or for the rights of some individual or group.

Public pressure tactics are not only related to television exposure; they include going public in any number of ways which disrupt normal services and routines. Two examples are letter-writing campaigns and sit-ins. In simplest fashion, an employee refusing a boss's work request goes public by stating his or her sentiments in front of the entire office.

Whether or not you approve of these new confrontational tactics is not the issue. The issue now is that anything can happen, so know this when going into negotiations.

WHAT NEGOTIATORS CAN LEARN FROM WATCHING PEOPLE BUY COMPUTERS

The newest scientific friend to humanity has been less than friendly to many consumers who own one. We're talking, of course, about computers. We can use the trends surrounding computers to demonstrate many illogical buying decisions. The circumstances in our computer example could happen in any negotiation, about anything. And, of course, the computers themselves are never the real culprit in these examples; *people are*.

FIVE LESSONS FROM COMPUTER SALES

What's really being purchased? Often, the buyer in a computer negotiation doesn't really know what he or she is buying. This reminds us that many negotiations can be concluded on the basis of indefinite future promises if a fad is at work.

Many buyers have purchased computers for which little software is available for their specific needs. A home computer program may identify nighttime stars, but what percentage of users really wants this function? Nevertheless, a little excitement in a seller's voice about "what this can mean to your children" can work wonders.

What's really needed? People feel excitement about computers. They feel the pull of the "me too" urge and curiosity to explore new things. Such feelings make logical price negotiation almost impossible. (Of course, not all computer buyers abandon logic.)

Often, computer buyers rely on outside experts who know little of the buyer's real needs. The expert may impose his or her views on the negotiation. As a result, the buyer may end up with a machine that is perfect for the expert, but not for anyone else.

How illogical negotiating mechanics emerged. Originally, the location and mechanics of a computer purchase negotiation were closely related to the manufacturer. Factory-trained service people and company-trained sales people and systems developers often converged on one location to work with prospective buyers. Today, the mechanics and location of a computer purchase can be quite different. Department stores, for example, may stock computers as ordinary shelf items. Computer franchises may be owned by people from such diverse fields as insurance or cosmetics. Thus, the mechanics of a sophisticated product purchase negotiation are often less logical than in the past.

Everyone's a computer expert. Unsolicited advice comes from all directions—family, associates, everyone who has a computer or who is interested in the field. People volunteer advice, and often what they say is completely unrelated to your needs. This illogical advice can come in such forms as—

- "You've got to get a computer. Everyone should have one."

- "You owe it to your children. Tomorrow's world will be a computer world."

- "I hear Jane got a great buy on hers down at the department store."
  No one says specifically what Jane bought. The emphasis is all on price.

- "Talk to John. He's a computer whiz; he'll set you straight."
  John may not know your needs. His knowledge may be specialized in an area unrelated to what you could use.

Would the real buyer please stand up? Often, a computer purchase negotiation is conducted by a third-party spokesperson for the real buyer. Parents or grandparents buy one for a youngster. A company executive will buy a computer system for other employees.

In any third-party purchase negotiation, the ultimate user's needs are often misunderstood. The result is that the new computer may never be properly used. In business situations, the cost of this problem can be great. Money is wasted on equipment which doesn't fill a need, and the organization suffers confusion and loss of morale, time, and effort.

RULES TO KEEP NEGOTIATIONS LOGICAL

Rule 1: Know exactly what you are buying. Resist persuasion based on hope, fad, fear, or excitement. Avoid self-delusions that confuse real value.

Rule 2: Keep advice from outside experts in perspective. Don't let them run your negotiations.

Rule 3: Be sure that the negotiation is at a time and place conducive to your concentration. Make sure negotiations are conducted in a manner that helps you understand everything involved—no legal boilerplate for you; no taking someone else's word for it, and no routines. Insist on special attention to all details and routines. Call on your own experts to clarify anything about which you are not absolutely certain.

Rule 4: Find ways to keep uninvited outside advice away from your negotiations. Since such free advice usually doesn't take your needs into account, it can only confuse you. Restrict gossip and the flow of information during your discussions. Talk about your plans only to people who are directly involved.

Rule 5: Don't let other people speak for you on issues that you are negotiating. Even your lawyer, banker, or accountant can confuse your needs and objectives. Better to have them present or available for limited purposes. Never rely on them to be your dominant spokesperson, unless, of course, you are in court or in an audit.

Of course, there may be times when you want to sell something using the same illogical persuasion points used to sell computers. If so, reread this section for ideas.

HOW MYTHS CAN BECOME REALITY IN NEGOTIATIONS

- In the World War II era, many of the world's most critical negotiations foundered due to myths about one of the negotiating parties. History revealed that the early myths about Hitler confused Chamberlain's negotiation with him for "peace in our time."
- We now realize that the early myths about Stalin set up many costly negotiating consequences.
- During the fall of France, myths about the old French leaders led to negotiating errors with these French allies. This lengthened the war and increased the Allies' risks immeasurably, as in Dunkirk.

Even in negotiations about life and death matters, we can be deceived by myths about the people with whom we are negotiating and what our opponents' true circumstances are. When this happens, the myths which we accept become our reality during negotiations and affect our negotiating results, as if the myths were fact.

TYPICAL MYTHS ABOUT OPPONENTS

- "He's a nice guy; I've heard it from a lot of people."
- "They don't have to sell; they haven't got a problem in the world."
- "I hear he's a tough buy. That's the word around."
- "They don't care about their people; everyone says they're selfish."
- "They're winners every time. That's what they say on Wall Street."
- "When push comes to shove, they can't handle pressure."
- "It's not in them to fight. It's not their style."
- "Everyone says this is the best time to do it."

WHAT TO DO ABOUT NEGOTIATING MYTHS

Every day and in every way, people complete negotiations based on myths about their opponents. Many people haven't learned what history teaches us about myths. Such people accept, at face value, myths about people and situations related to their negotiations. They refuse to ask—

- What says so?
- How do they know?
- What if they're wrong?
- How can I dig deeper?

Some myths may originate with our negotiating opponents themselves as they plant exaggerations or falsehoods to serve their own best interest. Why not promise ourselves to enter every negotiation expecting a few myths? This self-promise will help us learn not to be intimidated by myths. It will keep us flexible, so that we can respond quickly if a fact turns out to be a myth or if a myth turns out to be a fact.

TEN HUMAN NEEDS TO REMEMBER IN YOUR POSITIONING STRATEGIES

As you position yourself against your negotiating opponent, think about what your opponent might be feeling. Your insight might help you make your opponent's gut feelings work in your favor. Successful politicians realize that people vote their gut feelings in the privacy of the voting booth. Everything said before election day matters not when voters express their innermost sentiments.

We want our opponents to cast their ballots for us, and for this to happen, we must uphold our opponent's privacy. If we know our opponent's feelings are in our favor, we never say so directly. If a seller is afraid of his or her economic survival, we do not say, "You can't afford not to sell." To say this would destroy the privacy of our opponent's vote. It would embarrass, challenge, then anger our opponent, and perhaps turn any favorable feelings about us to feelings against us.

We should search out the human needs expressed in our opponent's negotiating positions. When we find them, we must be sure to keep our discovery from our opponent. Consider these ten common human needs. They are listed in the format of a memory tool to help you keep them fresh on your mind before and during a negotiation.

SHE DOES SIP: A MEMORY TOOL ABOUT YOUR OPPONENT'S NEEDS

- S...Survival feelings; the need to stay alive in a business sense.
- H...Hunger feelings; hunger not for food, but for other pleasures.
- E...Excellence feelings; the need to excel in something and to know that others are aware of this.

- D. . .Dedication feelings; the need to be dedicated to an idea, a person, or the memory of a predecessor.
- O. . .Ownership feelings; the need to control material objects or other people.
- E. . .Exploration feelings; the desire to explore, not for gain, but for intellectual curiosity.
- S. . .Sex feelings; which can affect your opponent's moods and behavior in hidden ways.

- S. . .Status feelings; the need to show our strengths and success.
- I. . .Imitation feelings; the need to copy social standards set by our peers and superiors.
- P. . .Pleasure feelings; the need to do things that are easy for us in an emotional or physical sense.

YOUR IDEAL NEGOTIATING POSITION IN RELATION TO THESE TEN NEEDS

- Your opponent feels no threat to his or her survival as a consequence of your demands.
- Your opponent feels that something he or she is hungry for will result from your demands.
- Your opponent feels that your agreement will preserve or increase his or her personal sense of excellence in something, and that other people will be aware of this excellence.
- Your opponent feels that agreeing with you will maintain or increase his or her ownership feelings about what he or she controls or owns. This could include space, a function, people, and other concerns.
- Your opponent feels your negotiating position will offer to him or her the feelings of excitement and exploration, new intellectual experiences, or new adventures.
- Your opponent feels complete in regard to sexual needs—no problems with the opposite sex; no unfulfilled hungers; no personality or behavior quirks related to sexual needs.
- Your opponent sees that agreement with you will maintain or increase his or her status feelings. Other people will still see the status symbols which provide this feeling to your opponent.

- Your opponent sees that one consequence of agreement with you will be that people equal to and above your opponent's social level will view him or her favorably.

- Your opponent perceives no threat to his or her feelings about pleasure. No part of your agreement will reduce pleasure; the agreement will not introduce anything that will strain your opponent in a physical or emotional sense. With luck, your opponent will enjoy more pleasure and fun as a result of your agreement.

KEY TACTIC: Target Your Efforts on Key Needs

In any negotiation, you may find and use several of the ten needs as active opportunities to pursue your goals. Thus, if an opponent is not threatened by eight of the ten needs, he or she may lack fulfillment in the other two. This is where you could concentrate your efforts.

For example, if the two problem areas were status and ownership, encourage your opponent to see how agreement with you would solve problems in these areas. Thus, you might arrange publicity for your opponent. Or, you might arrange to have him or her look good in the eyes of the opponent's family. Your effort doesn't have to be expensive; it should be creative. It should be imaginative. Play to someone's need for status by giving that person a more prestigious job title. Find a way to let someone retain control of something in a harmless way, such as allowing the previous owner of property to visit the gardens occasionally.

Even if you only offer to solve an opponent's problems related to unfulfilled needs, he or she will prefer to deal with you.

SECTION 10

HOW TO OVERCOME DIFFICULT NEGOTIATION SITUATIONS

SECTION 10

HOW TO OVERCOME DIFFICULT NEGOTIATING SITUATIONS

- Successful negotiators never cease trying to make their situation better.
- Successful negotiators improve conditions by finding ways to avoid difficult situations.
- Successful negotiators tune their ear to pick up on opportunities that will make bigger and better negotiations possible.

You can become an average negotiator or a superb one. The difference depends on how well you train your ear to spot discordant negotiating notes. Two people may go to the same concert. Both may be music lovers, yet the two may walk away with vastly different impressions. The person with a trained ear enjoys rewards denied the average music lover. The average music lover, sadly, never knows the difference.

In the same way, many people think of themselves as negotiators. They are, but they never discover the difference between average and superb. They never realize what they might have taken away from a negotiation. They think that things went well, and they never suspect how much more could have been gained had their ear been alert for better opportunities.

The purpose of this section is to tune your negotiating reflexes so that you may become a superb, not just an average, negotiator.

WHAT TO DO WHEN NEGOTIATIONS SLOW DOWN

Train your ear to hear opportunities in two areas:

1. The mechanics of the negotiation.
2. The human needs aspects of the negotiation.

HOW TO OVERCOME DELAYS CAUSED BY THE MECHANICS OF NEGOTIATION

Perhaps negotiations stalled because papers failed to arrive. Or, perhaps a person vital to the negotiations suddenly becomes unavailable. The times and places of your negotiations may make attending difficult for someone. Lawyers, appraisers, consultants, bankers, accountants, or other third parties may drag their feet due to a heavy work load. Uninvited spectators can slow talks down by offering advice, interrupting, or confusing the main purpose of your meeting.

You can avoid or minimize all of these mechanical holdups. You will improve negotiations by arranging in advance—

- *To use messengers instead of U.S. mail.*
- *To name alternates to key support people.*
- *To set times and locations carefully to accommodate everyone.* People often agree to the first location that comes to mind. Take time to find the times and places that are right for everyone.
- *To check outside professionals thoroughly.* How is this person's work-load and availability? Be sure that a lawyer can be ready when you say "go." List all of the outside people who will be involved and ask them to promise their 100 percent attention to your needs when you call them.
- *To make a security list of persons who need to know about your negotiations.* All others should be considered spectators. Try to reduce specta-tors' presence at your negotiations. Try to reduce the chance of

gossip about your negotiations. This encourages spectators to offer you or your opponent free advice.

- *To consider all tangential aspects of negotiations that might slow your progress.* Remove as many negative factors as possible before negotiations start. For example, you might feel that too much socializing between sessions would cause talks to drag, so limit activities at the end of each day.

EXAMPLES OF HOW AN OPPONENT'S HUMAN NEEDS CAN STALL NEGOTIATIONS

In addition to watching for possible mechanical problems that may slow down a negotiation, we must enter every negotiation alert to possible hang ups related to our opponent's human needs. Such influences are often hard to predict and may require rapid adjustment on our part. Consider the variety in these examples of what we may confront:

- An originally enthusiastic buyer or seller gets cold feet as the closing date approaches.
- An originally reasonable opponent suddenly turns mean due to a circumstance unrelated to your negotiation. The cause could be anything that affects emotions.
- A personality conflict arises and suddenly the relationship between two or more negotiators becomes abrasive.
- Your opponent suddenly feels that something about the proposed agreement will cause loss of status.
- Some aspect of the proposed agreement becomes threatening to your opponent's sense of worth and to his or her feelings of excellence. The same threat may apply to how the agreement will appear to other people.
- Your opponent may fear selling out on an issue to which he or she is very dedicated.
- Your opponent feels he or she is sacrificing ownership or control of something. Usually, this feeling has nothing to do with money. It could involve loss of control over people, loss of physical access to old surroundings, or replacement of a function toward which he or she felt a sense ownership.
- The agreement may, in your opponent's eyes, cost your opponent the chance to be part of a social group. People sometimes hesitate to sell if they feel that doing so will make their peers or superiors think less of them. The same can be true for buyers or decision makers in organizations.

- Your opponent sees something in an agreement which will cause him or her pain.

Thus, any part of the agreement which your opponent suddenly perceives as being difficult, less fun, or damaging will jeopardize the entire agreement. If you sense any of these problems, slow down your negotiations. Review the earlier sections of this book which discuss ideas for coping with human needs in negotiations.

WHAT TO DO WHEN YOUR OPPONENT HAS SECOND THOUGHTS

A very successful negotiator remarked, "The greatest danger in any negotiation is the fact that so many people are not at peace with themselves, and they are subconsciously churning all of the time. This lets irrational emotional fears upset even perfect details."

Second thoughts about negotiations can be as great a danger after a negotiation as during one.

EXAMPLES OF SECOND THOUGHTS

- A buyer returns a product that he or she loved yesterday, but feels uncomfortable with today.
- An employer hires a new person with great enthusiasm, but before the new employee reports to work, calls to tell the job applicant, "Sorry, I just couldn't work things out."
- A company owner signs a contract to sell the business, and then refuses to go through with the arrangement. The seller had been very anxious to be rid of the business, but now says, "I'm sorry. You can sue me if you like, but I just can't go through with the sale. I know now that it was a mistake."
- A three-month real estate negotiation cost all parties a small fortune in legal, appraisal, and permit fees, plus expenses for accounting and travel and hundreds of hours lost in executives' work hours. A day has been set for the closing, but the buyer calls to simply say, "We found that we couldn't raise the money."

HOW TO REACT TO AN OPPONENT'S FEARS

Rule 1: Don't ever believe the reasons given for a suddenly cancelled arrangement.

Rule 2: Don't ever expect to learn the truth about any sudden reversal in a deal. Sometimes the cause may be a better deal. In this case, your opponent will never tell you anyway. More often, the reasons are something that even your opponent does not understand.

Rule 3: Always take early steps to protect yourself against an illogical change in the agreement. For example, get a deposit that is large enough to hurt the someone who even thinks about breaking a deal. If you are being hired away from a good job, don't do anything about quitting your present position until the hiring party gives you a contract or a firm outline in writing. Even when a written confirmation is difficult, arrange to get your new employer to go on record in front of other people who can later verify your verbal contract. This permits the other person to realize that to welch would be embarrassing at the very least and possibly expensive legally.

As a reminder, always consult your lawyer about verbal as well as written contracts.

Rule 4: Do not count on payments related to any negotiation until the checks have cleared your bank account. This means never rely on future payments for current borrowings unless you can cover with some other resources in case the payments are not made.

Never oversimplify the problems and time caused by any legal actions necessary to make another person fulfill a contract. In other words, don't rely on what a contract seems to promise you. A top executive put himself deeply in debt to buy an expensive estate in the town where he had accepted a handsome new position. Within six months and after he signed a large six-figure mortgage, he found himself discharged. He sued, but long before his case came to trial, he lost the estate plus many other assets.

Rule 5: Structure any negotiations in a way that will embarrass an opponent who might have second thoughts about the agreement. This is a case of finding ways to replace an opponent's personal fears about an earlier arrangement with a greater fear about the consequences of welching.

The best strategy for creating a greater fear is arranging to have your opponent on record about your agreement and in ways that involve people who your opponent respects.

Thus, the fact that a neutral banker knows about your deal can often be more influential on a deal's fulfillment than a legal contract. You will always try to arrange the contract in any instance.

KEY TACTIC: *How An Opponent's Track Record Relates to Performance*

All of your strategies related to the possibility that someone else will go back on an earlier agreement require you to try to know your negotiating opponent's history in earlier negotiations. Yes, there is still value in a track record that reflects trust and good faith. Learning an opponent's history, however, is getting more and more difficult in our mobile society. This suggests that today's mature negotiators will still negotiate in good faith, but never in a way that rules out a worst-case scenario.

The trick becomes one of appearing to have complete confidence in your opponent's reliability, while creating diplomatic ways to protect yourself against the possibility of his or her second thoughts. As you implement strategies to protect yourself, look for strategies to reinforce the value of your agreement. You might have other people tell your opponent what a great deal has just been made. Be careful never to reveal your part in this flattery.

HOW TO MEET THE OTHER SIDE'S VALUE DISTORTIONS

The hardest part of any negotiation is to spot value distortions. Many people who pride themselves on their negotiating skills taught themselves to spot phony figures. But phony figures are the easiest kind of value distortion to recognize. For example, a sharp accountant may be able to see through a phony figure, but may never notice how a con artist's flattery persuades the accountant in emotional ways.

When we agree to something during any negotiation, we are ultimately placing values on many intangibles. For example, we place a value on how we feel toward our negotiating opponent. Likewise, we place a value on the consequences of that to which we agree. Concerning our future hopes, we ask if we have been sold a dream which has little real value.

CLUES FOR RECOGNIZING VALUE DISTORTION: TWO EXAMPLES

- The owner of a successful business brokerage which catered to the sale of small business franchises told us that the value a buyer places on a business is usually directly related to the buyer's dream of not having to work for a boss. "I always sell the worst dogs to otherwise sharp people," the broker said with a wink. What's his sales tactic? "I use the words, 'you will be your own boss,' over and over during our negotiations." The broker sends dreams across the negotiating table and the result is value distortion.

- The head of one of the world's largest business conglomerates told us his strategy for hiring the best executives available. "I pay them twice what they're worth, and then I give them four times the normal workload." This executive used "dollar flattery" to recruit executive talents who were otherwise unavailable. Of course, the executive never revealed in advance how heavy a person's workload would become. Through value distortion of the other executives' true worth, the head of the conglomerate made his deals irresistable.

Unfortunately for the newly recruited executives, the conglomerate head also confided to us, "Of course, I know that most of them will burn themselves out in ten years, but that's really not my responsibility. They all think the money proves they are up to any workload." This reminds us of our individual ability to make a deal based on a dream about ourselves which someone else deliberately suggested to us during a negotiation.

Despite these examples, the most costly value distortions in negotiations usually are the ones we make ourselves. We base such distortion on our opponent's strategies, which can be summed up as flattery. A clever negotiating opponent encourages you to sell yourself, and always in ways that prevent you from discovering that you have created and nurtured a valuation dream that your opponent planted in your mind.

A CHECKLIST FOR PREVENTING VALUE DISTORTION

The first step to prevent costly distortions about values which you perceive is to create a personal checklist about what you may need to guard yourself against. For example, you might begin by asking yourself these questions during any negotiation:

- Am I unduly impressed by the people with whom I am negotiating? Are they too nice or too important to me? Am I anxious to impress them for reasons unrelated to the actual negotiation? Am I unduly intimidated by their power or threats?

- Am I seeing value in what is being negotiated when the value is only a dream that I want to believe? Have my opponents slyly suggested dreams that are based on their personal wishes, but for which I will have to pay a high emotional price?

- Am I flattered by the surroundings in which we are negotiating? Do I feel like a big wheel because of how they are treating me?

- Are other people telling me that I have a great deal? If so, is someone using them to influence me through flattery? How would they really know what's best for me?

- Have I been brainwashed by flattery? Is it possible that my thinking has been guided by carefully planted dreams about what the deal will mean to my status, happiness, or wealth.

- Am I agreeing to something because I am overlooking the long-term costs to me because someone placed a short-term carrot under my nose?

- If I feel very excited about what has to be offered to me, am I caught up in an emotional promise that will evaporate after the deal is closed?

- Is it possible that I am a victim of a reverse sell? Have my opponents convinced me that they couldn't care less about my buying their deal?

- Am I in any way being intimidated by my negotiating opponent? Is intimidation causing me to fear not taking the deal? Is the fear I feel logical, or is it based on what my opponent said or implied to make me fearful without cause? Is it possible that I am being hurried through fear of an unknown which my opponent created to pressure me?

- Is my negotiating opponent trying to make me bask in feelings about his or her friendship? Am I agreeing to things simply because it's so nice to feel my opponent's warmth and interest in me?

In each case, your list should include areas in which you know yourself to be vulnerable. If you love numbers and statistics, perhaps a negotiation which is all numbers is keeping you from seeing some non-number problem, for example.

Remember, the greatest negotiating advantage you can have is when your negotiating opponent thinks you are buying his or her value distortions. When this happens, people get careless and will provide chances for you to add on all kinds of sweeteners to the deal. After all, an opponent who thinks you swallowed the bait will not be watching for your strategies. Of course, you always carry out your strategies in a way that preserves the illusion that you've been had!

HOW TO HANDLE NICKLE-AND-DIME DEMANDS THAT KEEP COMING

"Wear them down. Tire them out. Keep the pressure on all the way through!"

This is a commandment for certain types of negotiators for whom such tactics are a way of life. The tactics may clearly not fit a negotiating situation, but such is the habit of nickle-and-dimers. When you meet a nickle-and-dimer, don't expect to be able to change this person's habits. If you complain or try to use logic or even humor, these people think you are feeling the pressure, and they pour it on more.

RULES FOR COPING WITH NICKLE-AND-DIMERS

Rule 1: Never show your impatience.

Rule 2: Always act unhurried. The nickle-and-dimers want to put you in a time bind. They count on it, and when it doesn't work, they often get discouraged and impatient themselves.

Rule 3: Fight fire with fire. For every little demand your opponent makes, add two of your own, no matter how illogical or unrelated they may be. Remember, the demands of a nickle-and-dimer usually are not logical.

Rule 4: Use delay and even adjournment as a strategy for each petty demand placed in front of you. Smile as you say, "Let me have some time to check that point out." This will soon drive your opponent wild because you are expected to resist, argue, and get impatient. Instead, you smile and prolong talks.

Rule 5: Try to find out who or what the nickel-and-dime opponent fears most. Is this person afraid of not getting the best price or deal? Afraid of not appearing tough enough? Is this person deliberately trying to cause a shouting bout because he or she is afraid to match strengths and logic against you? Or, is your opponent afraid that superiors will think that he or she is weak unless you wilt under the pressure?

THE VALUE OF KNOWING WHAT A NICKLE-AND-DIMER FEARS MOST

You want to uncover what nickle-and-dimers fear most so that you can act as if they have you on the run. In most cases, it helps to keep telling this opponent that he or she is the best negotiator you've ever come up against. Like most tough guys, they will believe your flattery. They will believe that you are wilting, and then you have them because the next time you say you can't change your position or demands, they will feel you are now telling the truth.

If, for example, you find a nickle-and-dimer who is trying to look tough to a boss, tell the person's superior that you've never met a tougher negotiator. Often, this sets your opponent up for your next strategy. After all, now the boss won't think that he or she gave away the store. At this point, your opponent's guard goes down.

After you acknowledge a nickle-and-dimer's toughness, such opponents often get impatient themselves with your reciprocal tactics and good humored patience. They say, "Let's forget this nitpicking and wrap this up."

A *word of caution, however*: Some nickle-and-dime negotiators are not reachable. These people get a power feeling from grinding down an opponent. If you find one of these people across the table, try to have him or her replaced or just walk out. If you walk out, you lose nothing. You were not in a negotiation; you were in a psychiatric ward.

HOW TO GUARD AGAINST PARTIAL PAYMENT

"Sure, I'll take it!"

"Fine, I'll send it right over," a smiling retail store owner says to a customer. Yet when the bills go out, nothing comes in. Finally, the seller phones the buyer to ask about the missing payment.

"I'll send you something tomorrow," says the buyer.

A week later, a check for 30 percent of the amount due arrives. Two years later, at considerable cost to the seller in time, embarrassment, and collection fees, payment is made, but without interest.

Why should the seller go after interest at that point? It wouldn't be worth it, which, after all, is exactly what the partial payment customer counts on.

This simplest of examples happens and damages careers of negotiators involved in multimillion dollar negotiations, small business acquisitions, merger arrangements about sharing of powers, and in other negotiating situations. Everyone smiles as the negotiation ends. Then, when everything is signed, sealed, and delivered, one of the original negotiators or a proxy doing his or her dirty work emerges as a partial payment expert.

WHAT THE PARTIAL PAYMENT EXPERT EXPECTS FROM VICTIMS

- A partial payment expert knows that some people will spend a down payment or borrow against an entire deal. This makes it undesirable to reverse the deal or to get tangled up in legal battles.

- Some people will be too upset or too embarrassed to admit how badly they misjudged their opponent, and partial payment experts know this. People who get embarrassed or upset are at the mercy of an opponent who senses that they're too upset to fight back. Such an opponent knows that victims often kid themselves and say, "Oh well, it will eventually work out. I'll eventually get what was promised."

Some people will have found the original negotiations so tiring or difficult that they don't want to subject themselves to more of the same. So, they permit the partial payment expert to conduct a one-sided negotiation concerning how and when everything will finally be paid.

• Some people will agree to forgive some payments altogether in order to get most of their money sooner than they might through legal battles. They take less money now, even though they might expect all of the money plus interest later from legal actions. Many people hate to go to court for anything, so they settle on the partial payment expert's terms.

• Some people will rely on the partial payment expert's word instead of a legal document. When this happens, the partial payment expert usually pompously denies earlier promises and creates false agreements that he or she swears are the truth. Partial payment experts love to have a case of your word versus theirs. They have played this game so often that they almost never lose.

RULES FOR OVERCOMING AN OPPONENT'S PARTIAL PAYMENT STRATEGIES

Rule 1: Try to double or triple any money down amounts that a suspected partial payment expert offers. If you don't know who you are doing business with, consider this person suspect. Better wrong than sorry.

Rule 2: Have your lawyer handle everything that is to be given or paid to you after a negotiation. Do this before you hand anything over to anyone or deliver your services to anyone.

If you suspect a partial payment expert, have your lawyer put in special protections, such as extra penalties for failure to pay on time or special personal guarantees of your opponent's property or family members' property.

In accepting a new job, have your lawyer draft an employment agreement, including everything promised plus a high severance payment if you are asked to leave or if the promises aren't kept.

Rule 3: Never let intimidation or fatigue cause you to abandon a legal battle. Let your opponent know that you intend to have your lawyers negotiate in court to collect full payment. Knowing your intentions will often encourage your opponent to pay on time.

Rule 4: Always try to hold back something that the partial payment expert needs. Thus, you promise to deliver a key service, but hold up as long as possible to see if the check clears or that the legal papers arrive as promised.

Be creative in thinking about ways you can cause partial payment experts problems by giving them your own partial payment in one form or another!

WHAT HAPPENS WHEN A MEMBER OF YOUR NEGOTIATING TEAM GETS SELFISH

Since the days of Judas, the fair question has been, "Who can you really count on?" This question goes beyond cynicism to an understanding of human nature. Often, betrayal is not in the betrayer's true character. Instead, it can be an aberation of normal behavior caused by extreme pressures that overpower a person's dearest values.

WHY TEAM MEMBERS MAY BECOME DISLOYAL

Usually, disloyalty comes down to one dominant need, survival. When survival seems threatened, all other needs and values pale. Depending on what is being negotiated and who is on your team, someone on your side may compromise himself or herself. Suppose, for example, you are negotiating, and the other side ultimately becomes the dominant new force in corporate affairs. Do not be too surprised to find one of your most loyal team members building a bridge to your opponents during negotiations. It happens all the time.

AN EXAMPLE OF HOW A SLIGHTLY SELFISH TEAM MEMBER CAME OUT ON TOP

The leader of a dynamic electronics firm took his company from a five-person office to an operation with several thousand employees. Funds for much of this rapid growth came from stock purchases from outside investment-capital people. After several years of prosperity, the firm again needed an infusion of capital because of industry contractions. The firm's leader was confident that there would be no problem raising the cash.

"My executive vice president had been one of my five original employees, and I named him as one of six people on our new capital negotiating team. We visited several cities to meet a number of investment bankers. But, industry conditions were growing worse, and we struck out everywhere.

"My executive vice president suggested that we go back to our original risk-capital investors. This seemed reasonable, so I asked him to set it up.

"We succeeded in getting the money we needed from these investors, but what a surprise I had coming! One Sunday morning, my old friend comes to the house and says he has been offered my job as part of the new money deal. Of course, he hastened to explain that he hadn't accepted the job and wouldn't accept it unless I left voluntarily.

"I thanked him for his candor and, after a cup of coffee, he left. I thought I had been at every meeting this guy ever had with the risk capital people, and I sat there at home doublechecking my memory and my records. I was right. I had always been present. And, I know that my executive vice president would never have gone to a meeting behind my back.

"Of course, I got fired, and he got the job. I would never have stood in his way. But to this day, I still can't figure out how he got so close to them right in front of my eyes."

We suspect that the executive vice president was loyal, did not meet secretly or have telephone conversations with the investors, and did not consciously conspire to replace his friend. Nonetheless, we suspect that in small ways the executive vice president sent signals to the other side, and the message added up to a slightly selfish advantage over the current leader. It can happen, so be prepared.

HOW TO KEEP COOL WHEN AN OPPONENT IS USING SWEAT TACTICS

Sweat tactics are a prime area for your avoidance strategies. A tough negotiator once told us, "I never took advantage of a guy who wasn't asking for it."

We find no pangs of conscience or remorse in this statement; rather we interpreted it to mean, "Give me an opening, and I'll make it hard for you whenever I can!"

The people who use sweat tactics always search for an opening, a place to make you sweat that is based on a weakness you have revealed. This reminds us to try, wherever possible, to avoid providing our negotiating opponents with openings in our positions. Often, we can easily close any openings before negotiations start.

THREE TYPES OF OPENINGS TO CLOSE BEFORE NEGOTIATIONS BEGIN

Legal openings: If you are selling or buying something, you take steps before and during negotiations about the sale to clear the title and to establish legally exactly what is being offered for sale, plus any remaining service, guarantee, or contingency conditions so that you can avoid claims for nonperformance.

Remember, we live in a time when the number of liability suits has reached unimagined scope. You should always review any negotiation to determine how legal, accounting, or special regulatory conditions might affect you before, during, and after a negotiation.

You must think of breach of contract and discuss it with your lawyer. Verbal contracts have different legal interpretations from state to state. We recommend that you always review any important financial negotiation with your lawyer, accountant, and financial advisor. Ask these people to anticipate and explain to you all aspects of risk related to negotiations. Ask them to recommend steps to minimize the risk of legal action or claims from your negotiating opponents. Do this before you begin a negotiation, and do this whether you are the buyer or the seller.

Good-faith openings: As you try to clarify the legal aspects of any negotiations, expand your efforts in human relations, too. For example, it is foolish to take a new job only to learn later that what you and your employer think you agreed to is quite different. Employment arrangements must be reviewed to establish services to be rendered, prices, and any other areas that need to be clarified, such as noncompetition agreements. This also applies to promotions, transfers, and temporary salary reductions.

In hiring new employees or contractors of all kinds, the more you clarify, the more you gain. Exactly what do you expect? Answering this question helps you avoid another opponent's sweat tactics that are meant to embarrass or shortchange you. For example, an employee who resents you for what he or she considers a broken promise can cause you to sweat in countless ways, such as refusing to accept delegated responsibilities, distorting your key delegations to others, and displaying poor productivity.

KEY TACTIC: *Where Union Leaders Look for New Recruits*

Many union leaders have told us that their best way to get a foot in the door in recruiting nonunion employees is to find employers who have broken their promises. This means that even an employer who didn't break a promise can often seem to have done so if terms are not carefully spelled out and clarified.

Emotional openings: If you enter a negotiation feeling the emotions of anger, revenge, or anxiety, your opponent will see your emotional state and possibly use sweat tactics to make you look bad or negotiate poorly. Suppose you have a complaint you wish to negotiate, and you rush into your opponent's office making accusations of an emotional nature. You may threaten, name call, or disrupt the office surroundings. If other people are present to witness your emotional behavior, you could be exposing yourself to sweat tactics in the form of lawsuits.

The same thing can happen if you emotionally lose control in a letter you write to someone to complain about something. Here again, talk all punitive, threatening, or hostile ideas over with your lawyer before you take action. Losing your cool in a group negotiation can cost you the respect of everyone on both teams. This is not to say that you can't be tough. Sometimes it is necessary to be that way, but that is not the same as losing emotional control.

HOW TO RESPOND TO SWEAT TACTICS

Many times you do everything before and during negotiations to avoid giving your opponent any openings for sweat tactics, but your opponent gets mean anyway. When this happens, you may be able to do to your opponent exactly what he or she is threatening to do to you because you closed your openings earlier. Thus, if your opponent threatens to sue, you may have a winning case if—when your opponent threatens bad faith—you have written proof of exactly what was agreed.

If your opponent loses control of his or her emotions, you find ways to control yours. You may wish to cooly embarrass your opponent in other people's eyes. You may wish to respond calmly in ways that cause your opponent to be embarrassed in his or her own eyes. Or, you may wish to keep your opponent rattled to make clear thought difficult.

It is easy to stay cool when someone is using sweat tactics if you have closed your openings in advance. Approach every negotiation with this requirement in mind.

WHAT THE PHRASE "IN YOUR BEST INTEREST" REALLY TELLS YOU

An opponent expects you to accept certain terms because, according to the opponent, doing so is "in your best interest." This approach depends on one or more of these ingredients:

- *Friendship and flattery.* "I would only do this for you."
- *Survival.* "We need one another."
- *Fear.* "If you knew what I know."
- *Expertise.* "I've been doing this for ten years."

EXAMPLES OF "IN YOUR BEST INTEREST" APPEALS

- "You know that no one wants to take care of you more than I do."
- "We reviewed everything that might help you most and decided that this gives you maximum benefit."
- "I remember how hard you worked to get what you have. Few other people can appreciate what I appreciate about you. You can count on me."
- "I could have taken this proposal to other places, but I came to you first because you know how I feel about you."
- "Let's forget our differences. The fact remains that we need one another."
- "Business is one thing, but we have something more, something worth preserving."
- "There are factors to consider which only I know about. Without getting into details, let me say I am doing what's best for you."

WHERE TO LOOK FOR "IN YOUR BEST INTEREST" PEOPLE

- Lawyers often approach clients and adversaries with this tactic.
- Accountants often use survival and fear in their rendition of "in your best interest."
- Sales people love to build a confidential friendship bridge to their customers.
- Office politics could not exist without "in your best interest" appeals.
- Parents and people who act like parents to other adults count on the "in your best interest" approach to control other individuals.
- Members of the opposite sex will often use flattery to make you believe they think so much of you that anything they propose will be good for you. After all, who would hurt someone they love, respect, or admire?
- Doctors, scientists, governmental employees, mechanics, and most other varieties of experts tend to replace logical argument with this approach. They expect you to trust their expertise.

Many people find the "in your best interest" negotiating tactic almost impossible to resist. To them, we say, "Come on! Let's get logical and always ask ourselves the question, 'In whose best interest is it really?' "

If this sounds cynical, remember that most of these appeals are built on your opponent's cynicism. Such an opponent knows exactly what he or she wants to accomplish through this tactic and in negotiations with you. In fact, such an opponent probably chose this tactic because of a cynical attitude that all people are idiots. This opponent often feels superior to you. If you take the "in your best interest" bait, your opponent will see this as proof that such cynicism is a valid attitude.

WHAT TO DO WHEN YOU DISCOVER AN OPPONENT'S EMBARRASSING FLAW

- A number of promising careers floundered when people decided their boss was a fool.
- Sellers have observed many foolish product purchases and concluded that the buyers didn't know what they were doing.
- Some buyers laugh at their seller's stupidity.
- Many negotiations fail because one party feels superior to the other and gets careless.

You will help yourself a great deal if you learn to redefine the flaw you see in an opponent. Here are some guidelines.

- *Avoid drawing superficial conclusions about another person's speech, dress, or status.* Your opponents may be twice as sharp as you on the matters being negotiated.

  His or her appearance may be a deliberate strategy to make you careless. Ask courtroom observers about the unusual appearance and habits of the top defense attorneys in criminal courts, and you'll hear some bizarre stories about carefully contrived images.

- *Remember that even a stupid boss outranks you and greatly affects your career.* Could it be that the stupid boss has strengths that his or her superiors are aware of, but which you are overlooking?

- *When you find a seller who seems to be little match for you, look out!* Your best buy may also be the best sale for the seller who seems to be giving it all away.

- *Many so-called stupid buyers have a way of becoming very rich!*

- *Any truly gifted negotiator loves to have you feel superior.* The biggest wins are always from people who come away from a negotiation saying, "I cleaned them out."

That's exactly how you are supposed to feel.

Most embarrassing flaws in your negotiating opponents are actually smoke screens for what is really happening—to you!

SECTION 11

WHAT TO DO WHEN ALL SEEMS LOST

SECTION 11

WHAT TO DO WHEN ALL SEEMS LOST

No matter how well you do your negotiating homework, no matter how well you perform under pressure you will sometimes face overwhelming odds. You may be tempted to throw in the towel, but don't! This section presents some better alternatives. For example, you learn the value of leaving your opponents escape routes from their flat refusals. You'll see how one small business owner gained a major victory over an opponent who appeared much more powerful. And, you'll read why it sometimes really is wiser to fold your hand than gamble on a bad deal.

HOW TO STAY HOPEFUL WHEN ALL SEEMS LOST

- Only idiots kid themselves by blaming others for their negotiating results. There's no profit in it, and you always lose energy when you dwell on accusation and revenge.

  If a negotiation failed or is failing, blame no one, not even yourself. Say, "What is done is done. How, how can I negotiate something new to start me on the road back?"

- As long as you manage to keep your mental and physical health, any negotiation loss can be eventually replaced with a negotiating gain if you get going!

  For example, if you negotiate with your boss and get fired, spend no time blaming your boss or yourself. Begin by looking for a new way to negotiate about your future. Start with your boss. Any new negotiations here? If not, start to look for other new negotiating opportunities. Try anything! Just getting going is initially more important than where you're going. Anything may happen.

  If you are in the middle of a negotiation which you are losing, don't blame yourself. Find something new to negotiate. You may have little in mind when you start with new strategies and demands, but who knows where they may lead.

  A very successful business negotiator once told us three ideas about regaining hope:

1. "When things seem black, remember history."

2. "When things seem black, remember humor."

3. "When things seem black, get ready for tomorrow with a good night's sleep."

WHAT TO DO WHEN ONE PERSON HOLDS MOST OF THE CARDS

Earlier in this book, we discussed how to handle surprises in negotiations. In this section, we deal with the situation in which you know that your opponent clearly has the advantage before negotiations begin. We consider these four bleak prospects and learn how each situation was creatively transformed:

- A supervisor does not rely heavily on a particular employee. Simply stated, the employee is easily replaceable, but he or she wants to negotiate with the superior for more money, nonetheless. The employee seems to have few cards.

- An independently wealthy business partner suggests that both owners of a company take a deep salary cut to meet the firm's working capital needs. Many years before, the rich partner had needed a co-owner, but now if the poor partner walked out tomorrow, nothing much would change. The rich partner knows this, and the poorer partner doesn't seem to be left with many negotiating cards.

- A sales person's biggest customer calls to say that two competitors reduced their price by ten percent. Everything else is the same. Their product functions and quality are equal to the sales person's product. The customer wants the sales person to come over to discuss a new price. What, if any, cards might the sales person play against the customer?

- A small business owner needs the seller's product. The seller offers a lower price and higher quality than the competition. The seller's firm doesn't depend on the small business owner's volume to stay healthy, but the small business owner needs a price reduction to keep things going. The small business owner plans a meeting, but has few cards apparent.

HOW TO CREATE NEW CARDS FOR YOURSELF

Creating new negotiating cards usually isn't as hard as it might seem. The key lies in your psychology. There will always be times when you say to yourself, "I don't seem to have many cards."

As in our examples of imbalanced strength, the people in seemingly inferior positions appeared to have little hope of winning negotiations. Each case, however, had a happy ending.

The negotiators who turned things around against great odds did so with a positive outlook. They refused to be beaten. They said to themselves, "There must be something or some way to improve my position."

KEY TACTIC: Why a Positive Outlook Pays

You must have a positive outlook to get your creative juices flowing. You must believe that you have options, but don't expect a creative solution to always come to you right away. Often, it takes time for your subconscious to work out a creative problem. Never be discouraged because you're out of ideas at the moment.

If you believe in yourself, you do have a chance to find something or someway to make your situation less one-sided. As long as you believe, your subconscious will continue working on creative solutions. On the other hand, if you feel and accept emotional defeat, nothing can happen. It seems so basic, but unless you believe, you can forget it.

CREATIVE SOLUTIONS TO DISCOURAGING SITUATIONS

Perhaps we can bolster your faith in some future bleak-looking situation by explaining the creative solutions that the people in our earlier examples used to improve their positions.

Getting a raise: When the boss had no economic or political reason to give an apparently replaceable employee a raise, the employee did the following to change things in his favor. He spent time studying his superior's personal life. He found that his boss loved stamp collecting. So, he purchased a beginner's book on the subject and started learning about it. Then, the employee called his uncle in another city and asked a favor: "You know those envelopes you throw away every day in your job," he said. "Could you cut off the stamps once in a while and send them to me?" The uncle agreed. After all, he liked his nephew, the stamps cost him nothing, and his job at an international manufacturer meant he received customer orders in envelopes from all over the world every day. After a month of receiving envelopes from his uncle, the employee had a shoebox full of stamps from across the oceans. After work one day, the employee presented the shoebox to his superior. The boss was ecstatic and, with a rare smile, asked, "Where did you ever get them?" Upon hearing the employee's story and learning that the stamps would keep coming, the boss again smiled and said, "You were nice to think about me. That shows loyalty. And, you have a good mind to have figured out where to get me these stamps. Not many people are that capable."

Suddenly the boss began seeing his employee, who had once been replaceable, as *unique* among his other workers. The boss would not have promoted someone just for stamps, but the gesture had changed the boss's thinking about the employee from "replaceable" to, "Here's a guy who's different; he's energetic, and he has a sharp mind. The way he found those stamps—that was smart."

Yes, the once replaceable man got the raise and eventually a promotion. The last we heard the boss and the employee were both stamp collecting. They have a friendship based on a common hobby. The once replaceable employee's career looks brighter than ever.

Rich partner, poor partner: In our second superior strength example, a wealthy partner asked a poorer partner to share a mutual salary cut. Of course, the cut posed few economic problems for the rich man. But the poor partner had a problem, especially since she knew that a threat to leave would be ineffective since her departure would not affect the company's performance. So, she spent several days searching for a way to become more equal in this salary negotiation. Then, she discovered her answer.

She knew the rich partner was very anxious to become friends with another rich person who, although retired, was a well-known, highly respected business leader. She knew the man well from college days. She did not go to the rich partner and offer to set up a meeting because doing so would have been obvious.

Instead, she arranged to play tennis with the man her partner admired and aspired to befriend. Deliberately, she reserved a court next to where her partner would be playing.

The rich partner couldn't believe his eyes when he saw his partner's guest on the next court. Of course, after the court time expired on both courts, she introduced the rich partner to her retired friend, but only briefly.

A few days later the rich partner came into his less affluent partner's office and said, "Hey, that was great meeting Jock on the tennis court. I didn't know he was a friend of yours."

"We go way back. Maybe the three of us could have lunch someday," she answered.

"That would be great. Count on me being available any time!"

As the rich partner turned to walk out of the office, he heard his partner call behind him, "By the way, that idea about cutting our salaries. I'd like to hold up on it for the time being." The rich partner turned to smile benevolently. "Oh," he said, "that was just a crazy thought. Forget about it."

His negotiating message was clear: "Forget about the salary cut, but don't forget to set up that luncheon date with Jock." The poor partner found a way to come equal with the rich partner by finding out what really mattered to her opponent.

Same product, different price: In the sales example, the sales person faced tough odds. Two competitors with basically equal products cut prices ten percent and the sales person's biggest customer requested a price meeting.

After considerable thought and planning, the sales person devised a plan to come equal with the threatening competition. But his plan had nothing to do with a price cut! Instead, he brought one of his top engineers to the meeting with the customer. The engineer briefed the customer on a dramatic new product that the engineer invented. The product has nothing to do with what the sales person was selling at the time, but it could have meant a lot to the customer in the future.

The engineer's concluding remarks were exactly what the sales person rehearsed him to say, "Of course, we won't have this available until many months from now. Even then, we'll only be able to give it to a very few customers because there will be limited production capacity for a long time. But Henry [the sales person] told me that he insisted that you see it first and that you have first call when we finally start production."

The customer, beaming in appreciation, said, "Henry and I go way back. He takes care of me, and I take care of him." The meeting ended with everyone friends. The subject of a price cut on existing products was never even raised. Henry's tactic, a future promise, was more alluring to his customer than the price cut, even though it was in the indefinite future.

A price cut, please: Our final example was perhaps the most difficult. A small business owner needed a price cut from a supplier who already was under the competition with a product equal or superior to theirs. And, the small business owner's volume was only a drop in the seller's bucket.

The night before the negotiating meeting with the seller, the small business owner placed a conference call to seven other small business owners, all of whom he knew were in the same situation. They all bought relatively small amounts of the same product from the large supplier.

The next day, the small company owner sat down in the seller's office and negotiated a lower price by announcing that there was now a trade association composed of eight companies. He named the companies and said he had been elected to study the possibility of a consortium effort by the eight associate companies to build and manufacture the seller's product. He explained to the seller that he was inclined to stay with the seller if a price review could be arranged. The seller, no longer looking at a "drop in the bucket" customer, faced the possibility of losing the sales volume of eight companies. What's more, the creation of a new company would have meant a new competitor that could cut into sales from other companies.

You can bet that a price review followed, and one that gave the small company owner what he and the seven other owners wanted. The small company owner received a volume discount by placing one order to cover the needs of all eight firms. The volume discount permitted everyone to save face. No one really received a price cut; they had only earned a volume discount.

This was all possible because the small company owner created a way to become equal with the big supplier. The new price enabled him to ship the products purchased in bulk to each of the seven other small companies. Everyone shared in the savings, and the big supplier no longer had to worry about the specter of a new competing company being formed.

WHAT TO DO WHEN A NICE OPPONENT GETS MEAN

A negotiating opponent has been gaining your agreement through an "in your best interest" appeal. Then suddenly, this person drops the facade, or you see through it, and the gloves come off. Now the nice-guy opponent switches the negotiating approach from "courtship" to "rape." Now your opponent seeks to gain his or her purposes by attack and counts on the fact that things have gone so far that you have no negotiating escape. You are trapped and must accept the consequences.

HOW COURTSHIP TURNS TO RAPE: AN EXAMPLE

A real estate broker courts you like a bride or groom. When you put down a small, routine deposit, the courtship is in full bloom. Later, when you put down a really large installment and after the check has cleared, you have a few new questions for the broker.

"Sorry," you are told, "but you should have thought of this before. Now that the owner has a substantial deposit, you better not have second thoughts or you'll never see your money again."

Many people facing this situation will submit to their attacker by going through with the sale. The opponent often counts on this acquiescence. A better response when negotiation rape is threatened is to scream bloody murder. When you do, your opponent will usually run away from what he or she was trying to do to you.

WHAT TO DO IF THREATENED: A SIX-STEP PLAN

1. *Never really scream or lose control of your emotions.* If you do, your opponent may think you are afraid and be encouraged.

2. *An icy smile is always in order, as are the words, "Hold it!"*

3. *An unexpected action should come next.* Thus, excuse yourself from the meeting to make a phone call. (Your opponent wonders

who you're calling.) Or, if you are on the phone, say, "Hold it! I have to call you back." Say nothing more.

4. *When you come back into the room to resume a face-to-face meeting, or when you call an opponent back, say, "You'll be getting a letter from me; I don't want to discuss this verbally any more. You'll be getting my letter."*

    You haven't said who you phoned or why you got off the phone in the first place (assuming you were originally on the phone). Now, your opponent connects the events and wonders from whom the letter will be and what it will say. Now your opponent's feeling of attack are subsiding to curiosity, apprehension, and fear. Your opponent thinks you may be calling on others for help, but whom? Your lawyer? His or her boss? The public? A competitor? An accountant? An expert? Are you scheming some strong-arm tactic?

5. *Often, your opponent will start talking because you said you want to communicate only by letter.* When this happens, your opponent may try to get you to reveal to whom you talked, what the letter will say, and from whom the letter will be.

    Never answer such questions. Repeat yourself each time, "I said you'd get a letter." At this point, you haven't left; you're still with your opponent in person or on the phone. But you're silent, with an icy smile. Stay around long enough to give your opponent a chance to apologize and to begin to act in a reasonable way. Often, this will happen.

6. If your opponent doesn't back off after you linger in silence for a while, then leave. Consult whatever experts you need to write a letter on your behalf. Your experts will know exactly how to answer your opponent's attempted "rape." And when your opponent gets the letter, most times he or she will fold because you demonstrated that you are different than many people; you won't cave in to even the worst pressure! You will also have gained your opponent's respect, albeit begrudging respect.

UNDERSTANDING THE EMOTIONAL RISK OF A BAD DEAL

Some aspects of negotiations have nothing to do with financial deals, career paths, legal arrangements, or buying and selling. We are talking about how a deal affects your emotional well-being.

WHY THE ULTIMATE RISK IN A NEGOTIATION IS YOUR MENTAL HEALTH

To take chances based on reason in a negotiation is logical. To take chances based on emotion is illogical. You logically consider risk in such areas as—

- How much money down?
- Whose word can I trust?
- How long should the terms be?
- How valid is someone's credit rating?
- What's a fair return?
- What's a fair price?
- What could go wrong?
- What may go right?
- Who is winning?

All of these risks can cost you money. They can also cost you worry before, during, and after a negotiation. Some worry is permissible—a price you are prepared to pay. High anxiety, paranoia, and depression are never worth risking. Never gamble on your emotional stability.

People who take risks during a negotiation must continually ask themselves, "If the worst happens, can I handle it emotionally?" The question must also be asked in regard to loved ones. "If I could take it, could they? And if they couldn't, what would that do to me?"

TYPES OF RISK THAT CAN POSE EMOTIONAL DANGER

If you are disappointed in a price negotiation for a car, house, product, or service, you may worry, but you'll probably get over it. On the other hand, if you are worried about things which affect your sense of self, then you may be in danger.

Examples of dangerous risks are—

- Risk that affects the trust in a marriage or intimate friendship.
- Risk that dramatically affects your net worth. Thus, your financial risk should never cause you to question your ability to survive if you take a risk and lose.
- Behavior that causes you to feel shame, guilt, or loss of self-esteem if things go wrong.
- Risk that causes you to lose pride, reputation, or self-esteem if things go wrong.
- Risk that causes you to hurt others you love if things go wrong. You could experience the cruelest anxieties.

Some criminals can go to jail without feeling guilt. Their families may not feel badly. In such cases, the dangers of losing mental stability are not a real concern. On the other hand, we have seen scientists who sold their companies to people they eventually saw as promoters feel guilt, shame, and loss of self-esteem beyond logical explanation.

These situations remind us that everyone is different. We never dare to have someone else measure our emotional risks related to any negotiation. Only we know how we feel about the negotiation before and during the process, and only we can guess how we will feel afterward.

FOUR WARNING SIGNS TO TELL YOU WHEN TO GET OUT

- If you think you might be the kind of person who dives out of the window after a Wall Street crash, don't negotiate big financial deals.
- If you think you might lose your pride and sense of self-esteem if some risk proved you wrong, don't take the risk.
- If you think you couldn't handle hurting loved ones if your risk goes sour, forget the risk.
- If you think that any kind of risk anxiety about money, pride, or love will continue a long time, ask yourself, "Is the deal worth it?"

Take chances on anything that seems logical and reasonable. But never take chances on your inner well-being if in your heart you feel that the situation seems too chancy. Whether you are getting married or signing a big financial deal, no matter how late it is, pull out if your peace of mind is at risk.

HOW TO GET OFF OF THE NEGOTIATING JUNK FOOD DIET

Here are ten junk foods that you must keep away from your negotiating table:

- *Last-minute demands.* These may come from an opponent who expects you to swallow the extras because you've already had the main meal.

- *Extraneous advice.* Unsolicited opinions from spectators or friends of your opponent are to be avoided. Don't let your opponent swallow these extraneous opinions. Otherwise, he or she might feel sick about what you've already agreed.

- *Congratulations and flattery.* Never accept the wine of flattery. This can only blur your appreciation of what still has to be done to get the most from your negotiations.

- *Interruptions designed to upset your appetite.* Don't let your negotiating opponents take you on the town in ways that may make you less hungry during tomorrow's negotiating sessions.

- *Ridiculous demands of any nature.* If your opponent throws a ridiculous price at you, clear it off the negotiating table immediately or get up to leave. Usually, your opponent will brush away the crumbs he or she tried to offer.

- *Many little appetizers.* Your opponent offers to give you a lot of early goodies to spoil your appetite for the main meal. When this happens, put the goodies aside and say, "Let's have these later."

- *Overcooked arguments.* Don't let your opponent burn you with the same old issues cooked over and over again. Say, "Come on, you're giving me indigestion with that same old line." Smile as you say this!

- *A new menu.* You must always send back any new menu which your opponent presents to restructure or change the original negotiating agenda. When a new menu is presented for your approval, you say, "Hey, first we've got to digest what we had on our original menu. Put that away for now." Smile and say this with firmness.

- *Emotional appeals.* These can range from anger to a call for help. Tears of anger or of pleading can equally spoil the negotiating tastes for your opponent. Keep any kind of tears out of your eyes and out of your opponent's eyes. Or at least adjourn from the negotiating table until one or both of you are again under control. Remember, good negotiations mean both people have to "eat something" without tears.

- *A bitter taste.* All parties must leave the negotiating table with a good taste in their mouths. Remember, you both might want to sit down together again in a future negotiation. No one opponent should proclaim victory—no leering of satisfaction, no anger of loss. When you get up from the negotiating table, your winnings should be in your pocket and not on display for spectators to see. Your opponent must feel that he or she has some winnings to hide as well. Sometimes the atmosphere of a restaurant can go a long way to overshadow a bum meal. Always arrange the most conducive atmosphere for negotiations. Often, your opponent will find it easier to swallow a tough course if the music is playing, and the waiters are smiling, and the bill doesn't have to be paid now.

Everyone likes a pleasant dining companion. Everyone likes a pleasant negotiating opponent. Why spoil anyone's meal?

WHEN TO CALL TIME-OUT TO REGROUP YOUR LAGGING TEAM

During team negotiations, expect your negotiating opponents to apply different strategies to different members of your team. Their objectives will be to pick up some new negotiating advantage not earlier known to them.

TYPES OF INFORMATION NEGOTIATORS MAY UNWITTINGLY REVEAL TO OPPONENTS

- *Body language that hints of anxiety, fear, anger, or impatience.* Often, a member of your team may signal these emotions in regard to some issue in your negotiations. For example, a sleepy team member during a late-hour negotiation may be the sign your opponent needs to keep things going.

- *Team members who come under the spell of your opponents.* For whatever reason, be it brilliance, friendship, flattery, or something else, when this happens, your opponents will play more and more to the empathetic member of your team.

- *Some team members may start to rearrange the agenda.* They may introduce extraneous subjects or bring up agenda items out of sequence. Your opponents will quickly spot any such breakdown in team discipline and will try to use this to their advantage.

- *Passing information through idle conversation around the table.* It is not unusual for a team member to unwittingly pass along tidbits that are best kept in confidence. For example, an associate may mention that you have to be somewhere by a given time. This seems harmless, but a clever opponent now has a means of putting you in a time-bind.

- *Team members contesting one another at the negotiating table.* This is perhaps the most costly error when it is done within earshot of the opposition. Thus, a husband and wife negotiating a price on a new house may openly argue on some point that enables the seller to devise some new strategy besides lowering price. Even in the most sophisticated business team negotiations, ego causes members of the same team to get into arguments designed to show their status or brilliance to the opposition. When opponents spot an ego or personality rift in your team, what an opportunity!

THE VALUE OF PRESENTING A UNITED FRONT

The winning negotiating team always must appear united to the opposition. Likewise, members must defer to their leader in all actions. They must resist the other team's attempts to get into one-on-one conversations, even those of a social nature. This sort of discipline is hard enough to maintain when everyone is physically fresh. Often, fatigue and a few drinks can cause problems in controlling your team. Clever opponents may use social or dining breaks to get to your people because these are times when your team members may drop their guard.

Unless your team is 100 percent under your control, find a way to get everyone away from the negotiating table in a hurry. Don't resume talks until you have had a private team meeting to tighten discipline. Many times, the best thing is to replace the members of your team who have difficulty with your need for discipline. Or, you could simply arrange for this person to be absent when negotiations resume.

HOW GENERALIZATIONS GET NEGOTIATIONS OFF-TRACK

One divorce lawyer believes that most divorces come about because the marriage partners cannot overcome their habits of generalization. The lawyer explains, "Negotiations break down because the people aren't talking to one another about specific problems, instead they generalize about their feelings."

When a potential buyer says, "I don't think it's worth the price," this is not a negotiation until the buyer says how big his or her problems with the price are. In a flea market or Persian bazaar, the seller is expected to sell at a lower price, but this is not the etiquette of more serious negotiations. More than likely, such a generalization will cause the other party's guard to go up. The seller may walk away or at the least conclude that he or she is dealing with an amateur and act accordingly.

Top negotiators seldom generalize in making demands or taking positions, but we have seen many negotiators lose by using generalizations. A person who says, "We aren't going to let you push us around," is generalizing and probably won't be taken seriously. In contrast, a person who says, "Let me tell you exactly what will happen if you do that," is being specific. With a situation such as this, you have every reason to expect the negotiations to start moving.

TIPS FOR BEING MORE SPECIFIC WITH NEGOTIATING OPPONENTS

Rule 1: Be alert to your opponent's generalizations. They can come in many shapes and forms, as these examples show:

- "I have the feeling we're not getting anywhere."
- "You're trying to get me angry."
- "You must be kidding."
- "I think we should start all over again."
- "There's no way I could sell that."

- "We'll never see eye-to-eye."
- "You're not listening to me."

Rule 2: When you spot a generalization, ask a question that demands specificity. Questions that you might ask in reply to the example above are—

- "Not getting anywhere on what specifically?"
- "In what way do you think I'm trying to get you angry?"
- "Kidding about what specifically?"
- "On what issue, specifically, do you want to start all over again?"
- "No way you could sell what? And to whom?"
- "Exactly what can't we see eye-to-eye about? Why do you feel this way?"
- "Not listening to you on what subject? Why do you feel that way?"

Rule 3: Review and redefine each issue on your negotiating agenda. Nothing prevents problems with generalization better than your willingness to take the time to organize your negotiations into clearly distinct agenda items and to outline what you understand the topics to be. Do this before any discussion begins.

A COSTLY EXAMPLE OF NEGOTIATION BY CONFUSION

A business owner and union leader both had ample negotiating experience. The union leader had joined negotiations at the request of the local union members who reported, "Negotiations are at an impasse."

The issue at stake was a relatively small matter which had escalated into a wildcat strike. Plant operations were shut down, and the mood of the place seemed very angry. The hostility began after a night shift manager fired a female employee who was found in an embarrassing situation with a male employee. Within an hour of the firing, the entire plant was closed after workers walked off the job in protest of the dismissal. All subsequent negotiating attempts turned into shouting matches between management and labor representatives. This is why the company owner and out-of-town union leader began their talks.

The union leader's first task was to meet privately with union members, who shouted their contempt for management in a variety of generalizations. The union leader listened to their grievances, then asked for silence and said, "What specifically do you expect management to do?"

Emotional shouts resumed with a variety of anti-mangement generalizations. Again, the leader listened, then called for silence and asked, "What specifically is your complaint?" Eventually, someone offered a specific answer, and the union leader left to join the company owner in a private meeting.

"You won't believe it," the union leader said, "but I now have a specific definition of our problem. I had to fly in for this because your people and my people had been negotiating about two different things. Your people were rightly defending their decision to fire the female employee, and my people were upset about an entirely different issue."

"You've got to be kidding," the plant owner answered. "Think of what this cost the company in down-time and what it cost your people from lost paychecks! What is the issue?"

"Fairness. They want you to fire the man, too. They think you were unfair in firing just the woman," the union leader explained.

"Why didn't my people know this?", the plant owner protested.

"Your people didn't take the time to ask enough specific questions, and our people spent all of their time on general complaints that had nothing to do with the real issue.

"One other thing you might want to think about is to teach your negotiating people to ask the right questions about what's to be negotiated before they start talking," the union leader said. Usually, just a few specific questions can zero in on the specific aspects of your negotiating opponent's generalizations. Take the time to talk about one issue at a time. Also, take time to review the specific definition of each agenda item before the item is up for discussion. It pays!

WHAT MIGHT GO WRONG IN THE CLOSING PHASE

"Never keep talking after you've sold the shoes!"

This expression from retailing reminds us of how fragile many sales transactions are. Many things might well go wrong after a transaction is made. One side never knows everything involved with the other side's decision to agree to something. Both parties must always take care to maintain the other person's mood of decision, lest a change of mood cause something to go wrong.

SIX AREAS TO WATCH TO MAINTAIN A DEAL

Time: Do everything possible to keep the time lag between agreement and actual closing performance to a minimum. One car dealer personally drives the purchaser's new car to the home within 24 hours of receiving the order, assuming the car is in stock. A real estate broker pays a retainer to people to be available on instant notice to prepare legal, financial, banking, appraisal services as may be needed to speed up closing dates.

A tailor keeps twice the normal alterations staff to deliver a suit within hours of purchase. The tailor explains, "Many people buy expensive customer suits on impulse. When I cater to their impulse by offering same-day alterations, I feed their excitement about the purchase. I believe that many of our sales stem from our rapid delivery, not because the people really need the suits in a hurry, but because it makes it more fun to see the finished product in a short time."

The other person's psychology: This means that we must take steps to preserve a person's mood of agreement until the deal is complete. For example, a person agrees to something in a mood of fairness. Never display any unfair action to this person before the deal is completely signed. This would anger or disenchant the person. An investment banker once agreed to a multimillion dollar deal for an underwriting on the assumption that the other party was a fair person.

"Then I saw how this person crucified a secretary in a most humiliating fashion. What triggered it was a really minor error. I called this person the next day and cancelled the deal on some pretence. The fact is that I saw that my initial impression of the man's standards had been wrong. His actions revealed the true person and it cost him a bundle."

Environment of the agreement: Do not present a sharp change in environment between agreement and final closing. A changed environment can sometimes make one of the parties have second thoughts.

The owner of a small biochemical research business was regularly visited by a partner in a risk capital firm. The risk capitalist wanted to buy a substantial percentage of the small, but promising, company. Twelve months and over a dozen visits later, the small business owner decided to sell to the patient visitor. Both parties agreed on a price, and the closing details were to be finalized at the risk capital firm's bank in an adjacent city.

On the appointed day at the big city bank, the small business owner was given little courtesy and respect by many of the bankers involved with the deal. Usually, the bank expected the risk capital firm to be doing business with companies which needed funds. The small business owner was different, but the bankers failed to make the distinction. They acted superior and condescending with their out-of-town visitor.

"After two hours of this unpleasant treatment, I simply told them I was going home and had decided to keep all of my stock." The owner told us this years later, when the firm had grown to a dominant position in an expanding industry.

As it turned out, the company owner gained substantially more wealth by holding on to all of the stock. But money did not cause the earlier agreement to break down. The problem was the hostile environment at the big city bank. To this day, the risk capital partners regret their inability to close the deal, but they have no idea what really went wrong.

Chemistry of the negotiators: This factor must always be taken into account, especially during the lapse between agreeing and closing. The president of a large computer company sold her old friend on the advantages of an expensive computer system for the friend's medium-sized company. The president arranged to have a trusted employee visit the new customer at the customer's office. This employee was a brilliant expert who intimidated the customer with technical jargon and analysis of the company's needs. The company never went through with the deal to buy computers. Because the two company leaders were friends, the prospective buyer never revealed the real reason.

The computer company president should have accompanied the

employee to the first meeting. She could have spotted the chemistry problem and may have saved the deal by replacing the expert.

Professionals who second-guess: This type of person can upset even the firmest agreement between two other people. It is not unusual for an accountant, lawyer, banker, or some other advisor to upset an agreement by trying to intrude where he or she is not needed. This person may be trying to make his or her client certain of what the client really wants from the earlier agreement, but too often the professional's motive is simply to look good to the client.

For this reason, always restrict outside input to the negotiation phase, the time before the deal is made. Of course, always face outside professionals directly if they have to be involved after a deal is struck. Be present when any outside expert is involved with your deal during the lapse between agreement and closing.

Spectators around your negotiation: Spectators can be as big a problem as outside professionals. Spectators may give opinions without an invitation. Moreover, these opinions may be based on facts irrelevant to the deal. A spectator can be almost anyone—spouses, family friends, fellow workers, social acquaintances. They all have the potential to upset a deal with random remarks that make one or both of the original negotiators have second thoughts. Ask any real estate expert what he or she fears most after a preliminary contract of sale has been signed on a house. The answer will usually be, "When other family members come to look at the house."

A FINAL CAUTION: KEEP AGREEMENTS QUIET

In any kind of negotiation, one protection is to have both parties discuss outside influences and then agree to keep any final agreement to themselves until after the closing. Of course, this is another reason for keeping the time as short as possible between initial agreement and closure. The less time involved, the fewer outsiders who will catch up with what's going on.

HOW TO TURN A HOSTILE ATMOSPHERE INTO A SUPPORTIVE ONE

WHERE WE OFTEN FIND HOSTILE SURROUNDINGS

For many years, labor-management negotiations presented the classic example of a hostile negotiating atmosphere. More recently, we find our examples of hostile environments in unfriendly corporate takeovers by outside raiders. Other kinds of hostile negotiations relate to public issues such as nuclear protests, class action suits on behalf of consumer groups, employees, or public health.

On the surface, to suggest that hostile negotiating atmospheres can always be turned around sounds ludicrous. What is true is that much can be done to control even the most hostile situations and keep damage to a minimum.

IDEAS FOR CONTROLLING DAMAGE CAUSED BY HOSTILITY

- *Take a break when emotions are out of control.* Find an excuse for interrupting negotiations.
- *Insist on designated spokespeople.* This helps prevent everyone from shouting and posturing at the same time or at random. In other words, you insist on knowing who is calling the shots that are being fired at you.
- *Insist on a neutral negotiating location.* Don't let your opponent trade on the intimidation of an unfriendly location. Who needs to feel surrounded by the enemy?
- *Control your right to vote on when negotiations take place.* Don't let others force you into a negotiating session until you are ready. Being ready includes having your facts, having your people present, and being physically alert.
- *Set up public relations controls.* Establish the fact that you will not

tolerate one-sided leaks to the press or to any groups related to the negotiation. Where necessary, get a heavyweight public relations expert by your side.

- *Avoid letting your opponent's experts intimidate you.* This includes lawyers, accountants, scientists, or any other advisors. Be sure to match their experts with your own, not only in numbers but in quality of expertise. Don't sit down to negotiate until the number and quality of the players in the game is fair.

- *Insist on a written agenda long before any real negotiations take place.* Insist that the agenda be adhered to in every case.

- *Don't be hurried, and don't be afraid to stretch things out.* Sometimes an adjourned meeting is the way to change your negotiating climate for the better. Sometimes you need time to get new information or new ammunition.

- *Never get emotionally rigid.* Never allow yourself to become blind to new ideas about how to handle your opponents. Getting even makes no sense if it costs you a bigger victory that you can win by using an emotion-free, clear-eyed new strategy.

WHAT TO DO WHEN SOMEONE TRIES TO GO OVER YOUR HEAD

EXAMPLES OF THREATS THAT YOU MIGHT HEAR

- A customer comes in, makes a demand, and adds, "Or else I'm going to your boss!"
- One of your employees refuses to do what you request, saying, "I'll take this all the way to the top if you don't back off!"
- A fellow worker refuses to cooperate in a normal fashion and says, "I'm fed up with this system. If you know what's smart for you, you'll do it my way, or I'll tell people about you. They'll fix your wagon." In this case, you are being threatened with physical force by an informal hierarchy.
- A dissident stockholder tries to intimidate the company management by saying, "Mess with me, and I'll go right to the SEC."
- A child goes to Mother and says, "I'll tell Dad unless you do what I want!"

All of these examples are attempts at intimidation through fear. No negotiation should go forward under such threats.

SIX STEPS FOR HANDLING THE "OVER YOUR HEAD" THREAT

- *Step 1:* Show little emotion.
- *Step 2:* Calmly walk away or get ready to leave.
- *Step 3:* Try to find a witness to what is being threatened. Even saying that you need to call someone will slow the other person down as he or she wonders what strength you have up your sleeve.
- *Step 4:* Buy time. Walk away, make a phone call, or excuse yourself for a restroom break. Time often helps calm a tense, threatening person.

- *Step 5:* Say very little as you try to get the upset person talking in a calm manner. Feign confusion and concern and say, "Take your time and tell me what's going on. What's the problem?" Be willing to listen for a long time.

- *Step 6:* Postpone any decisions and adjourn the meeting. Talk the situation over with someone you respect. Often, a good choice is the person to whom your opponent threatened to talk.

HOW TO REPLACE A FLAT REFUSAL WITH NEW OPTIONS

"Value is in the eye of the beholder." This play on an old adage serves as a good reminder of what to do about a flat refusal to a negotiating point, including price. If this happens, immediately try to rearrange your position to look different in the "eyes of the beholder."

It seldom pays to restate the same arguments to a person who has given you a flat refusal based on those arguments. This could permanently damage your position.

IDEAS FOR GETTING BEYOND A FLAT REFUSAL

Look for creative ways to walk away from a flat refusal that permits you to live to fight another day. Consider some of these ideas:

- *Change the subject or arrange to take a break.* The object is to get your opponent out of an adversarial mood. A person may be calm and smiling while giving you a flat refusal. You can be sure that on the inside, the person is as keyed up as if he or she drew a line in the sand and dared you to cross it.

- *Remember that a person's position on anything is based on present conditions.* If conditions change, then the person's outlook can change dramatically.

- *Trade-offs are a key way to make things look different.* Often, a flat refusal can be modified later when you find a way to create something that your opponent now wants more than what was refused earlier.

- *Distraction can sometimes change your opponent's attitude.* One negotiation became hung up on a flat refusal of one key point. This took place during a World Series. The negotiator who received the flat refusal had a television wheeled into the meeting room. Soon, the opponent was caught up in the dramatic events of a baseball game. For more than an hour, the negotiating room became a grandstand. As the game ended, the person who issued the flat refusal earlier seemed markedly more relaxed. Negotiations resumed on an easier level. The mutual experience of the ball game drew everyone closer together. This doesn't sound logical, but then whoever said negotiations are always logical?

• *Check on your opponent's physical shape.* Many flat refusals result after one party to a negotiation "loses it" in some fashion. The problem may be fatigue, loss of emotional control, or a combination of both. When you suspect this to be the case, blame yourself as you smilingly say, "I've had a little bug this week, and I think I had better take a break. Nothing serious. I just need a few aspirins and a little rest."

This excuse for a break often engenders a bit of compassion from your opponents. At least it lets you wind up the meeting for the moment to let your opponents get in better physical and emotional shape.

• *Sometimes it pays to bring someone new into the negotiation.* One impasse between two forceful negotiators vanished when the recipient of the flat refusal invited a prestigious friend to join both negotiating parties for dinner. The invited guest was someone whom the refusal recipient's opponent valued highly, but had never had a chance to meet. The guest charmed everyone. After dinner, the guest left, and negotiations resumed. The "flat refusal" opponent's mood was dramatically different. This opponent was trying to look more reasonable in everyone's eyes.

• *Always provide an escape route for someone who paints himself or herself into a corner.* Many flat refusals result when people go too far in their posturing or their emotional displays. They create a position for themselves that they never intended to assume.

Negotiations of every kind fall apart when one or both persons paint themselves into a corner by words or emotions. This is why we must always seek to handle any flat refusal with care. Our response must be low key and indirect, never an escalating return salvo from us, never a matching flat refusal from our side of the table.

KEY TACTIC: *Learn to Provide Escape Routes*

In facing a flat refusal of any kind, we always seek immediate escape routes for our opponent, just in case the flat refusal was an accident or misstep. Respond with tactics which retreat from the direct challenge at hand, as if nothing that earth shattering took place. This does not mean we ignore what happened. Rather, we never show contempt for the other person's position. To do so would make your opponent more rigid and risk even greater escalation in your opponent's position.

The single best way to handle any flat refusal is to defer facing the issue by using one or more of the creative ideas listed in the last section. Avoid using the same arguments and same vocabulary when you reopen the subject. You are going after the same objectives, but now your motives are disguised with face-saving words and strategies. Your opponent may be painted into a corner, but you provide a way to go forward and reach agreement in the most painless way.

HOW TO PROVIDE AN ESCAPE ROUTE FROM A FLAT REFUSAL: AN EXAMPLE

The owner of a very lucrative antique car restoration business told us his greatest asset was his ability to handle a large number of highly independent craft specialists. "Our work is so specialized," he explained, "that some of our people are one-of-a-kind technicians and craftsmen. They are often irreplaceable."

Such artisans can often be prima donnas, as one of the owner's stories illustrates. The owner had a contract to sell an antique auto for a six-figure price. Only one person was capable of restoring the car's engine. This mechanic was in the owner's employ, but could be counted on to refuse to work on any assignment that didn't catch his fancy. His earlier employers told incredible stories about the man's short temper and strong-willed behavior. Once this person refused to do something, he never changed his mind. This was why he walked out on every previous employer.

As the owner approached the prima donna to discuss repairing the expensive antique, the mechanic was in a very bad mood. With all the other employees listening, the mechanic threw a temper tantrum and flatly refused to work on the critical job.

"The first thing I did," the owner said, "was to smile and walk over to another job that he had been working on. I distracted him by asking about some little thing concerning the other job. Before long, he calmed down and was enthusiastically discussing his present assignment. I acted very interested in everything he said and eventually drifted out of the shop. In other words, I got away from the subject of his original flat refusal.

"But I had a handsome profit involved in the car he had turned down, and I simply had to get him to change his mind. In view of his forcible refusal in front of all of his fellow workers, it seemed an impossible problem. I thought about it for days. Finally, I decided to try something that would give the guy an escape route from his original position. I knew that further argument might cause him to quit, so I decided to avoid any further discussion on the subject. Instead, I ordered the necessary parts, and one day I started to work on the car myself. I'm a fair mechanic, but everyone in the shop knew I was in over my head on this job. But I started out anyway.

"After a couple of hours, my prima donna employee stopped over to watch me at work. Before long, he started to give me a hand without saying a word.

"That's how the job got finished. Each day I would start to work on the car, and each day he would take over the hard parts without a word spoken. Finally, on the day the car was delivered to the buyer, one of the other people in the shop said to the prima donna, 'Nice job you did.' Without looking at the person who was complimenting him, my prima donna answered in a voice loud enough for the entire shop to hear, 'I didn't do the job. I only gave him a hand.'"

This clever negotiator came up with a creative way for his prima donna to save face as he broke a lifetime habit of never reversing a position once he had stated it.

WHAT TO DO WHEN YOU ARE OUT OF NEGOTIATING TRICKS

The manager of a large company's manufacturing department was negotiating price with the department's largest supplier.

"The supplier had a near monopoly on the market," the manager said. "They knew their quality was second to none, which was why they wanted to hit us with a really steep price increase. Of course, I resisted in every possible way. I used every tactic and emotional appeal that I could think of, and even said that the increase could cause us to go down the drain. After all of this, I saw that I was getting nowhere, and I didn't have another card to play."

The department head reached into a desk drawer, pulled out a calendar, shoved it across the desk to us, smiled, and said, "Take a look at that calendar. Notice the circled dates. Each represents a negotiating session with the supplier who hit us with the steep price rise. The dates span almost five months, which is exactly how long I was able to keep talking after I knew I was out of cards."

For specific ideas about what to say to keep talking, see the section of this book entitled, "How to Overcome Feeling as if You Are on the Ropes."

When you have played every card in your hand and have nothing left, keep talking without revealing your weak position. You should do this for several reasons, any one of which could turn the game in your favor. We think of these reasons as invisible cards. As you continue to talk, one of these invisible cards may surface.

1. *Impatience in your opponent.* Impatience can result in an unexpected reversal in your opponents' position simply because they want to wrap things up.

2. *Opponents' time-binds.* You may know nothing about a time restraint which may be exerting pressure on opponents to make a deal, even if it means reversing an earlier position. Money is often a key to putting your opponents in some kind of time-bind.

3. *An outside change that affects negotiations.* A sudden change in markets, interest rates, competitive availability, your opponents' own organization, your resources, or your opponents' resources are among the possibilities in this category.

   For example, the company of the negotiator who stretched talks out for five months used that time to discover its own manufacturing potential and began producing the part that had been the subject of negotiations.

4. *Surprising new information.* As you talk, you may pick up helpful information. Your opponents may inadvertently open doors for you by revealing something about their position.

   For example, a small company owner had tried everything to lure a bright executive from a competitor. Nothing worked, but despite being fresh out of ideas, the owner kept talking for another ten months. Lately, their meetings had turned into a lunch or outing with spouses after work. During a theater evening, the executive's wife told the small company owner, "Our son has been looking for a job for six months, ever since he graduated from college. He can't seem to find what he wants, a chance to break into advertising."

   This was the new information the small company owner had been waiting for for ten months. He sensed that the parents were as frustrated as their son, and he moved quickly on the new information. The owner offered the executive a package deal. The owner artfully negotiated to get the son an outstanding job with a prestigious advertising firm, provided that the father agreed to leave the competitor and work alongside the small company owner. The owner's victory was possible because he stayed alert for new information.

5. *Your opponent's fatigue.* Fatigue is the invisible card most widely pursued by sharp negotiators. For example, suppose you offer a person your highest price at 11 A.M., only to be turned down. Over the next several hours, you try many tactics and variations of the deal. Still, your opponent holds firm in refusing your best offer. It is now 4 P.M. You have managed to keep talking despite having played every card to no avail. But you keep talking! At 4:45, your opponent suddenly says, "I'll take your price."

   Why? You may never know. Even your opponent may be unaware of the reason. We suspect that metabolism can play a role in many negotiations by changing your opponent's perspective.

   To understand this point, consider the old question, "Is

the glass half full of half empty?" Fatigue can make the same person regard his or her glass differently at different points in a negotiation. A fresh combatant may greedily perceive the glass as half empty. Later, when fatigue sets in, the same person may be grateful that the glass is half full and grab the very deal he or she earlier rejected.

SECTION 12

HOW TO PLAY YOUR HUNCHES

SECTION 12

HOW TO PLAY YOUR HUNCHES

In negotiating or even considering the possibility of negotiating, we instinctively rely on hunches much of the time. A hunch combines our best guess about the facts of a situation with our intuitive feelings about the people and circumstances surrounding a negotiation.

For example, if we see an item advertised for sale in the newspaper, we may wonder if the price is negotiable. We make such a guess based on what we may know about the current marketplace for the item that is for sale. When we superimpose another estimate on top of our guess, we add our intuitive feelings about the seller. Thus, if an advertiser is a large company, we rely on our feelings about the company's image to suggest the value of the item. If the advertiser appears to be a fly-by-night operation, we may intuit that the price is more negotiable than a more established-looking company's price might be.

Out of this combination of our best guess, which is based on facts, and our intuition, which is based on emotion, we come up with a hunch about how best to proceed in our negotiations. This section will help you learn to recognize and cultivate hunches about negotiations. Our goal in doing this is to avoid two common errors:

- Limiting our guesses about facts to only the surface circumstances.
- Going with the first intuitive feelings we have.

For example, many people instinctively like or dislike an opponent based on physical appearance or mannerisms. The roots of this behavior may lie with another person in a situation long ago. Such preliminary judgment based on intuition in the present is silly and possibly quite costly!

THE TEAM APPROACH TO CHECKING-OUT HUNCHES

Your guesses and intuitive feelings should be checked out with other people. Ask their opinions with such questions as—

- Based on your experience with this sort of thing, am I overlooking any facts?
- Having told you my gut feelings, could I have gone overboard with my emotions?

In assembling a team to address such questions, always include two types of confidants: (1) people who are close to the negotiations; and (2), people who are far removed from your immediate activities.

Ask yourself—

- Whom do I trust most in my negotiating environment?
- Can I expect this person to keep quiet if I reveal my negotiating hunches?
- Will I really listen to this person or am I simply expecting agreement?
- Whom do I trust and respect most outside of my immediate activities? My spouse? My friend? A lawyer, banker, or accountant?
- Am I being really candid with the people to whom I go for opinions about my negotiating strategy? Am I slanting the facts to gain their agreement with what I already decided?

In addition to asking opinions and advice from others, you sometimes can ask some of these same people to dig up additional facts or hearsay about your negotiating opponent. Maybe one or more of these people you trust can give you information that your opponent assumes is not available to you. The kind of information you want at this point is not available in credit reports, letters of recommendation, or public relations blurbs. You want to unearth hard facts that your negotiating opponent hopes you never discover. You won't always come up with such hidden information, but it never hurts to ask the people you trust to help you look.

HOW TO PLAY YOUR HUNCHES ABOUT AN OPPONENT BEARING GIFTS

Everyone has weaknesses and areas of susceptibility. If your negotiating opponent knows about these, you may expect your negotiation to include gifts from your opponent which are designed to appeal to these known weaknesses.

QUESTIONS TO HELP YOU ANTICIPATE YOUR OPPONENT'S MOVES

- Where do I appear weak, in need, or susceptible to my negotiating opponent?
- Do I appear open to money offers?
- Do I seem to want power offers?
- Will my opponent think that I am a setup for flattery?
- Do I seem to need to impress my boss, other superiors, or someone else?
- Will I seem to be impressed by professionalism?
- Do I seem vulnerable to sex appeals?
- Am I open to appeals to my loyalty to certain things or people?
- Am I susceptible to gossip and inside information?
- Do I appear to respond to fear?
- Do I display the need to be in charge?
- Am I perceived as needing to imitate what others are doing?

EXAMPLES OF CLASSIC NEGOTIATING GIFT TACTICS

- A boss who uses fear to intimidate most of the time, but then offers the gift of a smile when negotiating to increase your workload.

- A person who tries to get your agreement on something by offering the gift of flattery. Thus you hear, "If you go along with me on this, everyone will think you're a genius!"

- A negotiator who presents you with a gift of friendship. Thus you are told, "After this is all over, we should see more of one another because we have so much in common."

- A seller who suggests that you will be seen as powerful because you do something that the seller wants. The seller may say, "Buy this for your needs, and no one will be able to touch you!"

- Many buyers love to dangle the gift of a superior's approval in this way, "If you agree to my offer, this order can make you a hero!"

- All too often, the gift takes the form of an appeal to some loyalty: "If we can work this out, you will be protecting the values we both know are so important."

- Appeals to greed usually offer gifts in a direct fashion: "This proposal will make you a handsome profit!" (Many mergers are put together with people who fall for the profit appeal, but later realize that the offering price was way below actual value.)

- Perhaps the most widely used negotiating gift is the tactic of making you feel as if you are in charge of what's happening. In this case, your negotiating opponent pretends that you're calling most of the shots. Your opponent will often say things like, "We want you to be happy." Or, "We defer to your experience in these matters." Or, "Tell us what you need."

There is no better time to apply your guessing and intuition than when an opponent bears gifts. If you can anticipate what your opponent may see as your weakness and what gifts you will be offered, then you are in a perfect position to protect yourself. Many sharp negotiators not only guard against such gifts but also they go a step further by acting in a way which suggests that they are being taken in by the gift tactics.

If your negotiating opponent feels you are falling for the gift that is dangled before you, you can benefit by the carelessness which results when your opponent takes you for granted.

TACTICS THAT WIN THE BATTLE BUT LOSE THE WAR

Often, careless negotiators ride roughshod over their opponent's emotions without ever noticing a problem. Later, they wonder why negotiations were so difficult or why negotiations fell apart. They win a battle, but it costs them the war. We simply must use our intuition and guesses to avoid backing our opponent into a rigid position on an emotional level.

Asking ourselves the following questions can guide our guesses and intuition through the emotional mine field of a negotiation:

- Is any issue secondary to our negotiation threatening our opponent's survival in a business sense?
- Is any issue secondary to our negotiation threatening this person's feeling of excellence about something?
- Is any issue secondary to our negotiation threatening our opponent's loyalties or dedication?
- Is any issue secondary to our negotiation threatening our opponent's self-pride or feelings about status?
- Is any issue secondary to our negotiations threatening our opponent's relationship with the opposite sex?

Better to be oversensitive to people's emotional needs than to ignore possible insults. You can never guess or intuit too much about other people's feelings.

QUESTIONS TO KEEP YOU FROM SHOWING YOUR HAND

Many astute negotiators move relentlessly to convince you of the problems and limitations which they have concerning your demands. The better the negotiator the more he or she will try to persuade you to show your cards. After all, they showed you theirs, or so they try to convince you.

WHAT TO ASK YOURSELF ABOUT YOUR OPPONENT'S TACTICS

The more your opponent confides in you and levels with you, the more you had best ask yourself these questions:

- Why am I suddenly this person's closest friend? What does it mean?
- Now that they are supposedly showing their hand, what cards do they still have hidden?
- What cards can I show to go along with this charade without damaging my position?
- Is this my opponents' last-ditch effort to avoid giving up what is already lost? Are we playing the "level with you" game to protect their egos or to fabricate some excuse to explain to their superiors why negotiations didn't come out better?

WATCH ATTEMPTS TO LEVEL WITH YOU AFTER NEGOTIATIONS

Many people have to try to convince themselves that they have had a good negotiation. After a deal is final, many buyers try to review the entire negotiation on a "level with you" basis. Thus, the buyer says, "Now that it's all over, tell me what you expected to get."

If you tell the entire truth, the buyer feels cheated. So, always pretend to level as you give the buyer a price way beyond that which you received. Do this only if you are asked to level. If you volunteer this information, the buyer will feel uncomfortable and will think that you are complaining, which is never the way to conclude a negotiation.

USING INTUITION TO FIND A PRICE THAT FITS YOUR OPPONENT'S VALUES

For reasons of legality and efficiency, mass-market items are usually priced alike. Any price experimentation is done by test-marketing variations of the value versus price equation before the product is introduced. Further experimentation may take place later in the form of sales prices.

In face-to-face negotiation with another party, pricing tactics are quite different. The setting gives you a chance to know a great deal about your customer. You have the opportunity to modify the customer's attitudes during negotiations. In face-to-face negotiation, you can often redesign the product to match the potential buyer's personal values. Always do this before you guess at a price. Consider this example.

WHAT A CHILD CAN TEACH US ABOUT FLEXIBLE PRICING

A child has a roadside lemonade stand with a sign that says only, "Lemonade For Sale." Without intending to be a clever negotiator, the child had become one. A customer who loves children may drop a $1 bill into the coin box. If the child had a price sign of, say, 50 cents, this customer's feelings of goodwill might have been diluted.

The next customers may be young hikers who are thirsty but broke. They ask the child if they can buy the lemonade at 10 cents a glass. The child agrees. This way, the youngster sells a dozen glasses, but this wouldn't be the case if the sign had said 25 cents.

This example reminds us how unprofitable it often is to be too rigid about price. We tend to base price on our own estimates of what something is worth, but we should consider price secondary in our negotiating arguments. If we can encourage someone to thirst for what we have, price can be raised because the customer's desire has been heightened.

TIPS FOR FINDING THE RIGHT PRICE

Many people negotiate with a fixed price as though they were selling a mass-market item. They push a firm price out front and expect

the price to sell the customers. In one-to-one negotiating, the least important factor is often the price that you think something is worth. Of
course, you should always know what your break-even price—the minimum price you must charge to make any profit—would be. How much
over break-even can you go? But learn to save your guessing until the
potential buyer starts to reveal his or her values to you. This is particularly
true with impatient buyers. They often bid up their own price voluntarily
simply because you ask for time to think about their last offer.

Your job is to find ways to let potential customers fill in the blank
on your guess about what a fair price might be. Yes, you can sell refrigera-
tors to Eskimos if you take time to let them tell you how great they
are for keeping beer from freezing! (And you thought that it was just
keeping beer cold.) Listen to all that the customers will tell you before
you begin to fix a value on something.

USING INTUITION TO DEAL WITH YOUR OPPONENT'S CHANGING CIRCUMSTANCES

Between beginning and concluding a negotiation, the truth about the other party's world may change. For example, a new owner tells a purchasing agent about immediate plans to expand sales by almost 100 percent for three product lines. Accordingly, the purchasing agent calls in all key suppliers and begins to renegotiate purchase prices based on purchase volumes that have doubled. Most suppliers reduce their prices sharply based on volume discounts.

One or two suppliers react in a different fashion, however. They have been in business a long time and have long memories. One of them was a supplier to the Edsel; the other supplied the U.S. tractor industry. Both have seen expectations change what people consider to be the truth. Both refuse to raise their customer's volume estimates or lower their own prices.

Within a year, the new owner sells out. Sales go down instead of up. The suppliers who lowered prices are stuck with low profits on this customer, and the new owners refuse to even discuss raising prices to a fair level.

Lesson: Spend time looking at everything related to the people with whom you are negotiating. Don't rely on trust alone or even the trustworthiness of your fellow negotiators. After all, the purchasing agent in our example was an honest individual who negotiated lower prices in good faith. The only problem was that what appeared to be reality changed for the firm and its suppliers.

Spend a lot of time listening to your intuition about who tells you what. Ask yourself what the chance is that reality may change for your negotiating opponent.

USING ENLIGHTENED GUESSES TO CUT THROUGH A COMPUTER-GENERATED MAZE

With today's computer spreadsheets, we've become accustomed to an opponent dropping a heavy batch of paper in front of us with the words, "There it is, everything that proves our point. The bottom line doesn't lie!"

Many computer-based statistical and graphic masterpieces have won the day in important negotiations. Members of Congress have received dictionary-sized printouts of the President's proposed budget just a short time before they are expected to approve its contents. As one member of congress aptly put it, "Nobody could have read it in the time available, but it gave a certain aura of credibility to our actions to vote the new budget into law."

HOW TO SIFT THROUGH INFORMATION OVERLOAD

Many negotiators who would never have dreamed of lying with statistics now seem perfectly willing to mesmerize others with computer-generated tomes of statistics and graphics. How is a negotiator to plow through such a mess to reach critical issues? Many people accept computer output as the final truth. "If the computer says so," one negotiator was heard to say, "then who am I to question?"

There appears to be no better place for controlled guessing and intuition than with your negotiating opponent's computer-generated information. Don't waste your time on the computer hardware and systems involved; they are probably accurate to ten decimal places. Instead, concentrate on the owners and the keepers of the electronic beasts. Find out who feeds the computer and how accurate the diet is. Find out who gave what verbal instructions to the computer programmers and in what form they were delivered. Did the instructions say, "Find ways to make what I have already said valid."? Or, is your negotiating opponent too uninformed to ever question a computer printout?

WHO'S GOT THE LAST WORD?

Most negotiations can benefit from background statistics made available through computers and carefully checked in regard to method and intent. Never rely on a printout as the final authority on any negotiating point. Computers cannot ever take the risk out of future developments. This assessment still depends on human guessing and intuition about unknown circumstances. If you still have doubts, look at a list of computer companies that went belly-up by relying on their own forecasts of future product needs.

Lesson: We believe in computers, honestly we do. But negotiators misuse the power of computers when they rely on them as authority symbols that intimidate more than they enlighten. Learn to make enlighted guesses about any negotiating arguments based on computer-generated reports. Uncover the people and motives behind the paper printout.

QUESTIONS TO ASK YOURSELF ABOUT USING MONEY AS A MOTIVATOR

As our world becomes progressively more scientific, we look for more and more logic around us. Often, though, we find less and less of it, particularly when we look to logic to predict human behavior. When we search for reasonable ways to motivate others to do as we wish, one of our most illogical and widely misunderstood resources is money.

UNDERSTANDING WHAT MOTIVATES US BESIDES MONEY

There is little logic in the way people view themselves with regard to money. Logic would tell us that, in a capitalistic system, money should be near the top of everyone's priority list. Yet, as any top negotiator will remind you, life is not quite as simple as that.

For example, a recent survey of successful executives in their middle 30s revealed that most men were willing to move to a location that represented a better opportunity for their working wives. This may suggest that success for many people is not measured by strict monetary standards. These men indicated that their wives' sense of fulfillment figured prominently in their idea of success. The fact that male executives may now modify their career situations to accommodate their wives is a new motivational factor not present even a few years ago.

Researchers have long recognized that executives in large organizations display an age-related drop-out syndrome in their early to mid-30s. At this point, quality of life and philosophical beliefs cause many successful mid-career executives to make changes that have nothing to do with money.

These examples remind us that in negotiating with people of all ages money must not become an overrated negotiating weapon. Even in the mass marketing of cars, appliances, and electronics, it has been shown in dramatic fashion that the quality of certain imported products can command a higher price than expected because consumers look past money to other motivators.

WHAT TO ASK YOURSELF TO UNCOVER A PERSON'S NONMONETARY MOTIVATORS

In negotiations of all types and at every level, it pays to ask yourself questions related to money. Here are some examples of such questions:

- Does my negotiating opponent have emotional needs that go beyond money? Needs such as ego gratification? The need to be associated with quality? A desire to feel more freedom? A need for more authority, to be noticed, or to please a mate or other family member?

- Does my negotiating opponent measure other people in terms of money? Are there other ways to impress this person? Some possibilities are knowledge, contacts, friendship, integrity, loyalty, service, special skills, business and social power, challenge, curiosity, and a chance to explore the unknown.

HOW TO OVERCOME NEGOTIATING PROBLEMS RELATED TO MONEY

Money can frighten another person in unexpected ways. For example, giving a person too large a raise can trigger the overpaid person's fear that you overestimate him or her. In reverse, seriously underestimating someone can be interpreted as discounting the person's potential. Another problem results when people regard their money rewards as cold payment that is devoid of other appreciation. When a person feels as if he or she is only a commodity, fear and resentment grow no matter how good the money is!

On the other hand, when a negotiation involves money and you try to convince people that money doesn't really matter, they usually feel nervous. This happens because most of us are conditioned to expect that money always matters. As a rule, whenever discussions involve money, even when you can afford not to care about the sum, act as if money was, is, and always will be a serious matter.

In negotiations, talking about money presents a special opportunity to use your intuitive and guessing strategies. The more you can find out about the person with whom you are negotiating, the better will be your hunches. This suggests the value of getting your opponent to talk about as many topics outside of your business negotiation as possible. If you listen carefully, you may find clues about what matters most to the other person. What matters may have nothing to do with money.

ANTICIPATING RISK AND PLANNING AN ESCAPE HATCH: TWO TECHNIQUES TO COUNTERACT OVERCONFIDENCE

It is always desirable to approach negotiations in a positive frame of mind. But negotiations can be lost when confidence gives way to bravado. Too often, people think they hold more cards than their opponents, and this makes them careless by underestimating the risk in what they do. Typically, careless negotiators have not thought about an escape hatch, a plan to give themselves time to regroup and try again. These people are so confident initially that they cannot imagine the need to prepare for any unexpected reaction to their demands.

This is not the habit of one successful negotiator who told us, "I enter every negotiation convinced that I will be successful, but not always in the ways I expected originally. I expect to find risk that I didn't anticipate in areas I might have overlooked. But for every demand I make, I always keep an escape route open."

THE KEY TO FINDING AN ESCAPE HATCH

We asked this clever negotiator what the single best escape route might be. The answer was remarkably simple at first blush, but the more we thought about it, the better it seemed. "I always smile and maintain a low emotional level. I'm very relaxed as I begin a risky proposition with a 'What if' question. This way what I say doesn't sound like a demand that is cast in stone. I can always retreat gracefully while I plan a way to reopen the subject.

We assure you that this negotiator also spent long hours before any important negotiation trying to anticipate the riskiest negotiating areas and possible fallback positions in the event of a problem.

TIPS FOR ESTIMATING RISK

Each negotiating opponent is unique. One person's metabolism may cause him or her to be high-strung. Past experiences may have caused another person to live in a shell of cynicism. Still another person may feel that events have put his or her back to the wall. Something may seem risk free to you, but to such people it may loom as a major obstacle. When this happens, you find that your deal is in danger of coming apart where you least expected a problem.

So, why not always tread carefully with even the most risk-free undertaking? Expect that your guess or intuition might have missed some hang up in the other person that you had no way of knowing about in advance. Remember to do the following things:

1. Maintain a calm voice.

2. Keep a smile on your face.

3. Slowly begin any risky demand with the words, "What if."

4. If you run into surprise resistance, keep smiling and start to guess how the same thing might be restated to sound different in light of the hang ups your opponent has revealed.

5. You need not be flexible in your position, but you do need to appear flexible to your opponent.

6. Remember, a "take it or leave it" offer is never worth taking. Always leave the door open by at least saying, "I guess not." If you say this with a smile, you give your opponent a graceful way to back down. He or she sees you are still smiling and may be close to agreement. In reverse, if your opponent is rigid in his or her position, you can try again with a new slant on your arguments. Begin by remaining calm and continuing to smile as you repeat the words, "What if."

Spend a lot of preparation time trying to guess where the risks may lie. Then, prepare fallback arguments just in case. Always phrase these arguments to sound different than the rejected proposal. You'll never correctly guess what all of the risks are. Expect the unexpected, and give yourself an escape hatch by the calm manner in which you state your positions. Wherever possible, preface your words with a smile and the question, "What if?"

WHAT HUNCHES TELL US ABOUT SETUPS

Many people conclude a negotiation with good feelings about what they accomplished only to be sadly disillusioned later. Labor unions sign tough new contracts with glee only to discover their plants are being shut down permanently and their jobs are going overseas. Individuals force employers to give them raises only to learn years later that they have irreparably damaged their future prospects with this firm.

In corporate mergers, everyone is assured of executive continuity until the last papers are signed; then heads may begin to roll. Unwitting suppliers make substantial price reductions on the assurance of high volume purchases, then sit back as the promised volume fails to materialize.

Heard enough? Executives, consumers, buyers, and sellers can all tell of situations in which they were yesterday's winner but today's loser! Often, this is an outcome that was planned in advance.

Thinking the worst about any negotiation you are winning is always unpleasant. In most cases, the situation is as it seems. Nevertheless, a sharp negotiator must go through unpleasant self-examination by asking questions.

- Is it possible that my opponents are only buying time with their agreement?

- Is it possible that they will resent this agreement in ways that will cause me problems later?

- Am I being encouraged to rely on future promises that they have no intention of keeping?

- Is it possible that even legal obligations will be unenforceable due to bankruptcy, flight, or countersuit?

- Have the entire circumstances around the negotiation been window dressing for my benefit? Something designed to hide a purpose from me? Are they using this negotiation to test me?

Negotiation setups are all too common. Indeed, many people think setup in all negotiations all of the time. They live by the phrase, "A sucker's born every minute." The next time you are way ahead in a negotiation, try to guess why. Find out as much as possible about your opponent's track record. Do you discern any long-term patterns in how this person makes deals? Are there any parallels to your situation?

HOW NIBBLING QUESTIONS CAN ADD UP TO A GREAT BIG DEAL

Nibbling questions are the art of top-flight negotiators. Experienced negotiators keep finding ways to sneak in little extras that add up to a great deal.

Usually, the best time for nibbling questions is just before you reach agreement on a point that seems important to your opponent. When properly timed, the little extra concession you request appears inconsequential to the important issue your opponent wants. Of course, he or she never knows you would have agreed to the main issue anyway. Only the best negotiators ever pause to consider this possibility. These examples illustrate this concept in action:

- In a price negotiation about a large order, a seller who is ready to give the lower price says at the last moment, "Can we put ten in each box instead of five?" The buyer, excited about the possibility of a lower price, answers, "Why not!" The seller's nibbling cuts packaging and handling costs in half on tens of thousands of items, yet the buyer doesn't think twice.

- A home buyer poses several nibbling questions at opportune times: when the seller asks for a signature on a preliminary deposit agreement that is refundable if the buyer cannot secure financing; just before the financing deadline expires (the buyer nibbles without admitting that the loan is approved); at designated buyer inspection points; and as the lawyers are drawing up final closing paper, the buyer's lawyer surprises the seller by insisting on an escrow account.

In each case the nibbles are timed to make the seller want to keep the negotiation going, and the demands seem small compared to the overall deal. Here is a recap:

- The nibble at the initial deposit signing was for an extra half bath in the basement.

- The nibble just before the financing deadline was for six extra magnolia bushes in the backyard.

- The two inspection points were a week before closing and the day of closing. In each case, the buyer complained about little points, then traded these problems for two more nibbles. "How about putting water pipes up to the unfinished attic?" And, after worrying the seller by frowning all through the second inspection, the buyer said, "I need carpet in the attic and cellar stairs."

- As the attorneys drew up final closing papers, the buyer's lawyer said, "My client expects that you'll fill up the fuel tank before she takes title. That's the way it was done when she sold her house."

- At the closing, the buyer's lawyer adds the final nibble by announcing, "My client has had second thoughts about the landscaping that has been done. We want to reserve another $600 until the lawn is seeded behind the garage and two more rose bushes are planted on the garage trellis. We feel the house needs at least six or seven more pine trees at the entrance of the drive."

The seller went along with each of the small requests without noticing their cumulative effect until much later when an accountant pointed out that the nibbles cost several thousand dollars.

Whether buying something small or something large, keep asking yourself, "What else can I ask for when I know my opponent is anxious for a bigger point of agreement?"

WHAT TO REMEMBER ABOUT LOST NEGOTIATING OPPORTUNITIES

Watch a good negotiator throughout a normal daily routine. This person stays sharp and wins more by being alert to informal negotiating opportunities. Part of recognizing negotiating opportunities depends on the experience you gain from reflecting on opportunities you may have missed.

Let's pretend we are Jack Jones, and we are examining our business day for missed opportunities for informal negotiations.

- When my assistant came in to ask for two hours off on Friday, why didn't I ask him to balance the books in his spare time? After all, I gave him the time off, and he would have been more than happy to return the favor.

- Harry tried to pick up the check at lunch, and I insisted that it was my treat. Why didn't I ask Harry if he could cover my desk next week when I duck out for the ball game. It would have been a perfect time to ask him!

- When I stopped in to pay my car repair bill, it would have been the perfect time to ask the mechanic to check the rear window that doesn't shut tight. He would have done it without an appointment.

- When the boss called me in to discuss the extra reports I agreed to do, I should have asked for more clerical help. Now that the reports are finished, I don't have as much negotiating leverage.

- When my best customer called to ask me to put her family up for membership at the golf club, I should have asked her what she has heard about the Halley company. She buys from them too, and she may know something about the rumors we hear about the company's problems. Too bad I didn't ask! Any information would have been a boost to my boss and the plan to buy Halley. I blew it!

We could go on about Jack's missed opportunities. He walked past a lot more, but he learned from the mistakes because he paused to reflect on his day. It's easy to discipline yourself to think about opportunities. And, when you do something nice for someone, think about what that person can do to reciprocate. We don't recommend being crass or obvious, but rather finding discreet ways to make the most of informal negotiating opportunities.

HOW TO INSULATE YOURSELF DURING DIFFICULT NEGOTIATIONS

An important but difficult negotiation might be when you have a job review scheduled with a superior who is under tremendous emotional pressure.

WHAT TO ASK ABOUT A DIFFICULT OPPONENT

Questions to ask yourself when pressure is high are—

- How can I delay these negotiations? Can I be called away on important business?
- How can I monitor the circumstances? Who can be my barometer to tell me when the emotional problems are at a minimum.
- If I have to go forward in this difficult situation, what should I *not* do? Other people in the organization who witnessed this superior's bursts of emotions can tell me what seems to trigger it off. I can avoid similar pitfalls.

It seems so logical that everyone would want to search out the conditions and emotions surrounding any important negotiation, but few people do! Most people concentrate exclusively on the subject of the negotiation and ignore the people doing the negotiating.

These are important questions that people forget to ask themselves:

- What has been happening to this person's business recently?
- What is going on in this person's social and personal world?
- Who can give me insights into my opponent's current emotional state and work conditions?

WHY AN INFORMATION SOURCE IS SO IMPORTANT

Try to delay any important negotiation until you locate an information resource to alert you to the facts about your opponent. Customers, suppliers, bankers, lawyers, secretaries, mutual business associates, or friends are all candidates. Ask them simply, "Anything new you can tell me about this person?"

Most negotiators fail to take this step. They don't ask themselves or others about their opponent's behavior patterns and work and social state of mind.

WHERE TO SET UP OBSERVATION POSTS TO WATCH YOUR OPPONENT'S SIGNALS

Who's serving lookout duty for your negotiations? Most likely, the answer is no one. Too few negotiators arrange to have anyone watch for signals from opponents. Even in one-on-one negotiations most people are so busy detailing their positions that they fail to see what their opponent's are unwittingly telling them. This is too bad because a good deal of free information is yours for the asking if you cultivate the ability to read the other side.

For example, one negotiator successful in arranging mergers and acquisitions told us, "Give me a chance to see how someone handles subordinates, and I'll know pretty much how to handle that person."

Many top negotiators create a system for monitoring their opponent's signals. One man makes grammatical errors every time he comes up against a self-important opponent. "As soon as I deliberately sound uneducated, I can spot the ones who think 'It's going to be easy with this hick.' When this happens, they get careless and I go to town!"

The specifics of this tactic vary. We have seen negotiators change how they dress and intentionally appear to lose track of what's going on. However, this tactic is a calculated attempt to smoke out the opposition's signals about how they measure you.

Another tactic is to test an opponent's patience and discipline. For instance, your reaction to fumbling or interruptions can reveal your patience level.

Reading signals during negotiations can take many forms. It never hurts to test your opponents, then watch for clues about this person. Given a little luck, you will often be able to wind the other person's clock once you know what ticks inside.

KEY TACTIC: What You Can Learn from Perry Mason

Read books about top trial lawyers. See how they learn to read the jury. We guarantee you that after you start to read hidden signals you will not only have more fun during negotiations, you will have more success, too! It boils down to one question, "What can I do to get them to reveal more about their inner feelings?"

WHAT THE MASS MEDIA HAVE TO DO WITH YOUR NEGOTIATING STRATEGIES

Suppose you plan lower than normal salary increases for employees this year, but you must increase productivity. By carefully timing the announcement of your "leaner" policy to coincide with television news stories about plant closings and layoffs, you can make a big impression on your people. Your people may be relieved that your policy isn't worse.

In reverse, if all of the economic news of the day is upbeat, wait to implement your policy. Under the current conditions, your policy won't ring true with employees' media-influenced attitudes.

WHY NEGOTIATORS CONSIDER HOW TELEVISION INFLUENCES VIEWERS

The news media is a new negotiating tool, thanks to the impact of television. Not only do most of us spend hours viewing TV, we tend to assign high credibility to what we see. If people watch an event on television, even fiction, many of them reason that, "I saw it on television. Therefore, it is important."

We tend to feel heavy emotional involvement with television. It teaches us new information and often suggests different emotional attitudes. A Super Bowl game reminds us of the medium's ability to bring controlled hype to bear in an obviously self-serving effort to gain multimillion dollar advertising revenues. Most people forget the commercial reasons and climb on board for the fun.

TV fiction such as "Roots" and "Dallas" galvanize attitudes. Thus, television affects the moods and logic of large numbers of the population instantly! In this sense, television is a new negotiating weapon to be harnessed. We can relate to sudden mood and logic biases influenced by recent television shows. TV also gives us a new vocabulary. When someone asks a boss, "Why can't we be more like the people on that new show?", the reference serves as shorthand about values. A manager had best learn more about the show to learn more about his or her people.

HUNCHES DERIVED FROM WHAT YOU SEE ON TV

• *Hunches about popular stereotypes.* An anti-establishment TV show may cause people to copy what they see. In reverse, a popular pro-organization show may encourage people to be more cooperative. In either case, what you see on television can provide you with models to discuss with your people. Thank goodness "Mash" is in syndication because you can use any one of the characters to illustrate how you want someone to act or not to act.

Chit-chat about popular TV fare can be an ideal bridge with negotiating opponents. The bridge may relax your opponent and show that you have something in common.

• *Hunches about recent news stories or documentaries can often be relevant.* If you want to negotiate with your associates about a nonsmoking policy, what better time than following a scary documentary about new scientific findings on the subject. More and more, executives tape or purchase copies of television documentaries and reports to use during a negotiation on the subject.

• *Hunches about using television to influence negotiator's mood.* Watching a televised event can be fun and often highly productive. One tough labor negotiation was falling apart when the negotiator suggested a break to watch a national sporting event. A television, beer, and pretzels were brought in. After a couple of hours, negotiations resumed amid a much improved atmosphere. Eventually, the deal was brought to a successful conclusion.

In a slightly different example, a service business owner wanted more productivity from employees. Already, he had begun to apply pressure, and the employees were showing signs of resentment. So, the owner resorted to sports to show he was human. He knew his people loved to watch Monday Night Football, so he announced that everyone could come in an hour later on Tuesday after games. "Overnight," he said, "I was a hero, and they forgot all those extra hours I was demanding the rest of the week."

KEY TACTIC: Reasons to Stay on Top of What's New on TV

Television can provide a common bond with negotiating opponents. It can give you clues about people's attitudes and moods that may have been affected by something on TV. Just as a picture can be worth a thousand words, today a popular TV event can score a lot of negotiating points if you carefully apply what you observe on television to the needs of your negotiating opponents.

So, to the reader we say, "Don't negotiate like J. R. Be more like Bobby." If you never watched "Dallas," this advice will mean little to you. But over 100 million Americans will find it comprehensible, which is another argument for keeping in touch with popular TV fare. You need to keep up for reasons of communication and empathy.

SECTION 13

ANTICIPATING YOUR OPPONENT'S KEY MOVES

SECTION 13

ANTICIPATING YOUR OPPONENT'S KEY MOVES

Many opponents may concentrate first on building a sense of trust and rapport when you enter a negotiation. While these are worthy goals, too much trust and too friendly a rapport can blind you to the realities of negotiation. They can dull your reflexes and work to your detriment.

A better tactic is to say to yourself, "If my negotiating opponent gets hit by a car, are the agreements we have made still valid and enforceable?" In this sense, trust is replaced by logic, and you maintain your ability to be cautious. You retain the desire to look beyond the obvious circumstances to discover what your opponent may be planning next, or what situations may develop that are beyond your opponent's control.

For example, you are negotiating to buy a new house. The seller is someone you admire and would normally trust. The house has a damp basement which the seller agrees to repair. Yet the seller wants to wait several months until the next rainy season to complete this work. You trust that this person is sincere in the promise. Emotion tells you to go ahead with the deal, but logic dictates that you ask yourself, "What if the seller gets hit by a car before the rainy season?" Now you think to ask the seller to set up an escrow account and legally agree to correct the problem. This protects you no matter what may happen to the seller, or what this person may decide to do.

QUESTIONS TO HELP SNIFF OUT A HIDDEN AGENDA

- Do any facts reveal possible hidden objectives behind the stated points to be negotiated?

    Can it be that we're really talking about something that the agenda is rigged to disguise?

- If my opponent is talking about wanting to help me, is this really a way of saying what he or she needs to help his or her goals?

- Even when a formal agenda is in writing, can there be hidden motives, such as—

    1. Testing someone's ability or performance under pressure?

    2. An excuse to hold a meeting simply to appear busy?

    3. An excuse to embarrass someone in front of others?

- Who in my opponent's organization may be calling the shots on the agenda? Is there a hidden player behind what is being formally discussed? How might this person feel about key issues? Any chance that my opponent is really doing someone else's bidding? If so, how might this affect how I handle the situation?

Sometimes a hidden agenda emerges when your opponent expects that you know more than you really do. For example, a boss may ask your opinion on a subject because you are expected to know the boss's opinion and agree with it. Unless you are alert to such a hidden agenda, you may give an opinion that goes against the strong wishes of your superior. In such a case, he or she may retaliate in the future, if not immediately.

TIPS FOR COUNTERACTING AN OPPONENT'S ATTEMPTS AT BRAINWASHING

A special cause for alarm in negotiations is a tactic designed to compromise your ethical position. Negotiations can involve the use of tactics intended to brainwash you, and this is quite different from mere offers of gifts which cater to your known weaknesses. Brainwashing is an attempt to completely change your negotiating positions based on some new dream which your opponent plants in your mind. When this tactic is successful, your opponent encourages you to become enamoured of this newly created fantasy. For example, the owner of a small business told us that over 100 employees believe they are going to be part owners some day.

ONE OWNER'S UNETHICAL SCHEME

"Every time I have a problem with someone who might want more money or a lighter workload, I simply take the person into my private office and confide that these normal demands can't be met because this person is one of the few individuals who I consider worthy of someday owning part of the business. Of course, I pledge each person to secrecy concerning my plans. Each person thinks that he or she is unique in the choice I have made. It works every time," the owner boasted.

WHEN TO RELY ON INTUITION AND A GOOD GUESS

A good time to rely on guessing and intuition is when your negotiating opponent asks you to share a secret. The moment you feel some unexpected excitement in what your opponent has surprisingly told you, watch out! This is the exact time to be wiser than normal. Use controlled intuition. Before you start to fall for the game, ask yourself how you feel about this person. Try to guess what the offer might really cost you in the long run. Whenever you feel excitement from a direct or implied promise from your negotiating opponent, remember the 100 people who are still waiting to become part owners of a business. They will not discover the truth until it is too late.

WHAT TO DO ABOUT AN OPPONENT'S POWER PLAY

During most negotiations there comes a time when the other person explores the use of power against you. Thus, even the kindest parent smiles and says, "I'd hate to have to spank you."

In negotiations, power doesn't always get applied so lovingly. A boss may display temper or threaten you with an icy ultimatum. When a power play is made with a smile, the expression usually masks hostility.

QUESTIONS TO ASK YOURSELF ABOUT A POWER PLAY

Use your intuition and experience when you sense a power play. At the first sign of trouble, ask yourself—

- Is this threat for real?
- Is it possible that this happened because of an emotional reason?
- Should we try to take a break in negotiations to cool things down?
- If the power play seems calculated rather than emotional, what makes your opponent think it will work? What does this person consider your weaknesses?
- What can we say to shake up their estimate of our weakness?
- How can we get more information? Should we pretend to be nervous? Should we simply ignore what we've just heard? Should we pretend to walk out? Or, should we act dumb by laughing, as we say, "You're some kind of joker."

THE BEST DEFENSE FOR A POWER PLAY

Most power plays are not what they seem at first blush. But, many work if unchallenged. The power play relies on surprise, and for this reason you can best defend against it if you guess and intuit before negotiations begin. In this way, when the power play emerges, it causes you less emotional damage. Instead of reacting in fear or confusion, you will say to yourself, "I thought this might happen, so now I'll respond carefully."

As you respond to a power play, use intuition to feel your way. Ask questions of yourself. The key is to do this controlled self-questioning without becoming emotionally rattled. This is why you prepare beforehand by anticipating the kinds of power plays that you might face.

WHAT YOU CAN LEARN WHEN YOUR OPPONENT COMES FISHING FOR INFORMATION

Never permit yourself to relax completely during a negotiation. Of course, you can seem relaxed, but this is only a contrived mood for your opponent's benefit. Underneath, your eyes and ears are alert for signals that your opponent is fishing for information.

A good time to use intuition and guessing is during the more relaxed moments of any negotiation. This is a two-edged sword, however. Be on guard against revealing too much of yourself, and look for ways to get your opponent to reveal more about his or her vulnerable points. Asking ourselves questions is helpful when an opponent starts a fishing expedition.

WHAT TO ASK YOURSELF WHEN YOUR OPPONENT GETS CURIOUS

- Is the tone of this negotiation too friendly? Am I being lulled into a careless, relaxed mood so that I will unwittingly reveal my negotiating positions? Is someone counting on my happy nature to condition me for agreement?

- Is the mood of this negotiation artificially hostile? Is my opponent pretending to be angry as a way of testing me for fear and capitulation? Is this a prelude to the good cop/bad cop routine which would set me up for an act of kindness designed to make me start talking?

- Is the setting of the negotiation supposed to impress or dazzle me, so I forget the real reason that I came? Has my opponent brought in people or dropped names to see if I am awed?

- Are the breaks in our negotiations being used to make me careless? Are we having too much fun? Too much booze? Too much fatigue?

- Is my opponent using time to test me? Am I being hurried? Is the other side deliberately stalling to see how I react? Is my opponent probing to see if I am vulnerable about time in some way or if I become impatient?

- In group negotiations, are they using tactics to gain information from people on my team?

USING THE INVERSE RULE TO SPOT FISHING ATTEMPTS

Many of your negotiating opponents will be less than artful in trying to fish for information. You will easily spot such crude efforts. But real pros are something else. They usually succeed in gaining tips about your negotiating position, unless you watch yourself all of the time. A very successful negotiator told us about an "inverse rule." The better a negotiator feels about any negotiation, the greater the possibility that some pro has figured him or her out by careful fishing. "When I feel good," the negotiator told us, "I always arrange a break in the negotiations to give myself time to guess what may be going on."

The best, smoothest deals are where you need to use guessing and intuition. Ask yourself some questions. Why is this happening? Is it because the other side tailored its position to information I unwittingly revealed?

WHEN TO USE YOUR HIDDEN POWER PLAY

A seller may have a hidden price that is only revealed after hours, days, even months of negotiations. Everything that goes before is simply acting that builds up to the optimum time and method for making the real price offer. Similarly, a buyer may precede his or her power price with a great deal of false negotiation designed to condition the seller for a carefully timed offer.

We use our intuition and guessing to learn the timing and method in which our power will best be applied. We rely on hunches about what will please our opponent and what will drive this person wild. For example, medical science classifies people as "A" types or "B" types to predict their susceptibility to stress-related illness. It is not too difficult to size up your opponent in similar fashion. You learn to time your power plays for driving "A" types differently than for the more placid "B" types.

People differ in more subtle ways as well. But sadly, many negotiators fail to take the time to make guesses about these differences. Thus, a hard-nosed boss may always use the same kind of intimidation with the same timing on all employees. This is silly. For a while it may succeed in gaining more and better work from some employees, but it may completely alienate others and thus lower their productivity.

You must sense how best to apply your power to different types of people. You must learn to recognize the best time to assert this power. The following questions present a road map to direct you to the best method and timing of a power play for a particular person.

QUESTIONS TO IMPROVE YOUR TIMING AND TECHNIQUE

- Is my opponent a driving-achiever type?
- Am I dealing with an easygoing opponent?
- Can I use my opponent's impatience as a weapon?

- Whether I am dealing with an achiever or a more relaxed type, what seems to motivate this person? What might his or her hidden needs be? How can I relate these needs to how and when I use my power?
- Am I up against a real pro, or can I expect to read this person's signals easily and clearly? (If I sense a pro at work, I had best spend more time than normal on my guesses and intuition.)

HOW GUESSING AND INTUITION WORK IN NEGOTIATIONS: AN EXAMPLE

A seller had three houses of the same size, style, and value for sale on the same street. Many sellers would have put their best power price on the houses and thereafter sold them for that price. But this seller used intuition and guessing to sell each of the houses above his power price.

To the first buyer: He sold a dream based on his correct guess that this buyer would pay more for nice neighbors. He timed his selling effort for this customer to put price last and neighborhood first. He devoted 75 percent of the conversation with this buyer to finding out the kind of neighbors the buyer desired, and then showed that the buyer's dream was possible in this house. Only after the seller guessed that the buyer bought the dream did he even begin to talk price. Finally, the seller lowered the price to a sum well above his original power price.

To the second buyer: This time the seller's approach was quite different. At first he had trouble finding what the couple valued. So, he stayed away from price discussion and kept up a general banter about subjects having nothing to do with the house. He talked about the weather, sports, and news events, quickly jumping from topic to topic until the buyers revealed something about themselves. The clue came when the husband said, "I don't keep up on things as much lately," and the wife said, "That's because you spend your whole life in your workshop."

The seller now spent most of his time getting the husband to describe in detail the furniture work he loved. The seller also discovered that the wife was really very proud of her husband's hobby despite her teasing. Now the seller knew exactly how to proceed. As he walked the buyers through each room of the house, he speculated about what the husband might consider appropriate furniture. In each room, the husband would describe furniture that he had or could make that would be perfect. When the tour was over, the husband and wife had mentally decorated the house. The seller correctly sensed that he had made a sale even before they negotiated a price (which also turned out to be more than the seller originally planned to ask).

To the third buyer: Again, the seller adjusted his strategy for the specific buyer. The third buyer was a hard-driving executive who had been recently transferred to the area. His wife and children would join him when he'd purchased a house. His primary concern was completing the job of house-hunting.

The seller guessed that the buyer was interested in this specific house because it was in a good school district. Playing this hunch about this buyer, he spent most of his time talking about availability. He stressed the fact that he had only this one house left and he didn't plan to build any more this season. "I expect this house to be sold shortly. I have some people due here later today," he said.

That did it. The impatient executive whipped out his checkbook before any serious price discussion took place. Again, this house sold far above the seller's original power price.

A CHECKLIST FOR USING GUESSES AND INTUITION

1. Be flexible in using guesses and intuition during negotiations.

2. Even if you think you have a hidden power, such as price, be prepared to recognize a greater power that may be revealed in a person's needs or dreams.

3. Avoid following the world's habits concerning power. Just because many people emphasize money or price doesn't mean you can't discover a stronger motivation by using intuition and guessing. Base your inferences on information revealed during negotiations.

4. Always hold back on what you expect your power advantage to be. This permits a stronger power advantage to emerge. Don't be lazy and rely on traditional power expectations. Keep digging.

5. Impatient negotiators may give more just to save time. Take your time.

6. Other people's values may differ from yours. Their dreams may give you more power then you originally estimated.

7. No two people have identical needs and, therefore, no two people have identical values. Think of your hidden power as variable, never certain. Vary how much power you use and when you use it, based on flexible, never habitual, guessing and intuition.

HOW TO SEE THROUGH FALSE DEMANDS AND SMOKE SCREENS

Most people are very obvious when they make false demands. Often, the situation resembles children at play when one youngster says to the other, "Give it to me or I'll go home!" Neither child gives the threat much credibility.

In adult negotiations, each party expects some posturing through idle threats or demands. When this happens, negotiators continue their business just as children continue their play. Everyone knows that nothing has really happened or will happen.

WHEN TO PAY ATTENTION TO FALSE NEGOTIATING DEMANDS

A second kind of false demand, however, warrants more scrutiny. Some negotiators think they are strengthening their positions if they deliberately ask for more than they expect to get. This kind of demand is usually not an idle remark, but is instead a carefully planned tactic. Even so, most people present such false demands in an amateurish way. Their body language or voice tone reveals exactly what they're doing. But unlike the demand that everyone disregards, you must always pretend to take this demand seriously.

Neither laugh nor ignore your opponent's latest request. This is the first situation in which to apply your intuition and guessing. Ask yourself, "Just how much time must I spend on this obviously false demand to convince my opponent that I take it seriously?" In other words, you ask yourself how much acting is required to show that you believe the false demand.

Start guessing about how to find a matching false demand that you can make. Look for a demand that is as bothersome to your opponent, as his or her demand was to you. For example, a person insists on payment in ten days, not expecting to get it. You pretend to think about it while you guess the amount of discount that you will demand to make your opponent feel your pain. Make this new demand!

Then, guessing that your opponent may be willing to forget the original demand, you switch the conversation to another agenda item. Or, take a break of some sort.

If your opponent returns to the original false demand, it may not have been false after all. You may have misread your opponent's body language or voice tone. At least you have a matching false demand on the table. Now's the time to make that demand a real one!

A STEP-BY-STEP PLAN TO DISTINGUISH FALSE DEMANDS FROM REAL ONES

1. Use your opponent's body language and voice tone signals to spot most false demands.

2. Never let on that you have spotted a false demand, and act as if you are taking the situation seriously.

3. Guess what counter demand will give your opponent pain equal to the strain inflicted on you, and make this false demand at this point.

4. Arrange to change the subject or take a break.

5. If your opponent returns to the original false demand, be prepared to revise your assessment of it. Treat it as a real demand.

6. Reintroduce your matching false demand as a real demand on your agenda.

WHY IS YOUR NEGOTIATING OPPONENT SO ANXIOUS?

Many people will try to negotiate with you in a hurry. Some do this to put extra pressure on you. Others do this because they have personal needs or problems which make time important to them. Pay attention to people who fit into this second category because their behavior hints at strategies you might include in your game plan.

QUESTIONS TO ASK YOURSELF ABOUT A HURRIED OPPONENT

Ask yourself these questions. They will help you recognize opportunities to apply your strategies.

- Am I being hurried in any way? Are my opponents trying to control the agenda and discussion in the name of a time-bind?
- If my opponents seem anxious and in a hurry, what will happen if I deliberately find ways to slow things down?
- Is their anxiety about time or something else?
- Why not slow things down until I can find out more?
- Since this buyer is anxious, do I have a chance to raise my price? Will a little more delay on my part produce a higher offer without my having to ask for it?
- Since the seller is anxious, why not stall to see what else is offered?

BE ALERT TO QUESTIONABLE DELAYING TACTICS

Astute negotiators do not limit their use of delaying tactics to people who are initially anxious. Instead, they try to create conditions which will reveal anxiety that may have been hidden. A classic strategy is to wait until the conclusion of a negotiation to stall on some pretense. Then, of course, the negotiator studies the effect of the delay on the opponent.

A banker, for example, delays the mailing of commitment letters until long after he verbally agrees to the terms of a loan. He explains, "I like to sit back awhile just to see what will happen. Sometimes this costs me business if the customers take their loan someplace else. But many times I receive a phone call which gives me insight into the real situation. Such phone calls often lead me to revise my decision to go along with the earlier terms. I save a lot of bad loans by letting the pressure build during a delay. Funny how many people will reveal themselves under only a little pressure."

We do not agree with this man's ethics, but he illustrates a type of opponent you may meet.

WHERE TO LOOK FOR CLUES ABOUT YOUR NEGOTIATING OPPONENT

Depending on what and where you are negotiating, you may be able to find clues about your opponent's normal work and social habits. For example, a law firm with a reputation for being ruthless probably has individual members who are truly ruthless. In reverse, a law firm with prestigious corporate clients may have some members who are as concerned with high profiles as they are with high effectiveness. Such people may be susceptible to the threat of adverse publicity surrounding a negotiation.

A list of cultural clues could go on for pages. You must, however, learn to find clues yourself. Begin by asking yourself these questions:

- What are the people with whom my opponent works like?
- What are his or her relatives and friends like?
- What clues can I find from knowing my opponent's schools, clubs, hobbies, and associations?
- What kind of people seem to admire my opponent? For what?
- Any clues in his or her work surroundings? What kind of office? Is it neat?
- How does this person dress? Conservatively? In trendy fashions? Neatly? Indifferently?
- How about superiors? Are they afraid? Subservient? Independent?
- Which best describes my opponent's associates: power-oriented, people-oriented, oriented toward some political or social cause?
- Are my opponent's associates quality conscious?

Guessing about an opponent's work-related influences is a two-way street. The head of one of the nation's largest financial institutions has made million-dollar decisions based on how a person handled personal grooming. Rundown heels were a dead giveaway for stopping the deal.

Strange criteria such as this aren't as uncommon as a person might think. What this tells us is that we need to try to anticipate how our negotiating opponents might perceive us. Depending on who our opponents are and what we are negotiating, rundown heels might be just the right touch.

CREATING EVENTS BEYOND YOUR CONTROL AS AN ESCALATING WEAPON

Nibbling, discussed earlier, is one form of demand escalation. Another tactic for escalating demands is to base the attempt on surprise related to sudden developments which your opponent did not anticipate.

HOW THE SPECIAL-EVENT TACTIC WORKS: AN EXAMPLE

The owner of a small business was negotiating with a key person he hoped to hire. The candidate was being very coy and appeared to have already written off the business as "too small for his big future." The small business owner anticipated this possibility and had decided to take the candidate to his home for lunch. As the two men toured the owner's impressive wine cellar, the owner unveiled his surprise, a guest book which he asked the candidate to sign. Conveniently, the owner excused himself for a moment.

The candidate signed the guest book, then spent a moment browsing through it to see who else had visited the cellar. To his astonishment, he saw the signatures of two cabinet members, one Supreme Court justice, four leaders of industry, and two former United States presidents. Guess what—the candidate took the job.

This change of heart was no chance development, although it certainly appeared to be. The small business owner carefully orchestrated an event "beyond his control" to exert pressure on his negotiating opponent. This sophisticated example is a long way from the sidewalk vendors at carnivals who use shills to bolster their sales pitches. Still, the principle is the same: use outside developments to help pressure someone to act as you wish them to act. The key is to always make the event appear unrelated to you, beyond your control.

In any important negotiation, use guessing and intuition to help you find the right extra to add to your arguments. Your goal is to influence your negotiating opponent by using a surprise development to exert indirect pressure.

THE DOUBLE-AGENT VARIATION

We have also seen the double-agent routine used successfully as a persuasive tool. The double-agent play can take various forms, but the pattern is the same.

1. A person appears to come into possession of key information because another person on the opposite team slips and tells too much. Of course, the slip is always a deliberate, carefully designed tactic to influence the recipient.

2. The double agent never acknowledges making the slip. This is key to convincing the recipient of confidential information that it was an event beyond the perpetrator's control—although in fact the event was planned.

ADDITIONAL ILLUSTRATIONS OF EVENTS THAT APPEAR TO BE BEYOND YOUR CONTROL

- An uncashed paycheck of sizeable amount was left in plain sight on the corner of the business owner's desk. The owner was negotiating an exchange of stock to acquire another company. The check was dated almost two months before the current meeting. Leaving the check on the deliberately cluttered desk, the amount of the check, and the fact that the owner hadn't bothered to cash it created the impression of financial strength.

  The person staging this event was careful to leave the room several times, thus giving the opponent ample opportunity to see the check.

- More common versions of the "check revealed" tactic come in the form of confidential reports, graphs, charts, and memos. These documents, of course, are carefully arranged so that a negotiating opponent receives the surprise of privileged information. Again, the event always appears to be beyond the perpetrator's control.

- Buyers generally have trained themselves to expect real estate or car sales agents to talk about "someone else who is also interested in buying this." But if in using this tactic, the agent has a competing potential buyer actually show up during a negotiation with someone else, then this appears to be an event beyond the agent's control. In one case involving this tactic, a car simply pulled up. No one was introduced; instead the seller acted very anxious and surprised and said, "I see that the Joneses have arrived in their car out there. I never expected them to be back so soon, certainly not today."

Assuming that you want what the buyer has to offer, this tactic can influence the buyer to make a buy decision quickly before the Jones family gets another chance. Of course, the seller doesn't seem to have caused the surprise event.

- In a triangle event, a third party unexpectedly does something to influence a negotiation. One party, of course, doesn't realize that the other party instigated the outsider's action. This enables the instigator to manipulate the other party's negotiating position. For example, a banker calls you to say your credit line is being cut back at the very time that someone offers to buy something from you. Such a call can influence your decision to sell. If done with finesse, the party who is unwittingly influenced never sees the connection between the event and the negotiating opponent. This principle is widely used in negotiating big deals.

Tactics such as the one in the banker example are often more artfully applied than most people suspect. Be wary, too, of lawyers who seem neutral or even in your corner, but whose advice helps your opponent. This may happen when, for reasons unknown to you, your lawyer has other negotiations or contacts with your opponent's lawyers on business unrelated to you. Lawyers rarely blatantly sell you out, but they can influence your negotiating results.

Another example of triangular negotiation is when a friend or family member gives you advice which benefits your opponent. Your advisor probably is not aware of what is happening, but in some way your opponent has reached this person. During any important negotiation, watch carefully. You will often see an opponent's efforts directed at family members or friends who are not parties to the negotiation. Classic examples are often evident in media accounts about the influence of a President's family on our nation's leader.

- Another application of events "beyond our control" tactic came to light in recent SEC prosecutions for insider trading. Many people had bought and sold stocks from someone without realizing that subsequent stock price movements were carefully orchestrated. The prices looked like surprise events, but they were a clever means of rigging market negotiations.

Events beyond the negotiator's control are a two-way street. When negotiating an important matter, use your hunches in two ways:

- Spot the events that other people may be staging to influence you.

- Consider your own tactics to stage events to influence your opponent.

As our SEC example reminds us, however, don't break the law!

WHAT DO YOU SAY WHEN . . . A NEGOTIATOR'S SCRIPT BOOK

All of your negotiations will be unique one-on-one situations that succeed on the basis of your own words and your personal negotiating style. In any negotiation, however, there are times when you'd like to know precisely how to respond in a tough situation.

That is the purpose of this appendix. It shows you, word-for-word, what to say—and when—to solve negotiating problems and persuade your opponent to see things your way. Run down the following list of situations to find the dialogue that best reflects your circumstances:

WHEN THEIR "EXPERTS" SAY IT HAS TO BE DONE THIS WAY

They Say: Please understand that this isn't something *we* decided to ask for. It's simply a case of what our experts tell us is sound business practice.

You Say: Maybe they're right. Why don't I run this past my experts to see if we're all looking at this from the same angle?

They Say: But we don't want to delay things on this point. You know our experts' reputation. You won't have any problems if we go ahead on their say-so.

You Say: We don't want to slow things down, either. So let me make a quick phone call, and I'll get right back to you. If you'll excuse me, I'll make that call right now.

(Meeting adjourned, then resumed later.)

They Say: Did you reach your people? Do they agree with our experts?

You Say: My people feel that what your experts have asked for can wait. They suggest we go ahead without any outside opinions until we have our basic agreement worked out. Then, we can put your experts together in a room with our experts, and they can work out the details.

They Say: Well . . . this changes the way we like to do things.

You Say: I'm sure it will all work out for the best this way. Let's forget about the experts for now and try to button up Item 6 on our agenda.

They Say: Oh well . . . Item 6, you say?

A–2

"THAT'S ABSOLUTELY THE TOP PRICE I CAN PAY!"

They Say: That's it. We can't pay even one more cent. This is our last offer!

You Say: Okay, let's go with your price just for the moment. We want to change the subject and look at the surrounding terms and conditions.

They Say: What do you mean?

You Say: Well, if you can't budge on price, maybe you could help us out in some other areas. Could you give us payment net in ten days?

They Say: That sounds okay.

You Say: What about a letter of recommendation testifying to our way of doing business?

They Say: That sounds okay, too.

You Say: Now, what about helping us out by defraying some of our out-of-pocket expenses, like phone, travel and shipping?

They Say: That's okay, as long as you get our approval beforehand.

You Say: Of course. And if you don't mind, we'd like to talk over the interest we pay to maintain an inventory big enough to fill your orders within 24 hours. We need some help on these special borrowing charges.

They Say: You never raised that subject before.

You Say: We never had such a tight price before. . . ."

A–3

"IF YOU AGREE TO THIS, I WON'T FORGET IT."

They Say: Give us what we need in this matter, and you can be sure we'll send more business your way. You know we won't forget it.

You Say: Your word is good enough for me. But what happens if you get hit by a bus on your way home tonight?

They Say: What are you talking about?

You Say: I think we ought to spell it all out in writing, just for the record, in case anything happens to you or to me. That way, all promises will be kept on both sides.

They Say: What do you have in mind?

You Say: You know we can trust each other. So let's get a lawyer to draw up something that will protect both of us if something happens to us.

They Say: So you'll go along on this and give us what we need?

You Say: Absolutely—as soon as we get all of our promises down on paper. I'll call my lawyer now.

They Say: But you know you can count on our word.

You Say: And vice versa. But we both have to look out for those buses!

A–4

YOUR OPPONENT THREATENS YOU WITH A TIME DEADLINE

They Say: I've been patient enough, already. I want your agreement, and I want it by the end of the day!

You Say: Okay. Just let me write down exactly what you want me to agree to by the end of the day.

They Say: Why are you taking all those notes? Are you planning to sue us or something?

You Say: You're making some strong demands, and now you're insisting on a time limit. You're not negotiating, you're dictating—and I want my records to show it.

They Say: Hey, lighten up. We were only joking around. Forget the deadline and throw your notes away. We were only kidding.

You Say: I'm glad to hear it was just a joke. But I think I'll hang on to the notes anyway, just in case.

A–5

YOUR OPPONENT TRIES PERSONAL FLATTERY TO PERSUADE YOU TO CONCEDE WITHOUT HAVING ALL THE FACTS

They Say: We hope you'll take us under your wing. Your reputation is so well known that we'd be privileged to do business with you.

You Say: Thank you.

They Say: We'd be inclined to take your advice on most things in this regard, of course. After all, you've had so much experience.

You Say: Again, thank you for your confidence in me. Now, why don't we get down to business?

They Say: By the way, your friends at that bank felt that we should bring our business to you. They seem to have a lot of respect for your work.

You Say: Reminds me of a joke about never trusting a trust officer. Okay, I'd like to start by looking over the financials on the project you propose.

They Say: We know you work with one of the top law firms in the nation, and we would, of course, defer to their advice.

You Say: Of course. Listen, I'd appreciate it if you'd hold the bandwagon hype for the next guy. If we agree to this deal, it will be based strictly on the merits.

They Say: Sorry. We were just trying to give you the respect that's your due.

You Say: There you go again! Why don't we hold off on this matter for a month or two until all the flattery dies down?

They Say: You're kidding. Think how lucrative this deal will be for you.

You Say: I'm not kidding. No deal until I get some hard information. Right now, all you're giving me is empty words.

They Say: Now wait a minute—

You Say: Not a minute—a month. After all, you guys are top flight. It shouldn't take you that long to put your proposal down on paper.

They Say: Oh, so you're flattering us now.

You Say: Could be. But I'm sure you're smart enough to understand that we can't go ahead until you've done your homework.

A–6

NEGOTIATIONS ARE GOING NOWHERE AND THE CONVERSATION IS WANDERING

They Say: The problem with this country is that no one wants to put in a full day's work anymore.

You Say: I don't see what that has to do with the subject we're discussing.

They Say: We've been at it for two hours now. Let's take a break.

You Say: Sounds good to me. But before we break, let's make a list of the items we agreed upon so far.

They Say: Sounds good.

You Say: Why don't you start by giving me our first point of agreement?

They Say: Well, we were talking about so many things that it's hard to know where to begin.

You Say: Don't worry about the order. Just read me your list.

They Say: Well, it doesn't look like we've really agreed on anything so far.

You Say: You know, we should probably draw up a written agenda to keep us on-track. Why don't I put something together when we break?

They Say: Would You? That would be a big help.

> *Note:* By offering to prepare a written agenda, you can not only get wandering negotiations back on track but also give yourself a negotiating advantage: if you control the agenda, you also control the items discussed, and their timing and sequence.

A–7

YOUR OPPONENT TRIES PUBLIC CONFRONTATION

They Say: (*Shouting from their picket line*) Now everyone can see how you threw us out here in the cold!

You Say: You're all shouting at once. I can't hear you.

They Say: (*Shouting at the television cameras*) This company is a disgrace! The people we work for won't even talk to us! They asked for this strike, and they got it!

You Say: Look, you're talking to the wrong people. You can't make a deal with the TV cameras. We're the ones you have to deal with if you want to settle this strike.

They Say: (*To cameras*) Their contract is a farce!

You Say: Why don't we try this? You pick a spokesperson and put together a committee of five people, and I'll get five of our people to sit down with you in the conference room, where there aren't any cameras.

      (*Two hours later*)

They Say: Okay, we're here. And we're going to stay here as long as it takes to get some action!

You Say: That's fine with us. But let's get one thing straight—absolutely no more playing to the media. We wash our linen in private, or we don't wash it at all. Understood?

They Say: But you wouldn't have sat down with us if we hadn't gone to the media.

You Say: You never even approached us in private. And you won't get much support from the public if you act like a screaming mob in front of the TV cameras.

A–8

YOUR OPPONENT EXHIBITS CHILDISH OR UNREASONABLE BEHAVIOR

They Say: You should know better than that!

You Say: Come on, calm down. You sound like a parent scolding a child.

They Say: Shut up and listen to me!

You Say: Now you sound like a child. Let's take a break so we can all calm down.

They Say: (*Pounding the table*) Don't you try to walk out on me!

You Say: Look, we're not getting anywhere this way. Let's take a break until we can all sit down together and act like adults.

They Say: Don't you talk down to me!

You Say: We'll see you back here in about two hours.
   (*Standing up as if to leave*)

They Say: Oh all right, hold it. Let's keep talking.

You Say: You sure you're ready?

They Say: Yes, yes. Let's go ahead.

A–9

WRAPPING UP THE DEAL YOUR WAY

They Say: Well, that's it. All that's left now is to put the details together. It has to go to the lawyers first, then the accountants, right? See you at the closing.

You Say: Listen, I have a light schedule right now. Why don't I follow up on the details? I'll take everything over to the lawyers' office tomorrow, and I'll camp out there till they do the boiler-plate. Then I'll send it to the accountants in Chicago by messenger. Oh, and some of our staff people can handle the areas that need field work.

They Say: That's a big imposition. We can't ask you to do all that.

You Say: It's no trouble at all right now. I have a light schedule.

Note: Even if you don't have a spare moment in your schedule, it pays to be the one to take care of the details. Here's why: first, you can make sure the deal is wrapped up before your opponent has second thoughts; second, by overseeing the details, you can make sure they are handled to your satisfaction.

A–10

PROBING YOUR OPPONENT'S VALUES AND OPINIONS

They Say: I guess we should get right down to business.

You Say: (*Taking your time to get your papers in order*) Did anyone see the rerun of "Roots" on TV last night?

They Say: Are you kidding? I wouldn't watch that movie—it's all just anti-South propaganda!

You Say: I hadn't thought of it that way. Are you from the South?

They Say: I married into a Southern family, and you'll never meet finer people.

You Say: Well, anything seems to be fair game on TV these days.

They Say: The problem with TV is the long-haired writers behind the scenes. They want to change the values in this country, and we're being brainwashed all the time.

You Say: I gather you're not too pleased with the way things are going in this country?

They Say: This country is going to hell in a handbasket!!

You Say: There's an awful lot of truth in what you're saying. . . . Well, we might as well get on with it.

Note: Some judicious probing at the beginning of negotiating session can tell you a lot about your opponent: his prejudices, his temperament, his likes, dislikes, and moral values. This information can be valuable when planning and conducting negotiations. The exchange above unmasked certain rigid attitudes in a short-tempered opponent who can now be handled with care.

A-11

YOUR OPPONENT IS IN A HURRY TO WRAP THINGS UP

They Say: Well now, you've made an excellent decision, and we think you'll be real happy with it. Why don't we finish things up and sign this agreement so that we can protect what you bought?

You Say: Look, it's been a busy day. I just can't look at another piece of paper right now. Why not let me hold it until tomorrow, after a good night's sleep?

They Say: Well, okay. It *has* been a long day. Keep the agreement until tomorrow.

You Say: Wait a minute. I can't do it tomorrow. I've got an out-of-town appointment. We'll get together the day after tomorrow.

          (*The meeting adjourns, leaving your opponent anxious, and resumes two days later.*)

They Say: Have you got the signed agreement? We should really get it recorded today to protect you.

You Say: I have it right here, but I haven't signed it yet because I have a few questions.

They Say: I'm sure we can work them out. What seems to be the problem?

You Say: I guess I'd feel better if I had a little more incentive to pay all this money. A little something extra would make me feel I was making the right decision. Is there some allowance you could give me?

They Say: Well, we don't usually do this, but to make you feel more at ease we can give you a special three percent discount. That's a real savings for you.

You Say: That would help. (*Looking at watch*) Could you excuse me for a moment? I promised to make a phone call, and I'm a little late right now. I'll be right back.

(*Negotiation resumes five minutes later.*)

They Say: Welcome back. Everything seems in order, so we'll just adjust the agreement to show the three percent discount.

You Say: I just spoke with my technical consultant, and he says it has to be four percent.

They Say: Your technical consultant? I didn't know you had one.

You Say: Oh, it's a personal arrangement that I don't like to go into.

They Say: All right, let's just sign. We just changed it to give you four percent.

You Say: Thanks. May I borrow your pen? Oh, by the way, I assume that you pick up the recording fees and the other legal expenses?

They Say: (*Wearily*) Whatever.

A–12

YOUR OPPONENT EXPECTS YOU TO TRUST HIS INTEGRITY

They Say: We've been in business for 25 years, and one thing you can rely on is our reputation for honesty.

You Say: The people who sold Edsels were honest, too.

They Say: That's different. We have a lot of people who will take our word, no questions asked.

You Say: I was just kidding about the Edsel. I do respect your integrity, but I'd appreciate it if you'd respect my situation, too. I've been burned in business deals before, so now I make it a point to check out every detail. I have a couple of professionals who help me out, and they'll be in touch with you. That won't be a problem for you, will it?

They Say: Not at all. They're probably aware of our reputation anyway.

You Say: I'm sure they are. I hope you won't take any of their questions personally, by the way. It's just standard operating procedure. Believe me, we all know about your outstanding reputation.

A–13

WHEN MONEY ISN'T THE PROBLEM

They Say: I've been thinking this over, and I'm not sure now is the right time to sell.

You Say: You understand that we want you to stay with the company even after you sell it. We'll need to have you involved in the day-to-day operations to keep everything running smoothly.

They Say: That would be written into the sales agreement?

You Say: Of course. And there's another thing we'd like you to do, if you're willing. We think the time has come to set up a satellite operation in Europe. You'd be the ideal person to handle that, and it would give you and your wife a chance to do some travelling.

They Say: That sounds interesting. My wife would love it! But I don't know—

You Say: The other thing we're exploring is putting part of the sales proceeds into an endowment for your university. It would be used to finance a scholarship in your name.

They Say: What a great idea! That's something I've always wanted to do.

You Say: Well, we can take it up again whenever you're ready. You know, we're both so dedicated to this company. There just aren't a whole lot of dedicated people left, and maybe we should stick together for the time being.

They Say: You know, I've been thinking that maybe it's time to drop out of the rat race and start taking life easy. Why don't we at least start work on an agreement and see what we can come up with?

A–14

WHEN YOU THINK A NEGOTIATION MAY BE "SUBJECT TO. . . ."

They Say: Let's sit down and see if we can't work something out together.

You Say: Sounds like a fine idea, but first let's be sure we know who has authority, and for what.

They Say: What do you mean?

You Say: Well, I don't have to clear this with anyone—not my lawyer or my banker or my accountant or my wife. Do you?

They Say: It's our normal procedure to send any agreement to headquarters for final approval.

You Say: In that case, I reserve the same right to defer final approval until a later date.

They Say: But it's our policy to get your signature on an agreement before we send it in for approval.

You Say: No way! If headquarters doesn't approve it, we've completely wasted our time, and time is money to me.

They Say: What do you want us to do?

You Say: Call your headquarters and tell them I refuse to negotiate with hidden players. Tell them to give you 100% authority to approve a deal, or get someone else in here who has the authority.

They Say: This happened once before, and they sent in a consultant who had the authority.

You Say: Well, if that's what they want to do this time, send me his name, and I'll get in touch with my consultant. Then we can talk, when all the cards are out on the table.

They Say: Well, if that's the way you want it . . . but it may take a little time to arrange things.

You Say: Not half the time it would have taken if you and I worked out a deal that headquarters didn't go for.

A–15

YOUR OPPONENT IS NERVOUS OR AWESTRUCK

They Say: Uh, we haven't had much experience at this.

You Say: Neither has my five-year-old, and he beats me every time.

They Say: But there is so much money at stake here. I'd feel more comfortable about this if we called in an expert.

You Say: The only time you need an expert is when you aren't perfectly clear on something. Until that happens, you're your own best expert. In fact, calling in an expert may only confuse the issue.

They Say: Yes, but we're outnumbered here. You have a big team of people to back you up. It might be better—

You Say: Look, even in the biggest organizations, only a few top people really call the shots. In your case, you are the top people in your organization, so we're even. Numbers don't mean brains and ability, and you obviously have brains and ability, or we wouldn't be here.

They Say: All right, we'll go ahead on our own for now. But we'd like to be able to call in expert help if we need it.

You Say: Fine, but I'll bet you won't. Negotiations like these are pretty much a matter of common sense.

A–16

YOUR OPPONENT THINKS HE HAS YOU BEATEN

They Say: Just look at the facts. It has to be this way to make any sense at all!

You Say: I guess so. I have to admit I'm running out of arguments.

They Say: Then it's agreed? We do it our way?

You Say: Maybe—but I'm still not quite convinced. I'd like to make a quick phone call to check on a couple of things. Will you excuse me for a few minutes?

They Say: Who are you going to call? Is it something we should know about?

You Say: It's a personal resource, really—a private matter—but I think I may have something new for you after I make this call.

They Say: Suit yourself, but we can't see how one phone call will change things. Facts are facts!

(Negotiations resume ten minutes later)

They Say: Find out anything new?

You Say: I think so. And it's being mailed from the Coast tonight.

They Say: The Coast? Tonight? But you may not get it for a couple of days.

You Say: As soon as it arrives, I'll get back to you. The moment it arrives.

They Say: Exactly what have you got coming?

You Say: I'd rather take a good look at it first before I lay it on the table. I'll call you.

Note: If you think you're cornered but you're not ready to capitulate, a ploy like this one can buy time. Force your opponent to wait things out for a few days. In his nervousness, he may inadvertently reveal something you should know— and in the meantime, you may uncover new facts or come up with a counter-strategy.

A–17

YOUR OPPONENT HAS PRECONCEIVED NEGATIVE NOTIONS

They Say: Shall we begin, please?

You Say: Before we get started, could we please take a few minutes to clear the air?

They Say: We have no idea what you're talking about. Now may we please get on with this?

You Say: Look, I'm sure you've heard the rumors, and I don't want to go ahead until we've shed a little light on them. To begin with, there's some truth to what you've heard, but the problem is nowhere near as serious as you may think.

They Say: This isn't really necessary, you know.

You Say I think it is. I'd like to get all the facts on the table before we negotiate. Otherwise, the whole thing will be a waste of time, because you'll be operating under some false assumptions. Now, here are the facts. . . .

A–18

YOUR OPPONENT DEMANDS A BREAK AT A CRITICAL JUNCTURE

They Say: Maybe we should consider adjourning for the rest of the day?

You Say: We were planning to take you to dinner. That gives us three more hours before our reservations.

They Say: I'm really bushed. How about a catnap before we go to dinner?

You Say: If the company finds out we're sleeping at the switch, we're in deep trouble. We'd better keep going.

They Say: How about a 15-minute coffee break?

You Say: We're way ahead of you. We just sent out for coffee, and it should be here any minute, so let's keep working.

They Say: It's getting late. Maybe we should skip the tough items on the agenda and come back to them tomorrow.

You Say: They won't be any easier tomorrow. Besides, we agreed to follow the agenda sequence, which brings us to the next point, which is. . . .

A–19

YOUR BOSS TRIES TO PUT OFF A DISCUSSION ABOUT YOUR FUTURE

Note: This is the true story of a young accountant who ultimately became president of one of the world's largest companies. He embarked upon his career at a time of economic uncertainty, when many companies faced serious financial difficulties. His company was unwilling to promote him to a position that would raise his salary. Although his boss thought highly of this young man, his hands were tied.

Faced with a difficult situation, this young accountant was determined not to let his career and ambitions suffer. He used a novel negotiating ploy to get the promotion he was after—and in the process, he earned the gratitude of his boss and the respect of the entire company.

Boss Said: Sorry, I just can't talk to you now. I'm so far behind I don't know what I'm going to do.

He Said   I'll make it quick. I just wanted to give you a book on rare coins that I found in an out-of-print bookshop. Thought you'd like it for your coin collection.

Boss Said: Wow! This is great! Sit down, sit down. Let me take a look at this!

He Said: No. I can see you've got a lot to do, and I don't want to hold you up. But maybe you can suggest a good time to get together? What if we met for an early breakfast?

Boss Said: I can't thank you enough for this book! And breakfast is a great idea. Let's do it a week from Friday at 7 A.M. at Harvey's Diner?

He Said: Sounds great. Talk to you then.

(The following Friday)

Boss Said: You made it! Come on over, I've already ordered your coffee.

He Said: I really appreciate your meeting me this way, on your own time.

Boss Said: Think nothing of it. I told my wife I was meeting the guy who gave me the book, and she understood completely. That's a terrific book, by the way.

He Said: I'm trying to locate an earlier version the bookstore told me about.

Boss Said: Great, and if you do, be sure to let me pay for it this time.

He Said: Absolutely not—it would spoil my fun. And besides, I figure if I give you enough books, you've got to give me that promotion.

Boss Said: Which is why we're here, right?

He Said: Not entirely. Come on, you're a good friend, and I hardly ever see you anymore now that you're working 24 hours a day.

Boss Said: Okay, I admit it. I *have* been ducking you, and it's because I'm getting a lot of heat on next year's budget. The cost of money at the banks is going up, and we're supposed to hold back on any promotions that will cost us money.

He Said: So that's it! I wondered because you brought up the subject a couple of months ago, and I haven't heard anything since.

Boss Said: Now you know why. Look, I'll tell you what. I can't make any promises, but I will go in and fight for a raise for you. I'm not optimistic, but I really need you in that new spot.

He Said: Hey, I can read the papers. I know the problems with the economy. If you stick your neck out right now, you might get your head handed to you. What if we held off on the raise for now? What I really want is the job.

Boss Said: I can't ask you to take on more responsibility without a raise to go with it.

He Said: Let's defer the raise for a year. If things improve, I'll be glad to take retro pay or some kind of bonus. In the meantime, how about an important new title for my resume in case the raise never comes through?

Boss Said: You've got it. Congratulations, and thanks. Wait til management hears about this.

APPENDIX B

A TREASURY OF QUICK-REFERENCE CHECKLISTS FOR NEGOTIATORS

As you prepare for an important negotiation, mentally drill yourself on the ideas in this appendix. Let these concepts serve as a refresher course. Just as airline pilots rely on preflight checklists, doublecheck yourself before critical moments and in critical areas.

These checklists highlight the areas most prone to problems during negotiations. They will remind you of big concepts and little details, both of which you need for a winning edge.

CHECKLIST FOR KEEPING A GIVE-AND-TAKE APPROACH IN NEGOTIATIONS

Remember what a negotiator is.

- Traditionally, dictionaries emphasize that the negotiator is a trader.
- Too many people regard negotiations as a one-way street and enter into them intent on winning everything.
- A top negotiator spends as much time finding issues to give as issues to win.
- The better you understand your opponent's thoughts and emotions, the more you will find issues to trade against your goals.
- Always negotiate in an adult frame of mind. Too many people enter a negotiation in the posture of a parent or child. In the parent mode, they lecture and intimidate. In the second case, they emote and demand.
- The trick of productive negotiation is to be an adult yourself. When you find an opponent in a child or parent role, refuse to adopt a corresponding response. Instead, take steps to bring the other person into an adult frame of mind.
- As you walk through any negotiation door, do so with a personal resolve to be patient. Often, your opponent will sorely strain your patience. This is the key test of your maturity as a negotiator. To get maximum negotiating results, you must always pass the patience test.

B-2

STEPS FOR AVOIDING
PRENEGOTIATION PANIC

Make yourself have high aspirations in every negotiation.

- Many people who want to sell themselves, a product, or an idea panic even before negotiations begin. When this happens, they mentally lower the value they attach to themselves, their product, or their idea. This sort of self-depreciation usually stems from prenegotiation anxiety.

- It is normal, even healthy, to feel pregame jitters, provided that you do not turn these jitters inward as self-doubt.

- Good negotiating opponents always move slowly and wait to see if you are uncertain of your price. Never be awed or panicked by an opponent's silence. It is a tactic to put pressure on you.

- Don't let a smooth, fast-talking operator make you panic by moving at a rapid pace that makes it easy to yield to your panic.

- A top negotiator told us that he has never been impressed by anyone in the golf club shower room. "There's something very leveling about nudity," he explained. "So, in the early stages of any negotiation, I imagine what the other person might look like in the nude. It works every time to lighten any dark mood or doubts I might have had about myself. For some reason, the humor of my exercise washes away my possible awe of the events about to take place."

- Nudity fantasies may not be for you, but this example can remind you not to let any situation intimidate you.

B-3

CHECKLIST FOR RECOGNIZING THE "TELL ME HOW I CAN HELP YOU" APPEAL

This comes in many forms, but the mechanism is always the same.

- Your negotiating opponent says something intended to pass the ball to you.
- Your opponent hopes that now you will voice all of your problems and demands.
- Your opponent sits back in silence and uses the silence to put maximum pressure on you.
- If you permit this pressure to hurry you, if you simply list all of your demands in one fell swoop, then you give your opponent a tremendous advantage. You have not had a chance to test your opponent's problems and needs.

Your response to this tactic must always be a relaxed generalization accompanied by a smile. Never get specific immediately. Buy time as you throw the ball back to the other person by saying something like, "I think there is a good chance we can help one another in many ways, and I'd like your view on things." Then, you sit back in silence. After all, he or she may be more impatient than you. Also, you will uncover your opponent's anxieties before revealing yours.

At the very least, you are now equally in control of what will be discussed and when. Always reveal your demands slowly, one at a time, and throw the ball quickly back to your opponent for reaction.

B-4

CHECKLIST TO KEEP YOU FROM GIVING IN TOO EASILY

Whenever you are about to agree with a demand, make it seem to be a big deal.

- In any negotiation, your opponent is watching you like a hawk. He or she measures how you measure everything. If you quickly accept any demand, you cause two things to happen:

  1. Your opponent will accelerate the number of demands made on you, and

  2. Your opponent will worry that he or she could have gotten more because you agreed so easily and quickly.
  Remember, negotiation is trading. If you permit a demand that you are meeting to appear to be of little importance to you, then you will not be able to trade much for what you are yielding.

- Every negotiation has a rhythm about it. Your opponent may try to get you to easily agree to a number of little things to get you in the rhythm of agreement. Don't let this happen. In the beginning, your opponent may suggest a time and place to meet. This is a good place to start to assert yourself nicely as you counter with a different time and location. Of course, you always do this diplomatically, saying there are reasons beyond your control. But when you do it, you assert the value you place on yourself, and you demonstrate that you can't be steamrolled into the rhythm of an easy agreement.

- Never agree to something without first searching to locate a demand of matching value which you can make on your opponent. Always do this diplomatically. You might say, "I can see how this is important to you, and in a different way, let me tell you what's important to me. I need. . . ." Then, you present a demand equal to or in excess of what your opponent asks.

- Time is on your side in yielding to any demand. Take plenty of time, every time!

- Remember that whether you are buying or selling, the other person never feels comfortable if it's too easy.

B-5

STRATEGIES FOR RECOGNIZING AND AVOIDING BRINKMANSHIP

- "Take it or leave it" is never a good tactic. You can be strong on a point, but always stay short of issuing an ultimatum.
- Attempts to intimidate an opponent are forms of brinkmanship and are usually not productive negotiating strategies. Intimidation risks high emotional response that takes away negotiation and replaces it with dictatorship or war. Both are to be avoided, especially legal war!
- Most brinkmanship occurs when you or your opponent lose emotional control. So, monitor the emotional level at all times, and take a break when things get too hot.
- Some people use and need brinksmanship all of the time. These people are not playing the negotiating game; they are playing an ego game based on their own sick emotional needs. Walk away from such individuals, or they will make you sick, too!
- Whenever you make a demand, have a graceful retreat phrase or tactic, such as a smile, to keep your opponent from assuming that you are playing the brinksmanship game.

CHECKLIST OF TIPS TO HELP YOU RETAIN CONTROL OF NEGOTIATIONS

Watch out for paid professionals.

- Pay equal attention to lawyers, bankers, accountants, consultants, and other experts on both an opponent's and your team. Professionals are often unable to understand fully what is being negotiated. They may get involved in ways that muddy the water or change the intent of the primary parties. The key is for you to control them, not vice versa.

- Some experts can be like arms suppliers. They don't want easy agreement; they want problems to continue, which will require their services. Again, you must limit their activities in a manner that prevents them from taking over your negotiating function.

- Of course, when the other side brings in experts, you always match them with experts of your own who perhaps exceed the strengths of your opponent's outside consultants.

- Perhaps the most important thing you can do is to resist being impressed when your opponent quotes an opinion that he or she has supposedly gotten from an expert. Always respond by saying, "Of course, my advisor experts will want to comment on that view.

- Many people are so trusting that they happily let their opponent's experts represent their interests, too. This is asking for trouble. Don't take this easy way to try and save a buck. It could cost you much more later.

B-7

CHECKLIST FOR PREVENTING NEGOTIATION BURNOUT

Burnout is the problem of trying too hard.

- Your emotional makeup and the importance you attach to a negotiation determine your capacity for burnout. But rest assured; everyone is susceptible to the syndrome at one time or another.

- Signs of burnout include sudden new anxiety levels and near obsession with your negotiation. If you can't get things off your mind, if you can't leave your business at the office, then you are too involved for your own good.

    When you find yourself approaching burnout, try to put time and distance between you and the negotiations. This may take several days, a lot of exercise, or a new landscape. Whatever it takes, you have to find a way to lighten up, not only to protect your health but to give your creative subconscious mind time. Walk away from any tense situation, and your subconscious mind will often come up with effective solutions. Yes, stress seems to help produce more creative ideas, but not the undue stress of burnout.

- The best measure of how close you are to emotional burnout is how you relate to people you love and those who are close to you. After all, they often see you under pressure and can judge your irritability and moods. They will tell you when you are exceeding your own norms. And when they do, listen and stop negotiations until your fires again burn brightly.

B-8

QUIZ FOR MAKING SURE YOU ARE NEGOTIATING WITH THE RIGHT PERSON

Are you spinning your wheels, or is your negotiating opponent really the person with authority to decide the issues the two of you are discussing?

- The key to answering this question is to try to find the person or persons to whom your situation is most important. Many people will try to handle your problems or needs even though there is no mutual need. Why argue with a service manager if the owner will find you more important to his or her needs?

- Often, lawyers, bankers, or accountants will come between you and their clients. You are not an important player in their future, so don't waste time with them. Do you make a habit of going to the person to whom your position is most important? You should!

- Often, especially in selling or buying a product, it is difficult to find out who will be most responsive to your situation. A real estate agent may claim to have full authority, but it may be a sham. A buyer may claim to know what is needed by an organization, but is this the case? It always pays to take time to see who is in the loop of decision making. Who has the most clout, and for what reason? Tailor your negotiating strategies to the people with clout, while diplomatically going through the motions with people who are less important in this situation.

B-9

CHECKLIST OF TIPS FOR FINDING MORE NEGOTIATING STRENGTH

Try to make good things happen for others.

- When you find a way to help another person solve a problem or fulfill a need, you are negotiating from maximum strength.

- Too often, people enter negotiations assuming, not knowing, what the other side wants. This happens because someone suffers from laziness or blindness to other people's needs. It never makes for highly productive negotiating results and can often be the reason for negotiations breaking off completely.

- Consider all the people directly and indirectly involved in your negotiations. Seek ways to make good things happen to as many of these people as possible. In effect, if you can relate your goals to people's needs, they become members of your negotiating team.

- One important benefit of searching out what others may need is that doing so creates negotiating opportunities. For example, suppose a secretary tells you that everything is hectic today because the boss's dog is lost. This is your chance to be helpful in ways not earlier available. You may call friends to help find the dog, for instance. You may not actually come up with the animal, but you'll at least get credit for trying.

- If you go through each day learning more about people's needs, you will discover more and more excellent ways to help. For each way you help others, there will be a potential negotiating advantage for you, now or in the future.

B-10

CHECKLIST OF REMINDERS THAT FACE-TO-FACE NEGOTIATION IS ALWAYS PREFERABLE TO OTHER OPTIONS

- A poor telephone connection can ruin a deal, as can a lost or late letter.
- Voice tone over the phone can be misunderstood. One sentence in a letter can be misinterpreted.
- Your opponent's ability to concentrate on your discussion can be spoiled by circumstances, such as interruptions to a phone conversation, or the conditions under which a letter is opened.
- In any important negotiation, there is no substitute for reading the other person's facial expressions, body language, and mood as you argue on behalf of your negotiating goals.
- Nothing is as warm as compassion and a broad smile delivered in person.
- Despite trends for using conference calls, computer bulletin boards, instant transmission of letters, and cellular phones, keep meetings face-to-face. Of course, we endorse these technological innovations, but not for key negotiations. Meet in person, and you'll win more!

B-11

STEPS TO MAKE YOUR VOICE A PRIME NEGOTIATING TOOL

- Sharp negotiating opponents pick up on voice tones which reveal your emotional state. Your voice may sound tense due to anger, but an opponent may misread this as fear. When this happens, a lot of time is wasted before your opponent gets the right signal. Pay attention to your voice.

- Three or four minutes before beginning a negotiating session, do some deep breathing. This will give your brain more oxygen and will ease your tension.

- Keep a glass of some nonalcoholic beverage nearby, and take a sip from time to time, especially before you begin to talk. This will eliminate dryness in the throat caused by nervousness.

- Rehearse a few of your key points in front of a friend or into a tape recorder. You want to seem confident but not tense. Of course, being confident does not mean being unduly forceful. Listen to make sure you have a confident conversational tone.

- In large meetings where you want your voice to carry, quietly hum to yourself. This will prepare you to bring your voice forward. Try it at home, and see how a hum gets you ready to really project your voice.

- Whatever you do, avoid a phony or self-conscious speaking style. Be yourself—unless you are usually pompous.

- The subject of voice tone is as important with close associates and family members as anywhere else. In fact, when negotiating with people close to you, be doubly aware of your voice, because these people can read you best!

B-12

CHECKLIST FOR RECOGNIZING SELF-DECEPTION

- People are very good at self-deception, especially if it postpones pain. (Self-deception never cures pain; it is always only a way to postpone it.)
- Psychoanalysis has been called the study of self-deception. A lot of people believe what they deceive themselves into thinking!
- When you enter a negotiation, be prepared to hear and see the realities of the situation. Don't kid yourself to postpone the pain that the reality suggests. Many a spouse has negotiated to continue a marriage when reality clearly spelled divorce.
- If you want something badly, you may overlook anything to get it. Remember that the cute cottage that looked so desirable in the summer still should have a good heating system for the winter. If you buy the house in the summer and kid yourself about what is to come, you may feel the pain of frostbite during the next cold spell.
- People become poor negotiators by going against their own common sense when they want something badly. We suppose this is perfectly fine if they see what they are doing. But how many really do?

B-13

QUIZ TO HELP IDENTIFY OPPORTUNITIES FOR UNPLANNED NEGOTIATIONS

- Whenever you spot what may be a problem for people, do you regard it as an opportunity to bargain? You may find that people are willing to talk to you about how you might solve their problems.

- Do you understand that a person in conflict with someone may be willing to talk to you if it helps resolve the conflict?

- Did you ever consider that people who want to learn something from you might often be willing to trade something in return? They may not have ever thought they had anything you wanted, but who knows what you might come up with?

- Are you influencing people in a way that makes them want to negotiate with you? People who buy an image you deliberately create to impress them will often be willing to negotiate with you about what you want from them because they want to become part of your world.

The world's wealthiest negotiators usually negotiate with people who never planned to bargain with them. Big time negotiators find a way to whet appetites after searching out hidden needs in people. Thus, a three-generation family company is not for sale, *until* a smart negotiator finds a way. Consider today's merger and acquisition mania. What started it? Sharp people with the ability to open negotiations when no one planned to negotiate with them.

This is not to suggest that everyone begin stalking everyone else for negotiating pay dirt. But it can be easy to find negotiating opportunities that other people overlook. Many people voluntarily do favors for others with no thought of a payback. These people build up grateful contacts who are later potential negotiating opponents. For what? Who knows the reason, but someday they may find a way to use a past favor as an opener in a negotiation.

B-14

CHECKLIST FOR AVOIDING CYNICISM

- Even as we train ourselves for difficult negotiating opponents, we must recognize that, in most of life's negotiations, everything is really quite aboveboard and pleasant.
- Most people need friends and colleagues, for we are social beings. Because of our need to be social, most of us are willing to negotiate in most instances, since the very fact of community living requires compromise.
- Most people have to work with groups to survive economically. This, too, requires compromise.
- Most people are conditioned to trade their wants and needs when compromise is required. In most negotiations, habit favors finding common ground.
- In working conflicts out with other people, look for a way to marry some of your ideas and feelings to some of the other person's ideas and feelings. This goes a long way toward building trust.
- Always be a good listener. It never hurts to ask questions that encourage frankness from your opponent. In negotiating how to share, assign, or perform work, always be willing to try out something. Be flexible and allow time to work the bugs out of the new system. Most people who see you as fair and flexible will reciprocate.
- Strive to win acceptance from people surrounding a negotiation, such as fellow workers, family, and friends.

B-15

WHAT TO REMEMBER ABOUT NEGOTIATING ON THREE LEVELS: A CHECKLIST

- It's been said that, to win the hand of a mate, you should sell the person's parents, friends, brothers, and sisters. In other words, use your negotiating strategies on three levels.

- If you fail to negotiate on three levels, you can lose if someone from one of these unattended areas influences your negotiating opponent against you.

- Even if you ignore one or more levels of people around your opponent with some success, your agreements may come apart later because these unattended people begin to work against you and the agreement.

- People left unattended in a negotiation may not deliberately try to sabotage your negotiation agreement. Yet, they could end up doing so because they don't understand the new arrangements and unwittingly cause problems.

- Always take time to find out who may be important to your negotiating opponent on three levels. Try to win these people over in an emotional sense. Never ignore them in your courtesies; make them feel that they have your respect. For example, treat your opponent's employees in a manner that at least shows them that you are a sensitive, warm human being. This has nothing to do with any negotiating point under discussion with their boss, but it goes a long way to keep your deal going smoothly.

B-16

CHECKLIST FOR FINDING A FACE-SAVING FORMULA FOR YOUR OPPONENT

- Surround every point you hope to win from your negotiating opponent with face-saving strategies. This will make your opponent secure about how he or she will appear to you and to others if your demand is met.

- Let the other side posture and protest for awhile in case your opponent wants to tell someone, "I really tried not to yield."

   This charade can be played with high emotions that—you understand—mean little. You are expected to know that such drama is for someone else's benefit. Don't respond with matching emotions, although you may feign such feelings if you sense that this is what your opponent needs to convince a superior to make the deal.

- Perhaps the most important place for saving face is between your personality and your opponent's personality. If you gloat, intimidate, or flaunt victory of a demand just won, you may not win another issue all day. The desirable way to win a point is in a feeling of necessity and logic. This enables your opponent to feel that the facts created the need to yield.

   Thus, in a simple price negotiation, the buyer shows that cash is in his or her wallet, and the seller agrees to accept the amount so dramatically presented. In a complicated negotiation for an organization, a memo from some higher authority may be used to explain the inevitability of a negotiating demand.

   In short, the more you help your opponent feel that there are factors which neither of you control, the easier it is to gain agreement.

B-17

CHECKLIST FOR FINDING THE BEST TIME AND PLACE TO NEGOTIATE

- Too often, people start to negotiate at exactly the wrong time. Sometimes it is the wrong time for you; sometimes it is the wrong time for your opponent. The same applies to where negotiations start.

    It is silly to start negotiations at a time or place which finds your opponent emotionally on edge or socially embarrassed. It's silly to try to negotiate a long-winded subject with someone who has a plane to catch, or to force someone to make a decision when you know that that person has to clear it with someone else. It's silly to confront someone with a negotiation demand without requesting a meeting at a mutually convenient time. Nonetheless, people make these mistakes all of the time, to their detriment. Good negotiation requires patience, not only during the negotiation but also in finding the best time and place to meet your objectives.

B-18

CHECKLIST FOR LOOKING BEYOND OBVIOUS CONSEQUENCES

- If you're negotiating for a raise or a promotion, try to look beyond your immediate objective to see how this might affect your career.

What's the point of forcing a raise on your employer in a way that makes your boss vow to never give you another promotion?

- If you insist on winning every negotiating point, you may find that the entire negotiating process has blown up.
- If you win through fear, threat, or intimidation, how might this temporary victory cause you problems later? How will these tactics affect your reputation and other people's sympathies toward your opponent? Will the agreement stick? Will you lose productivity through resentment?
- If you win a particular battle, will it cost you the war?

A classic mistake is to sell something on credit to someone who lacks the ability to pay. This happens every day. In employment, a typical mistake is to negotiate to hire someone who isn't really ready to change jobs. You win initially, but eventually you may find a no-win situation because the new person is not motivated. With products, people tend to claim more than can be delivered. You win the sale, then lose on many fronts: complaints, service, time, and legal hassles.

Try to curb your impatience long enough to consider the consequence of what you impatiently want now. Try to consider not only the consequences involving your opponent but also the consequences with people who learn about the terms of your agreement. Wherever possible, ask people you trust and respect to review your demands by saying, "If I insist on this, how do you think it might turn out?" Often, another person will spot a consequence beyond what you considered.

B-19

A PLAN TO HELP YOU SAY WHAT YOU MEAN

- Often negotiations get nowhere because one or both of the parties gets hung up in ego gratification. These people like to hear themselves talk. They may start a posturing, strutting, barnyard dance to establish a territory. Sometimes, one or both parties uses a negotiation as an excuse to fill time or to embarrass someone. And there is always the chance that someone will try to show off brillance or toughness to an onlooker. Ego gratification has nothing to do with top performance as a negotiator.

- A frequent danger is confusion. This results when one party assumes an opponent knows as much about a subject as he or she does. Thus, a car sales agent tells a customer all about gear ratios, and the customer thinks the car sounds too complicated to drive. Or, an accountant starts to talk about terms which cause his or her opponent to feel inadequate and therefore afraid to continue discussion.

- Fit what you say to whom you are saying it. If you sense an information gap, relate examples in everyday terms to make your point clear.

- Avoid cliché examples and expressions that may not express what you want to say. Often, a negotiating opponent will pretend to understand the intent of your cliché but will privately question what you said. This unsureness can blur an opponent's ability to hear your next point.

- Do your homework about the points you want to make. Organize these issues before you go to a negotiating session.

- Never let emotions blur what you are saying, including the emotions conveyed by your body language. Many people manage to keep their voices calm but move around like stalking animals. Of course, this makes the other person very nervous and unable to concentrate on what the speaker says.

- Many people cannot carry too many facts or arguments in their minds at one time. Thus, it pays to always present one argument at a time, slowly and clearly, then pause before going on to the next point. Some negotiators throw out all of the facts at once in staccato fashion to overwhelm their opponent. This is just another form of attempted intimidation; it never pays in the long run.

- More and more negotiators are impressed with how spreadsheets and computer graphics dazzle opponents. Sometimes they work, but in most cases such efforts should be explained with a few clear ideas and simple gestures toward the dazzling materials. If you expect the other person to really get into details, you will confuse the rest of your negotiating plan by encouraging digressive questions, contesting opinions, and fatigue caused by noncomprehension.

- Remember that repetition aids recall. If you want to be sure that your opponent gets key points, find simple ways to state the ideas over and over. This doesn't mean that you always say the same words; it does mean that you arrange to say the same thing in different words again and again!
- People who write reports and memos often develop an artificial speech pattern in negotiations. This can be deadly boring and usually quite pompous. Remember, you are speaking, not writing. At all costs, make what you say sound fresh, not canned.

B-20

CHECKLIST FOR KNOWING WHEN TO TALK AND WHEN TO LISTEN

Choose your words carefully during a negotiation.

- Avoid words like deadbeat, selfish, unfair, or cheater.
- Use words such as dignity, mutuality, respect, or friendship.
- Words can go a long way toward predisposing people to your objectives and demands. Words can help you appear nonthreatening and sensitive to the other person's needs. Ill-chosen words can make you seem authoritarian, cold, or superior.
- Words can be used to fit the person or group with whom you are negotiating. To some people, a country vocabulary might be more appropriate than a city vocabulary. Always find words that function in two ways: they clarify and avoid talking down to an opponent.
- Snarling, snide, or accusatory words never help, and often they cause your negotiating opponents to become rigid. Foolishly, the people who practice intimidation rely on such words. Such words never make for good negotiations, plus they hang around after a negotiation like ticking time bombs that can upset future events.

- When you organize your negotiating strategies, organize the words that you will use to put your best foot forward, instead of your mouth!
- Different kinds of negotiations require different strategies. Some require a little acting or publicity. Some call for a little commotion.
- In most cases, the biggest negotiating gains come from quiet, thoughtful use of your time.
- Telling others of your negotiating problems and needs may help your ego, but it is like telling others about a broken love affair. They don't understand. They don't feel what you do, and they can't help!
- If this seems obvious, ask yourself why so many negotiations occur in public areas of plants and offices with many bystanders. Or, why so many negotiations leak to the media? Why do so many family members get involved in arguments best left to the privacy of the bedroom?
- Keeping many of life's negotiations from turning into shrill shouting matches in front of audiences takes considerable discipline. But the discipline is worth the effort if you want better negotiating results.
- Choose quiet thinking over shrill bickering, and you may get shrewd ideas about your negotiations. Fighting is an inefficient way to bargain.

B-21

CHECKLIST FOR GAINING BETTER UNDERSTANDING OF YOUR OPPONENTS

Understand how age affects negotiations.

- Older people can usually relate to younger people.

- Younger people find it very difficult to relate to the feelings, experiences, and needs of older people.
- When negotiating with an older person, it is easy to build bridges of understanding.
- When negotiating with someone younger than yourself, be prepared to have difficulty building bridges of common feelings. If you say, "I know how you feel—I was there once myself," you are telling the truth, but the younger person will have trouble believing you.
- In Japan and some European cultures, age is a prime negotiating advantage. In the United States, it often pays to match people of comparable ages.
- Age takes on a secondary role when the older person has some other power.

Try to discover the other person's mood and react accordingly.

- Support defensive people by empathy.
- Try to hear the other person out before beginning your strategies.
- Try to negotiate problems instead of demands.
- Do not heed Mark Twain's adage, "Negotiation is give and take. Give one, take ten!" Remember that poor agreements break down.
- Remember the three emotional roles that people assume: parent, adult, and child. The biggest communications problems occur when one party to a negotiation acts like a parent or child. The other party usually responds in the role opposite to the role the opponent used. The key in such situations is to put yourself in an adult role and refuse to play the parent-child game.

B-22

CHECKLIST OF IDEAS TO ENCOURAGE AN OPPONENT'S POWER FEELINGS

- A recent advertisement described the feelings of power as, "More seductive than sex, more addictive than gold." This could be right when it comes to encouraging power feelings in your negotiating opponents.

- The best way to another person's power feelings is through flattery. Flattery comes in many forms, some obvious and others subtle. Some people see your good manners as a sign of respect, and this gives them power feelings. To other people, you might have to say over and over, "You're the greatest."

- In using flattery, don't grovel or sacrifice your dignity.

- Some kind of flattery always helps. The key is to use it in ways that do not cause your negotiating opponent embarrassment or make you appear phony. But don't worry since most people are so busy enjoying the power feelings that flattery produces that they don't look for your excesses.

- One negotiator says this about power: "The way to take control of any negotiation is to take control of the other person's power buttons. Push them properly and you'll be given the keys to the kingdom because he or she feels so good about giving you exactly what you need."

Cynical? Maybe. Worth trying? Definitely!

B-23

CHECKLIST FOR IDENTIFYING FACTORS OTHER THAN MONEY THAT MATTER TO AN OPPONENT

- Learn what a person already has, and what he or she considers important.
- Dare not disturb those things most important to your opponent.
- People will place less value on something that poses risk to what they already have or what they consider important.
- As a rule, people will pay a high price for that which promises to protect what they already have or that in which they believe.
- Installment sales people never talk total price. To do so might suggest risk to a person's stability. Sales people talk about modest monthly rates to avoid threatening what a person already has.
- When you sell brand names or service guarantees, you take the risk out of purchases and can therefore get a higher price, in many instances, than with a comparable but unknown product.
- When you ask someone for more work, don't rely on money to gain agreement. The person may feel incapable of doing as much extra as you request and may fear losing his or her present position by not living up to the new higher expectations.

    Better to base your appeal for extra work on the logic of preserving the organization's competitive health, and therefore continuity. Remember, people want first to protect what they already have. Also, the use of a vague increased work norm as a test will cause less fear among your people.
- When a purchasing agent fears you may cause problems with quality, poor delivery, or related concerns, no amount of price reduction will cause the agent to risk a superior's rebuke or loss of professional reputation or income.
- Save all cost appeals until your opponent sees everything else as a way to protect the status quo.

- Any extra benefits can only be effective if there is no perceived risk to existing benefits.

- If you are trying to hire an executive away from another company, money will do little for you if the executive doubts that his or her current values will be realized in your new situation.

- Offering money far in excess of a person's expectations can cause anxiety about his or her value. The contradiction between your offer and expectations might cause the person to turn you down!

- Products and services are worth different things to different people. A negotiator must know a lot about a person's values and present situation to peg even roughly the individual's money values.

- In pricing your worth to an employer, you will be worth more if you seem to help the employer protect what he or she already has and considers important.

    Assuming that you pose no risk to your superior's status quo, any additional values that you contribute at no new risk may increase your worth. What people who are important to your superior think of you can give you another value boost in your superior's eyes.

    A job offer from a respected competitor, like a mentor's recommendation, may make you appear more valuable to your boss. On the other hand, a job offer from a company your superior looks down on may not help at all.

- A con artist never says, "Do you want to take a chance?" A con artist always says, "Do you want to get in on a sure thing?" The con artist knows that even greed is tempered by most people's fear of losing what they already have.

- A good rule is to always shoot higher than necessary on a new service or product. Usually, you'll find you end up with more.

B-24

CHECKLIST FOR IMPROVING
NEGOTIATIONS BETWEEN INTIMATES

This discussion applies to people who live or work together. So many of our daily negotiations are with such individuals that we had best perfect our skills in dealing with them.

- To an outsider, it makes no sense. One partner says, "Do you want to have Chinese food tonight?" The other partner answers, "Yes." But the first partner responds, "Why don't you feel like Chinese food tonight?"

    An outsider might hear words, but what mattered most to these intimates was the tone of the message. Thus, "yes" can mean "no" in a close relationship.

- If you are the outsider to a negotiation between two close people, you can usually do little to understand what is really taking place. This means you can contribute little, especially during emotional negotiations when neither party has the time nor the will to explain what the words really mean.

- If you are one of the people who are close, you can encounter considerable difficulty if you forget to say what you really mean. Using the Chinese food example, a straightforward "no" would have left no room for hidden anxiety. But if you said "yes" in a way that the other person knew meant "no," then the other person feels anxious and worried about your lack of honesty.

- Many negotiations between close people flounder because one of the parties forgets how well the other party knows him or her. Thus, even a white lie may be spotted and interpreted as having deeper meaning than intended.

Outsiders cannot help in personal negotiations between people who are communicating through tone and body language. When you are negotiating with someone to whom you are close, say what you mean. Avoid white lies and avoid being preoccupied because both of these factors can begin a circle of doubt with the other person. They cause the other person to be afraid to say what is on his or her mind;

then the other person gets matching anxieties. Communication falters and spirals toward total misunderstanding.

B-25

QUIZ: ARE YOU OVERLOOKING KEY NEGOTIATING STRATEGIES?

Before a negotiation, do you look for what you have in common with an opponent?

- People often react on the principle, "The enemy of my enemy is my friend."
- If you can find things which you and your opponent dislike, you have a bridge to your opponent.
- Other people will often be more willing to give you what you want if you suggest that by so doing your negotiating opponent will also be asserting a value he or she feels strongly about or is using to get even with someone.

During a negotiation, are you willing to switch goals if necessary?

- Everyone knows the benefit of establishing a negotiating agenda in advance, but few know how to switch to a new agenda if talks turn out differently than expected.
- In a deadlock on an important issue, look for a way to save the day. If the boss refuses to give you a raise, maybe you can negotiate another week's vacation. If that fails, you might still win a reserved parking space. After all, you're there negotiating. Use the moment despite your earlier disappointment.
- Another advantage of switching to new goals when facing a deadlock is that you keep talking about something. If you keep talking, the other person may surprise you with something new. Your boss, for example, may give you the reserved parking space and a company car! The parking space discussion may trigger the boss to think about the car. It pays to keep talking!

Are you becoming a victim of your own game? Don't let yourself be destroyed by the very tactics you are trying to use against others.

- Remember, if you start to play tough, they may play tougher!
- If you deceive, your opponents may play the same game.
- Leak information and they may out-leak you.
- If you befriend their enemies, they may form an alliance with yours!

Depending on the kind of negotiation and its stakes, you may be tempted to get nasty in one way or another. In most cases the nasty approach will be met with equal nastiness and often cause any chance of agreement to vanish. After all, negotiation suggests reasonably civilized behavior most of the time. Think long and hard before crossing the line.

After a negotiation, are you prone to go soft on a bargain? After a negotiation, the other party may approach you in an effort to reopen some subject.

- Do not agree to give back what has been agreed.
- If you go soft, the other party will lose respect for the rest of the agreement.
- If you go soft, all the people who know about the earlier agreement will lose faith in you and the entire agreement.
- Sometimes when your opponent comes back to ask that you give something back, you may see an opportunity to make a new demand for yourself. In such a case, start a new negotiation to arrange a trade. This is quite a different situation than a one-way give-back. Always avoid it.
- If you use someone's give-back appeal to open a new negotiation about something else you hope to win, make sure that everyone who knows about the old negotiation understands that your new situation is a new negotiation, not a simple give-back.

INDEX

A

Accusations
  reducing negative effects of, 6–8
  why to expect, 6
Acting techniques, opponent, 101–2
Adult-to-adult communication, 232–33
Agenda, setting up of, 234
Agendas
  formal agendas, 192
  hidden agendas, 165–67, 383
  loaded agendas, 9–11
Ambivalence, understanding opponent's
    ambivalence, 266–67
Amnesia, as short-change artist trick,
    31–32
Angry negotiators, dealing with, 255–56
Anxiety game, 114–16
Anxious opponent, 223–24
Arm's-length tactics, 86–87
Authority symbols
  blunting impact of, 145–46
  use of, 144–46
    basic rules, 144–45

B

Bargain rationales, 258–59
  examples of, 258–59
  planting seeds of, 259
Biased experts, 60–63
Bluffs, 52–54
  handling failure of, 53–54
  passe bluffs, 52–53
Body language, 96–97, 330
Boxers' options, to negotiations, 135–37
Brainwashing, opponent's attempts at,
    384–85
Breaks, in negotiations, 216–18

Brinkmanship, avoidance of, 431
Burnout, prevention checklist, 433
Buyers
  anxious buyers with casual airs, 114–
    16
  compared to sellers, 219
  speeding up buyer's close, 219–20
Buyer-seller-agent triangle, 81–83

C

Career promises, indefinite, 44
Caring individual stereotype, 120
"Cash on the table", examples of, 196–
    98
Casual game, 114–16
  winning at, 115–16
Child-child communication, 232
Closing phase, 219–20, 335–37
Clues, planting false clues, 64–65
Communication
  adult-to-adult communication, 232–33
  child-child communication, 232
  parent-child communication, 232
    negotiator's script for, 412
Con artists
  going along with, 125
  how to con, 126–28
Confusion
  avoidance of, 153
  confused opponent, dealing with, 75–
    76
Conspiracy promises, indefinite, 43
Contrived protests, 237
Control, retaining control of negotiation,
    432
Curiosity
  exploitation of, 172–73
  of opponent, 388–89
  role in reverse sell, 154–55
Cynicism, avoidance of, 440

D

E

F